Volume 2

Life & Godliness
for Everywoman

Edited by Sheila Jones

Life & Godliness

Volume 2

for Everywoman

A Handbook for Joyful Living

DPI
DISCIPLESHIP
PUBLICATIONS
INTERNATIONAL

Life & Godliness for Everywoman – Volume 2
©2001 by Discipleship Publications International
2 Sterling Road, Billerica, MA 01862-2595

All rights reserved. No part of this book may be duplicated, copied, translated, reproduced or stored mechanically or electronically without specific, written permission of Discipleship Publications International.

All Scripture quotations, unless indicated, are taken from the NEW INTERNA- TIONAL VERSION. Copyright ©1973, 1978, 1984 by the International Bible Society. Used by permission of Zondervan Publishing House. All rights reserved.

The "NIV" and "New International Version" trademarks are registered in the United States Patent Trademark Office by the International Bible Society. Use of either trademark requires the permission of the International Bible Society.

Printed in the United States of America

Cover Design: Jennifer Matienzo and Christine Nolan
Interior Design: Christine Nolan
Cover Photo: Laura Meyer

The women in the cover photo are disciples in the Boston Church of Christ: Cindy Wilson, Judith Tauriac, Karen Arsenault.

ISBN: 1-57782-163-7

Dedication

To Irene Gurganus

A pioneer of faith, courage and sacrifice
for all of us to follow.

CONTENTS

LIFE

Introduction   9

Teen and Campus
1. Relationship with Parents   *Elizabeth Laing Thompson*   13
2. Girls and Guys   *Brian and Mary Scott, Sheila Jones*   24

Single
3. Single and Happy in the Kingdom   *Pamela Roy*   31

Wife
4. God's Plan for a Wife   *Sheila Jones*   35
5. No Longer Two   *Sheila Jones*   37

Mom
6. A Godly Atmosphere in Your Home   *Shelley Metten*   40
7. Friendship with Adult Daughters   *Mary Lou Craig*   43

Difficult Pregnancy
8. Choosing Faith over Fear   *Lisa Morris*   49

Single Mom
9. We Can Do It!   *Debbie Rosness*   54

Special-Needs Children
10. Special-Needs Children: FAQs   *Gail Ewell*   59

'Working Women'
11. Hospitality for 'Working Women'   *Sheila Jones*   68

Eating Disorders
12. Chasing After the Wind   *Melanie Breitenbach, R.D.*   73

Abortion
13. Abortion and Forgiveness   *Kay Summers McKean*   83

Aging Parent
14. Facing Reality   *Theresa Ferguson*   87
15. As Our Parents Age   *Sheila Jones, Linda Brumley, Gloria Baird, Donna Western*   92
16. Letter to Momma   *A Disciple*   108

Physically Challenged

17. Temptations and Opportunities
of the Physically Challenged *Linda Howard*   112

Sexually Transmitted Disease

18. Sexually Transmitted Diseases *Claudia G. Trombly, M.D.*   140
19. Living with Herpes *A Married Disciple*   150

Death of Husband

20. God Is Faithful *Joyce Conn*   154
21. My Grief Will Turn to Joy *Jayne Ricker*   159
22. God Knows What He Is Doing *Melanie Cicerchia*   164

Codependence

23. When All I Can Do Is Not Enough *Brenda Leatherwood*   168

GODLINESS

Health

24. Your Body Is God's Temple *Barbara N. Campaigne, Ph.D.*   175

Emotions

25. Dealing with Emotions *Sheila Jones*   180
26. Controlling My Emotions *Gail Frederick*   186

Relying on God

27. God and Only God *Lynne Green*   188
28. Be Still and Listen *Vickie Boone*   191

Ordered Life

29. Using Time Well: The Noble Path *Gail Ewell*   194
30. Order in Your Home:
Ordered, but Not Obsessive *Helen Wooten*   196
Consistent, but Not Compulsive *Geri Laing*   199

Women's Role

31. The Role of Women in the Church *Douglas Jacoby and
Pat Gempel*   204

Other Helps

32. Contents Page from *Life and Godliness
for Everywoman — Volume 1*   213
33. Suggested Reading for Parents *Lea Wood*   215
34. Things Not to Say to Single Women *Sheila Jones*   218

Contributors   221

Introduction

Life and Godliness for Everywoman

Everywoman is you. Everywoman is me. She is all of us. She is each of us. She is on a journey through life, with many stages, changes and challenges along the way. She laughs, she cries, she falls down, and she gets back up. God loves Everywoman, and Jesus died for Everywoman. This book is written to help her have life and godliness, to make the journey all the way to heaven…and to make it joyfully:

> His divine power has given us everything we need for life and godliness through our knowledge of him who called us by his own glory and goodness. (2 Peter 1:3)

Life

The "Life" section of Volume One of *Life and Godliness for Everywoman* spoke to many issues in the lives of women, and Volume Two will do the same: Everywoman is a teen, a college student, a single woman. She marries a husband; she loses a husband to death. She is physically challenged; she is trying to be a good steward of the body God gave her. She is dealing with an eating disorder, the guilt of having an abortion, the agony of having a sexually transmitted disease. She is making decisions about the best way to support and care for an aging parent. She is desperately trying to find her way out of a codependent relationship. She has questions about the best way to be faithful in each of her stages, changes and challenges. Her God has the answers, and her spiritual siblings will help her find them.

This section will help you to know yourself and to be proactive in your faithful responses to life. It will also help you to know your friends, your leaders, your mother, your daughters…and to encourage them in the context of that knowledge.

Godliness

The second section is entitled "Godliness." We all need to grow in our character; we all need to become more like Jesus. That means we need to learn to trust him more in prayer, to not be tyrannized by our fears and emotions, to rely on God and not ourselves, to live an ordered life in an ordered home, and to gladly accept our role in the church.

Great and Precious Promises

Take a moment to read through the "contents" page of this volume (and of Volume One on pages 213-214). Remind yourself that no matter what happens in our lives, God has given us "everything we need for life and godliness through our knowledge of him who called us by his own glory and goodness"—*his* glory and *his* goodness, not our own. We do not have the power on our own to navigate the ups and downs and rights and lefts and jerks and bumps on the journey of life. He gives us his promise that he will be with us and he will sustain us…and enable us to participate in his nature:

> Through these [his glory and goodness] he has given us his very great and precious promises, so that through them you may participate in the divine nature and escape the corruption in the world caused by evil desires. (2 Peter 1:4)

Trying to live life our own way brings "corruption." Making the decision to trust God and live life his way (the way of the cross) will bring us life to the full.

The women who have graciously contributed to this book are sharing with us the surety of the promises of God. These promises will not disappoint us; they will give us clear direction for our journey. The writers share with tears, with humor, with candor and with hope. It is my prayer, and theirs, that you will reach out in faith, no matter what is happening in your life, and take hold of these "very great and precious promises" of God. And don't ever, ever let go! You will be eternally grateful…and that's a promise!

Sheila Jones
August, 2001

Relationship with Parents

> Children, obey your parents in the Lord, for this is right. "Honor your father and mother"—which is the first commandment with a promise—"that it may go well with you and that you may enjoy long life on the earth."
>
> Ephesians 6:1-3

High atop Mount Sinai, with the Israelites trembling at the base, God delivered the Ten Commandments to his faithful servant Moses. "Honor your father and your mother," God began the fifth commandment, "so that you may live long in the land the Lord your God is giving you." The first command with a promise attached, God states clearly the importance of a respectful attitude toward our parents.

The Bible is absolutely clear on the relationship between parents and their children. Children are to honor, respect and love their parents, and parents are to love, discipline and train their children.

The teenage years are notoriously the time when many teens begin to rebel against their parents for the first time. Suddenly, they feel as if their arrival at adolescence has made them so brilliant, experienced and even spiritual that they can discern what is best for their own lives. They think they know better than their parents do. Teenagers' complicated emotions don't help the situation—and unless both the teens and the parents are spiritual, adolescence can be a time that severely damages or even destroys these relationships.

Honoring Our Parents

When God commands us to honor our parents, it means that we should love and respect them with all of our hearts. We should listen very carefully to them, be obedient to them and genuinely admire them. Children should be their parents' biggest fans!

When I was three and four years old, I loved the television show, *The Incredible Hulk*, which stars an extraordinarily muscular, green monster. One day I walked up to my dad and permanently won his affections by declaring, "Daddy, the Incredible Hulk is big like *you* are!"

Many of us had this respect and admiration for our parents when we were younger, but have lost it. We are either too critical of them to see anything good in them, or we are too prideful to admit how much we really do respect them. I talked about my parents to my high school friends all the time, and they were amazed to hear about the relationship that we had. They thought it was really cool, and some of them were jealous!

Perhaps my proudest moment in high school was when my father was able to speak at my baccalaureate ceremony before graduation.

If you have not already figured this out, let me clue you in on a mind-boggling fact of life: Your parents are not perfect. They, like you, are sinners! Many of us have completely unrealistic expectations for our parents. You may have thought that they were perfect when you were a child, and you still expect them to be perfect now. There is not a perfect parent anywhere on the planet. Give your parents a break, and let them be normal human beings with weaknesses just like you. They are going to mess up, hurt your feelings and say stupid things to you or to each other, but this is all part of life.

Even though our parents are imperfect, God still commands us to honor them absolutely. As we mature and begin to see flaws in our parents, we must make decisions about how we will respond. Many teens handle this realization by choosing to become critical and ultimately losing respect for them. They may even rebel outright. They feel that God's laws about respect only apply when the parents in question are perfect or sinless (and also nonexistent)!

Just seeing sin or weakness in your parent can be quite a shocking and unsettling experience. I remember some of the times when I realized that my parents had weaknesses and sins just as I did—and that we actually share many of the same sins! I didn't know what to think or feel. Part of me felt scared by the realization, part of me felt guilty, and then another part of me became critical of them at times. It is not wrong to notice that our parents have weaknesses, and even to feel hurt by their sins. It is very wrong if we hold our parents' weaknesses and failings against them and become critical and judgmental of them.

I did not initially deal well with the realization that my parents were imperfect. Instead of having the same kind of mercy on them that they have had on me throughout my entire life, there were times when I criticized them and held their sins against them. I especially had to deal with this in my relationship with my mom. Adolescent girls tend to struggle at times in their relationships with their moms. Many of us can be "daddy's girl" but have real problems with our mothers. This stems from pride, competitiveness and insecurity, all rolled up in one ugly package.

There were several times that I deeply hurt my mom because of critical feelings I confessed to her. I cringe even writing this, because I now realize how arrogant, hypocritical, ungrateful and unmerciful that was of me. My mother was the one friend I had throughout my rough years as a young teen, loving and forgiving me when I was an absolute jerk. She had been patient with me when other people would have written me off as a complicated, annoying head case. Yet when I saw little things in her, I became critical and judgmental. Who did I think that I was? Even now it brings tears of anger and regret to my eyes when I remember having those feelings and thoughts.

It is disgusting to God when he sees us behave like that. In fact it infuriates him. In Deuteronomy 21:18-21, God commanded the Israelites under the old covenant to have the elders stone to death any rebellious, arrogant children! If you have allowed yourself to harbor critical, resentful or judgmental thoughts toward your parents, you must repent of these thoughts immediately. Confess them to someone who can help you, and apologize to your parents with all your heart.

I remember weeping as I told my mom how sorry I was for my arrogant behavior, and writing her cards to let her know just how much she meant to me. I spent extra time in my quiet time thanking God for all the wonderful things I saw in my mom, and even wrote all those things down for myself so I could fully realize what an incredible woman she is. The most amazing thing I saw in her was her willingness to forgive me so completely, even when I had hurt her. Because she was forgiving and did *not* treat me as I had treated her, our relationship was quickly restored, and we once more became best friends as we had been before.

If you are realizing as you read this that you need to repent of attitudes toward your parents, I encourage you to deal with them quickly. Don't allow another day to go by in which you are not close to your parents (as you need to be).

Just one other thing about respecting your parents: Ask yourself what you sound like when you talk to your parents. Some of us speak to our parents in the most appallingly disrespectful ways—even as Christians. We whine, complain and argue. We are sarcastic and obnoxious; we are know-it-alls who dismiss every word that our parents say as absurd and outdated. Taking these tones with our parents is absolutely sinful. Such talk should never emerge from our lips to anyone, under any circumstances, least of all to our parents. Some of you would never speak to your friends, or even your teachers, the way that you speak to your parents—and this is completely displeasing to God. If you are not sure whether or not you do this to your parents, ask them—they'll tell you! Or ask your siblings or your friends (friends who will tell you the truth) how you come across.

Honoring Is Obeying

Another key way that we must honor our parents is by obeying them. God commands obedience, as we have already seen in Ephesians 6:1. Colossians 3:20 reads, "Children, obey your parents in everything, for this pleases the Lord." Does he say we should only obey when we like what is being said, or when it is convenient for us, or when we can still look cool just like all our friends? Nope! It says that we should obey our parents in *everything*—whether it be concerning a curfew, whether or not we are allowed to date, or where we are allowed to go with our friends.

The teenage years are an awkward time because we have more freedom to make decisions about our lives, and there are many more options open to us. Many of us can drive; we are old enough to be interested in dating; we have some say in the classes we take; we can choose whether or not to play sports or be involved in clubs, and most importantly, we can make our own decisions about our relationship with God.

Adolescence is an exciting time, but it is also the time when many people abuse their new freedom and end up sinning very seriously—and in that sense, it can be a scary time! You may feel old and mature once you hit high school, but you must realize that there is a lot in life that you have absolutely no clue about. Even though your parents went through adolescence many years ago and probably wore some really ugly clothes at the time, they still know a great deal more than you do about making it through adolescence. Let them help you! They are not out to ruin your life when they make suggestions or lay down rules for you. They are simply trying to protect you. It might not be fun to have an earlier curfew than all of your friends, or to not be allowed to date yet, but instead of resenting your parents, you should appreciate how much they love you and are concerned for you! I know very few parents who make rules just for the twisted pleasure of ruining their teenagers' lives.

And guess what? In the same way that adolescence is a new experience for you, it is also a new experience for your parents! You've never been a teenager before, and they've never dealt with you as a teenager before—so none of you knows exactly what to expect. They are probably scared to death! All of a sudden, you look more like an adult, you act more like an adult, you have hormones and crazy emotions that make you cry at the drop of a hat, and—heaven forbid—you are attracted to the opposite sex! You were much easier to deal with when you were a little girl, and now they have no idea of how to deal with you. If you are the oldest child in your family, like I am, they *really* don't know what to do with you. Their first instinct is probably to lock you up in the house all day long where you can't get into any trouble, nobody can mess with you or hurt your feelings, and no boys can come after you! So hey—if you get to go out at all, even if your curfew is 7:00, you're doing pretty well, and you should thank your parents big-time! If you aren't allowed to date but are allowed to at least speak to guys, at least your dad isn't standing guard outside your house all day long with a shotgun—this is a big step for him.

I know I am joking around a little here, but seriously, we have to understand that adolescence is a new thing to our parents, too. And since they're not perfect, sometimes they'll mess up—just as we will. So be

TEEN AND CAMPUS

patient, and let them learn, just the same way you expect them to be patient with you as you grow up. If they are a little overprotective, don't resent it. That just proves that they care deeply about you and want to protect you from getting hurt.

My parents have always been a little more protective than some of my friends' parents, but I really appreciate that. I feel so loved and cared for. They always encouraged me to get in bed at reasonable hours, and whenever I went out, we agreed upon a time when they could expect me back so that they would not worry. I was not allowed to ride in a car unless I was wearing a seat belt, which was a very good thing, considering the way some of my friends drove in high school. Even when I was in college, my parents were still concerned about me and told me what to do at times. When I went home for the summer and Christmas holidays, I still tried to be in by a decent hour so they didn't worry, and I still checked with them before I made plans.

If you prove yourself to be obedient and trustworthy, your parents will probably give you more and more freedom as you get older. I was allowed to do many things by my senior year in high school that I never could have done as a freshman. Don't spend high school fighting with your parents and making your lives miserable. Just decide to be a great daughter no matter what.

Also, don't let yourself off the hook by just obeying your parents grudgingly—doing what they say, but rolling your eyes, making faces, sighing despondently, slamming doors or stomping off in a huff as you do it. That's so immature. Grow up and get out of preschool! Consider Paul's words in Philippians 2:14-15:

> Do everything without complaining or arguing, so that you may become blameless and pure, children of God without fault in a crooked and depraved generation, in which you shine like stars in the universe. (Philippians 2:14-15)

What do you do if your parents ever tell you to do something that you feel is wrong? What does God think about that? It really depends on the situation. God would never have us break his commands because of what another person tells us to do, but few of us ever encounter a situation in which our parents actually command us to sin. Sometimes we may not like what they tell us, but often it is just a matter of opinion, not of right and wrong. If something your parents ask you to do violates your conscience before God, then you need to first pray for wisdom, and search it out in your Bible to see if there is a Biblical command about it. You can humbly mention your concern to your parents, and ask them to help by explaining their thoughts about the matter to you. This should clear up most issues that you may have. If they are Christians, then they probably have a good explanation for why they are thinking as they are.

If you still feel unresolved about the issue after talking with your parents, or if it is a particularly sensitive issue, you may need to seek some advice from another Christian. I would recommend talking to someone like your discipler or one of the teen leaders at church. They can help you decide what the wisest approach would be to your particular situation.

Honoring Is Openness

Teens tend to have the bizarre idea that once they hit adolescence, they should no longer be close to their parents, because it's not cool and because their parents probably wouldn't understand them anyway. What a stupid idea! Whoever thought of it should be flogged or something. Our teenage years are a time when, because we are older, we actually have more in common with our parents than ever before. These are the years when you can have not only a parent-child relationship, but you can truly become friends.

Although we had bumps here and there, my relationship with both my parents during high school was characterized by a deep closeness and best friendship. As I have grown older, we have become even closer (which was hard to imagine!), building on the groundwork we laid at that time. My mom and I can talk to each other for hours on end and not become bored. Whenever I go home, I have to make rules for myself about not going downstairs until I have read my Bible and prayed. Otherwise, Mom and I will spend the entire morning talking, and I'll miss my time with God! We talk about everything—from our relationship with God, to our dreams, to the details of my dating life (before I was married, of course). It's so much fun, and I have learned so much about life, God and the ministry just by hanging out with her.

In the same way, my dad and I have such a special relationship, unlike any other in my life. He is my hero of all time, and the model for the kind of man I wanted to marry (and did marry). We share so many of the same passions and can understand each other's interests in even the seemingly most insignificant things. When I was in college and went home for spring break, we had an opportunity to spend an unexpected morning together. We had an absolute blast! In a matter of about thirty minutes, we discussed everything imaginable—from our mutual passion for writing and history, to politics, to the history of God's kingdom. When we returned home, we both teared up as we talked about how much we just loved being together.

Please open up your heart to your parents. Let them be your friends. Don't put on an act in which you pretend not to need them. Be humble and vulnerable, and let them know the real you. Talk about your feelings, thoughts and struggles. Your parents can help you so much at this time in your life, and most of them really want to be close, but so many times it is the teenagers who refuse to allow them into their hearts. Consider the admonition of Paul:

> We have spoken freely to you, Corinthians, and opened wide our hearts to you. We are not withholding our affection from you, but you are withholding yours from us. As a fair exchange—I speak as to my children—open wide your hearts also. (2 Corinthians 6:11-13)

Open wide your heart, and let your parents in. Remember that love is not a feeling, but a decision and an action. Don't wait for your feelings to be just right before you act—do what you know is right, and God will work on your emotions as you go.

What about those whose parents have not made efforts to become as close as they would like to be? There are certainly many teens who would love to be close to their parents, but do not feel they can be because their parents are not warm, loving or receptive. My own father had a very difficult time getting close to his dad. His dad had a great sense of humor and really loved all of his children, but he also had a bad temper that scared my dad. He died when my dad was only twelve, and they never had the chance to build the kind of relationship my dad had always wanted. My dad felt hurt and deep regret for many years, until he learned to allow God to be the father he needed, and until he was able to remember all the ways his father had sought a close relationship with my dad in his own way. Imperfect people can never substitute for God's role in our lives— only he can provide us with the security and unconditional love we need.

If you have a difficult time getting close to one or both of your parents, don't be discouraged by that. You are certainly not alone! It may be that you need to change a lot in yourself, and it may also be that your parents have not made the effort they should have to be close to you. If this is the case, study how Jesus treated people who treated him unjustly and unkindly, and look at how much he loved them in spite of their actions. It will not be easy by any means. Maybe if you take the first step in seeking a closer relationship, or in making yourself vulnerable to them, you can break through some of the barriers that separate you from each other. You have to start somewhere, so don't be discouraged if things don't change right away. It may be that your parent or parents never knew how to be close to their own parents, and so they honestly don't know that things should be any different.

Honoring Is Gratitude

So many of our problems with our parents could be solved if we would simply appreciate our parents and all that they do for us. Teens are notoriously ungrateful for the blessings in their lives, but especially for their parents. Your parents are imperfect and have surely done innumerable things wrong. They have probably even hurt you at times. Even if your parents are not expressive and have not made all the efforts they should have to be close to you, God expects you to appreciate them.

I encourage you to do something this week to let your parents know how much you appreciate them, and to do such things often. Write a card, give a gift, give a hug or just tell them in person.

Even if you don't feel thankful right away, expressing your gratitude has a way of making you feel it more strongly. If you struggle with criticizing your parents or if you have a hard time being close to them, then you especially need to do this! Take some special time to write down for yourself all the things you appreciate about your parents, and keep that list so that you can look at it whenever you are tempted to have a bad attitude, criticize them or simply take them for granted. It will do you a lot of good and will probably transform the way you view them.

Kingdom Kids

This discussion of gratitude leads me into a very important area, and I want to address "kingdom kids" for a moment—those of you who have grown up in the kingdom of God with Christian parents, and especially those of you whose parents have been leaders in God's church.

We are some of the most fortunate people alive. Most of us have absolutely no idea how blessed we really are to have been raised as we have. Having Christian parents is, besides salvation itself, the greatest blessing God could possibly give us. We are spared so much of the heartache and suffering that so many others endure. We were born with salvation sitting in our laps, waiting for us to pick it up. Our parents are godly, spiritual people who have raised us the way God would want us to be raised.

We should therefore be the most grateful people alive. Not a day should go by when we do not thank God for the life we have led. Yet I am sad and ashamed to say that we are often the people who appreciate God's kingdom the least. We act as if we deserve salvation and special treatment, when we should be falling all over ourselves searching for ways to serve and show our appreciation.

I have definitely been ungrateful many times for my parents and my life in the kingdom. As I have seen more of the world and studied the Bible with countless women who did not have a family or life like mine, I have come to appreciate it so much more. I am in awe that God chose me to have the family I have and the life I have had thus far. I would not trade it for anything or switch places with anyone.

While we need to grow in our gratitude and continually remind ourselves how blessed we are, we should not feel guilty because of the life we have had. Some of us can feel so unworthy and can beat ourselves up in an effort to try to deserve what we have—and sometimes other disciples can make us feel guilty, because they wish so much that they had the same opportunities we have had. There is absolutely no reason to feel guilty for our lives. We should simply be overflowing with gratitude and should let that thankfulness compel us to share our faith that much more. We cannot give other people our childhood or our family, but we can tell them about what life is like when God comes first in a family. We should be the most evangelistic people in the kingdom!

We can also be unselfish with our families, enabling them to help others. My family loves it when any of us brings a friend home, and our friends are invariably amazed at the love in our home. A number of people have become Christians after seeing God's power at work in the relationships within our family. Other disciples, particularly other students who have grown up in families that are not close, are similarly amazed and inspired by spending time with our family. We serve as their family if they do not have a close one of their own, and they catch a vision for what they can one day build for themselves.

One final thought to kingdom kids: If you are especially close to your parents, that is great, and something you should be proud of and thankful for. However, it cannot be that you only allow your parents to disciple you. You must allow other people into your life to train and help you spiritually and not allow your relationship with your parents to serve as an excuse for being independent from others whom God wants to use in your life.

Being in the campus ministry was a challenge for me my first year, because it was the first time when I had ever really let anyone besides my parents into my life. I had to learn to be humble and to accept advice, challenge and help from other disciples and not go running home to my parents all the time. My parents are an incredible help to me, but I had to decide that they would not be a spiritual crutch for me. I desperately need other people in my life as well—people who are a bit more objective than my parents and who may have a different view of things.

I have had to learn that other people may even do things differently than my parents do, but this is not necessarily bad. My parents do not know everything (nor do they claim to!), and it would be foolish for me to limit myself only to their opinions in my life. I appreciate having many different points of view to help me to grow spiritually.

Non-Christian Families/Challenging Family Situations

Some of you reading this may be having a hard time knowing what to do with it because your parents either are not disciples or because you have a difficult family situation. Perhaps your parents are divorced and you only live with one parent, or you have one or more stepparents, or perhaps you have never even met one or both of your parents.

These can indeed be very challenging and sometimes very hurtful situations. There is no way that I can list all the possible family situations you may be involved in and provide specific advice, but I can tell you some principles to keep in mind.

The most important thing you must do is believe with all of your heart that God has an amazing plan for your life and that he has called you to follow him at a young age for that very reason. His goal is for you to be around Christian families while you are still in high school, so that one day you will know how to build an awesome Christian family of your own. You must also remember that your security and your source of unconditional love must be God, not your parents. Some people spend their entire lives unhappy, insecure and unfulfilled because they do not feel loved by or close to their parents. Read everything you can in the Bible about God being your father, your caretaker and your shepherd.

If your parents are not Christians, it is crucial that you help them to feel great about your involvement with the church. That responsibility falls primarily on your shoulders, not on those of the teen workers or other disciples in the church—although they do need to help you in whatever way they can. If your parents are open to the idea, set up opportunities for them to spend time with Christian parents of other disciples. It will help your parents to feel good about the church if they see that other parents also want their teens to be a part of the church. That way, adult disciples will have an opportunity to share with your parents and perhaps help them become Christians themselves!

At my old high school, a girl named Susan was recently baptized after being reached out to by one of the guys in the teen ministry. She brought her parents to church, and they loved it. They became friends with some of the married couples at church and began to study the Bible as well. Within a few months, both of her parents became Christians. Her dad shared at his baptism that the thing that helped him the most was seeing the lives and relationships of the teen disciples.

Regardless of whether or not your parents are supportive of your involvement in the church, you must be especially careful to be very responsible. You have a responsibility before God to set a great example at home, not to preach at your family or tell them that they are going to hell, but to be a great servant, daughter and sister. Your family should be amazed by your attitude—especially by the way you serve.

TEEN AND CAMPUS

Be very careful always to communicate very clearly with your parents about your attendance at church-related functions. Be responsible about finding rides, and always be home when you say you will. If your parents feel that you are reliable and responsible, they will be far less likely to prevent you from being involved. If a situation ever arises when your parents do not want you to attend something at church, be very wise in the way you handle it. Do not pout and make a scene. You can humbly and calmly let them know what you would like to do and why, but then you have to let it go. Trust that God is in control, even of situations like that.

Another thing that would be very helpful is for you to keep the teen workers in touch with your parents. Your parents need to know the people who look after you at church so that they can trust them. It would help to even have a friend who works in the teen ministry spend time hanging out at your house every once in a while, just so your parents can get to know them. Your parents have a right to be concerned about who you spend your time with. Also, let your parents get to know your friends in the teen ministry. They will be impressed by your friendships and will want you to remain friends with such respectful, responsible teens.

Your high school years will fly by before you even know it. A class period may seem to last an eternity, but do not be deceived. Just as you finally feel you've gotten the hang of being a student—you've figured out your way around school, you've learned all the cool slang, figured out where to sit at lunch, and more importantly, you've gained confidence and conviction as a disciple—it will be time to order your cap and gown. These four years will most likely be the last ones you will spend at home with your parents. They are such a special time, a time that will never come again, no matter how much you may want them to. One day soon you will pack off for college, and your life will change for good. You will still have your parents, but it will not be quite the same. You won't be able to run downstairs every morning to get one of your dad's bear hugs, or go grocery shopping with your mom, talking and giggling the whole time.

Do not squander this time. Draw close to your parents now; spend the extra time with them now; open your heart now. Then when you move on to college and the rest of your life, you will look back with tears in your eyes, treasured memories in your heart, and the kind of relationships that will only grow closer and richer in years to come.

Elizabeth Laing Thompson
Atlanta, USA

This material is reprinted from *Glory Days* by Elizabeth Laing Thompson (Billerica, Mass.: Discipleship Publications International, 1999), 118-134.

Girls and Guys

When boys are no longer annoying little pests and girls are no longer "cry babies," a whole new awakening happens in teenagers' lives. They begin to actually *like* members of the opposite sex. They are fascinated by them, but also confused by them. They are drawn to them, but also afraid of them.

The following three sections offer practical suggestions to help you understand more about what your relationship with guys should be...now and if you marry in the future.

They Are Not Weird—Just Opposite

From the Guy

I (Brian) was sitting with the boys talking about life, dealing with the homework assignments, making plans for the weekend and the game Friday night, reliving the last joke played on somebody, rating teachers, discussing parents' odd behavior, music...and of course, girls. What I knew about girls would have fit in a Dixie cup, but there I was, passing through puberty and trying my best to sound like an expert. I remember the summer my friend John got a girlfriend. He just disappeared, and I got an attitude over it—which hurt our friendship for years.

Girls were a mystery. While they could be a lot of fun, they were often difficult to talk to, difficult to understand and increasingly difficult to avoid. Face it, they were *different*. They had emotions I didn't even know existed and possessed an innocent, but somehow brutal, honesty. Passing comments from girls about what they liked in a guy could leave me feeling insecure for days.

Girls might make me feel awkward, embarrassed or even elated, but their presence always made life much more complicated than I thought it needed to be. It was *us* and *them*, even to the point of sitting on opposite sides of the room at parties with only a few socially gifted kids attempting to bridge the gap.

From the Girl

From kindergarten on, I (Mary) was aware that boys were different from me. And who could figure out why they did what they did, and why they liked to discuss gross things and torture the girls? At five years old, I developed my sprinting abilities by running away from boys as they'd try to catch the girls to kiss them.

Guys can get all wrapped up in their "acts," not being open about their real feelings, which are often insecurity, self-consciousness and rebellion. In high school, I developed some very close, pure relationships with a few guys. From their outward appearance, it was not obvious that they even cared about other people's opinions. They teased the girls and called each other horrible names. By accepting them and listening, I began to understand that guys are sensitive and can be hurt easily. They teased others unmercifully to keep everyone from seeing how tender their own feelings were.

Both girls and guys are silently screaming out for acceptance. Girls usually express this in a totally different way than guys. For example, in our house growing up, we had a five-minute limit on the phone (this was before call-waiting was invented). I would talk to my friends for an hour by alternating calls every five minutes. I wanted to have someone know *everything* I was thinking and feeling. I wanted to be completely understood and used a lot of words to make sure my meaning was clear. I was so self-conscious that I would think through an entire conversation before I said anything so I wouldn't make a fool of myself—but I often did anyway!

Accept One Another

Sometimes the opposite sex can seem a bit like the demoniac in Mark 5:1-20. Jesus spoke and listened to the man and "Legion" who had possessed him. He didn't complain that the man hadn't showered or didn't listen to the kind of music Jesus did or that he wasn't wearing clothes from the Gap. Jesus loved the man right where he was and knew that he could change.

As disciples of Jesus, we're not allowed to just write off the half of the population that is different from us. We must look at each other with acceptance and vision, remembering that we all want to be loved. God created men and women to be different and to complement each other's strengths and compensate for each other's weaknesses. Thankfully, men and women disciples are spiritually gifted with the power to see through gender differences to the person—the soul—on the other side. Paul writes in Romans that we are to "accept one another, then, just as Christ accepted [us], in order to bring praise to God" (Romans 15:7). Think about what Jesus has accepted in you and imitate him in your relationships with the opposite sex. And have a great time enjoying the difference!

Brian and Mary Scott
Boston, USA

Questions

1. When was the last time you became friends with a Christian of the opposite sex? Do you have a great guy friend who helps you understand the opposite sex?
2. Are you open with your discipler about your questions concerning the opposite sex?
3. Where do you go to develop your opinions about the opposite sex—school, your friends or the Bible?

What Is Your Motivation?

Brian was my girlfriend's big brother. One summer night when I was thirteen, he offered to walk me the two blocks home. As we walked, he talked about how silly guys and girls can be about each other. I agreed.

Then he said, "Why do girls freak out because a guy touches them?"

I replied, "I don't think that's a big deal."

The next thing I knew, Brian had his arm around me. I was very uncomfortable but felt that I'd set my own trap by my words. I endured the walk home but made sure I never got into a situation like that again with a guy I didn't know very well.

Another time in college, I followed an attractive guy around for days. I would stare him down across the room until I could see that he was very uncomfortable, and then I'd laugh about it. When I finally was close enough to start a conversation, his voice was like Kermit the Frog. Everything I found attractive about him disappeared. I wasn't trying to get to know this guy; I was seeing who I could attract.

Check Your Heart

Have you ever been in a situation where someone acts friendly toward you at church, but when you see them at school, it's as if you don't exist? Have you ever been the person doing it? The world teaches us to use people to look better. The Bible teaches us to think about others first and build them up according to their needs (Ephesians 4:29).

How do you choose your friends? One of my guy friends from the world told me once that he was only friends with girls he found attractive. At first that thought disturbed me. But really, our friends are people we feel attracted to for one reason or another.

It may be that you feel free to be yourself around someone, so that freedom attracts you. Or it may be that a friend of yours always tells you the truth about yourself, so you feel very safe with them. You may have a friend with whom you've been very successful at a project or in sports.

As disciples of Jesus, we are called to be remarkable for our love for each other (John 13:34-35). We are not called to use one another to make ourselves feel bigger or better than we are. How often do you reach out to someone who is very different from you? When you speak with non-Christians at school, do you think about them in terms of teaching them about God, or just how attractive they are, or who is seeing you speak with them?

It is natural to respond positively to someone you find attractive. There is nothing wrong with feeling good because a guy is nice to you or speaks to you. But be aware that you may feel tempted to entertain a friendship with a guy and not tell anyone about it. Proverbs 16:2 says, "All a man's ways seem innocent to him, but motives are weighed by the Lord." Your own motives may be pure. Or they may not be. You may not be thinking anything impure, but that guy you are paying a lot of attention to may not have the best motives for being around you. If you're unsure what your motives are in a "friendship" with someone who is or isn't a disciple of Jesus, ask yourself some questions, and then ask another disciple who is more mature than you what they think.

As Christians, the "limits" have been lifted off of us. We don't have to "belong" to any clique. We can have friends from all different walks of life. Like Jesus, we speak and act in ways that call the other person to a relationship with God and to a relationship with people that is pure and useful (1 John 3:18).

Mary Scott
Boston, USA

Questions

1. Do you keep friendships to yourself or do you want everyone to get to know this great person?
2. Do you feel that you don't need advice about your relationships with people of the opposite sex? Do you actively seek advice about this area of your life?
3. Do you only make friends with people who will increase your social status? Where would you be if Jesus did that to you?

Are You a '1 Corinthians 13' Date?

Things to think about...

- If he has trouble communicating, are you *patient*?
- If he says something dumb, are you *kind*?
- If someone else got the date you wanted, do you *envy*?
- Do you try to get to know the other person, or do you center on yourself and *boast* about your accomplishments?
- Are you too *proud* to go out with certain brothers?
- Are you *rude*, interrupting others when they are talking?
- Do you always want to do things your way on a date (*self-seeking*), or after being honest about your preferences, are you willing to die to yourself?
- Are you *easily angered* and quick to get your feelings hurt?
- Do you hold it against someone if you don't enjoy the date (*keeping a record of wrongs*)?

Make the decision that you will believe in each other and encourage each other. Trust God in every relationship and on every date.

God's Plan for Sex

Sex is good. It is a gift from God to married couples to express their love and to have children who can share their love.

It is probably difficult for you to think of your parents having a sexual relationship. But you wouldn't be here if they didn't! It is understandable, though, that this thought might make you uncomfortable because most of what you see is the world's understanding of sex—sex outside of marriage. Sex without commitment. Sex to fulfill selfish desires and to be accepted by others. This intimate gift of God is used, abused and confused. Sex outside of God's will is sin. But sex in marriage is created and blessed by God:

> Marriage should be honored by all, and the marriage bed [the act of sex] kept pure, for God will judge the adulterer and all the sexually immoral. (Hebrews 13:4)

A whole book in the Bible actually describes in poetry form the joys of Solomon's sexual relationship with his wife (Song of Songs).

So, you should not be any more surprised that your parents have sex (or make love) than you would be that they talk together, sleep together or pray together. All of these activities are God's will for their marriage.

There's a lot of talk nowadays about healthy sex. Teens are advised, *Abstain if you can; otherwise use condoms. Know your partner's sexual past.* Not a very strong call to purity is it? True healthy sex is when two people commit not only their bodies, but their time, emotions and their lives to each other. God wants you to experience healthy sex—when it is time, when it is right, when it is in marriage. Then you are free to wake up in the morning, feeling clean, free of guilt and not regretting the sinful loss of control the night before or wondering if you may contract a killer disease or be pregnant.

Make the decision to trust God. He made us. He made sex. He knows what is best. Decide that you will be pure in your dating relationships, even when you're with the one you want to marry. Heavy kissing and petting (taking the freedom to caress and touch sexual areas of each other's bodies) is designed as a prelude to intercourse in the marriage relationship. If you don't plan to have intercourse, then don't begin the foreplay that will arouse your passions and take you where you don't want to go.

Guard your mind and your heart. Don't give in to acting out anything in your imagination that you would not want to act out with your bodies. Jesus very clearly said, "...anyone who looks at a woman lustfully has already committed adultery with her in his heart" (Matthew 5:28). This also applies to looking at a guy lustfully. And remember, just because a weird or sexual thought pops into your head, it does not mean you have sinned. Make the decision to take the thought captive (1 Corinthians 10:3-6). Purposely put pure thoughts in your mind, and don't allow false guilt to rob you of your peace in Christ. If you do sin in your thoughts or actions, repent quickly. Don't give up and fall into more sin. Be open. Be wise. Be pure. Get advice if you are beginning to feel something more than sister-to-brother love for someone.

Above all, remember that Jesus was a real man who experienced sexual temptation:

> For we do not have a high priest who is unable to sympathize with our weaknesses, but we have one who has been tempted in every way, just as we are—yet was without sin. (Hebrews 4:15)

Notice the last four words above, "yet was without sin." He is some-one who totally understands your feelings and temptations *and* has the power to help you not to give in to sin:

> Let us then approach the throne of grace with confidence, so that we may receive mercy and find grace to help us in our time of need. (Hebrews 4:16)

Feel free to talk with Jesus, with older Christians and with your par-ents about any nagging questions or concerns about sexual topics. No one should be more open and honest about the sexual relationship than those of us in the family of God—after all, sex was God's idea.

Sheila Jones
Boston, USA

Questions

1. Are you confused about any aspect of human sexuality? If so, ask an older Christian.
2. Do you think of sex as something dirty or wrong? How has this chap-ter helped you to change your view of sex?
3. Is there any sexual sin that you need to repent of? If so, decide who, besides God, you will confess to.
4. Has anyone touched you in a sexual way or in any way that has made you feel uncomfortable? If so, realize that this is not your shame; it is theirs. Talk to an older Christian about it so it will not stay hidden inside you. God can help you work through your hurt, fear, anger and confusion.

This material is reprinted from *Let It Shine* (Billerica, Mass.: Discipleship Publica-tions International, 1995), 109-116, 119, 123-125. (no longer in print)

Single and Happy in the Kingdom

I am a single woman and I can truly say, "I love my life! I wouldn't trade it with anyone." But, believe me, I've had my moments. Maybe you can relate...

I've had moments feeling like, "If I have to go on one more first date and answer the question 'So what's your favorite movie?' one more time I think I'll shoot myself." First dates are necessary, I know—but I want to get to the good stuff, get past the initial awkward "getting to know you" stage. I want someone to know *me*—that I get cranky when I'm hungry, that I'm a little obsessive-compulsive when it comes to cleaning and that I get a little competitive when playing games. And I long to know the idiosyncrasies of the man of my dreams.

I've also had moments of thinking, "If I have to go to one more wedding or wedding shower as a single, I'm going to die." You have to understand...I've been a disciple for fourteen years. So going to weddings means seeing all my longtime kingdom friends who are now living in suburbia with their spouses and children and who inevitably ask me that dreaded question, "So, are you dating anyone?"

I've had moments of longing, aching for that special someone, crying out to God, reminding him that it's not good for man to be alone. Surely there is some man out there who is alone...I can be his suitable helper. As God himself says, "Two are better than one" (Ecclesiastes 4:9).

I've had moments of feeling that life was supposed to turn out differently. I should be married and have kids by now. My twin sister has been married for almost eleven years and has two children. (She's been a disciple for thirteen and a half years.) Sometimes I've felt panic, fear that maybe I'll spend the rest of my life alone.

On a recent date, someone asked me how long I'd been a disciple, and when I told him, he responded, "And you've never been married?! How'd that happen?" Well, I decided to take that as a compliment.

The next question people usually ask is, "Have you ever dated steadily in the kingdom?" Yes, I have had that privilege once. I'm going to be vulnerable here. He was my first love. I dated in the world, but I never gave my heart to a man until I dated in the kingdom. We led a Bible Talk together and had a blast. We dated for five months and were best friends. I was convinced that he was my "missing piece." When God made it clear that we weren't meant to be together, I was crushed. It was the worst and the best time in my life—the best because I learned to cling to God like never before and the worst because my dream of true love had evaporated.

Psalm 23:5b-6 says,

> My cup overflows.
> Surely goodness and love will follow me
>   all the days of my life,
> and I will dwell in the house of the LORD forever.

Through all of this, I learned to look at the goodness that God had showered upon my life rather than looking at the one thing I didn't have that I wanted. I thanked God that he allowed me to love and be loved. I thanked God that the day after this relationship broke up, he gave me the gift of baptizing my dear friend Christine. I thanked God that I was surrounded by so many amazing friends who cared. I thanked God that he was teaching me to be compassionate for others going through heartbreak.

Isaiah 53:3 states that Jesus was a "man of sorrows, and familiar with suffering." I had to see this time and any similar time in the future as a call to know Jesus better, to embrace God and let him be my fortress. As I prayed to God for strength, he helped me have a devoted heart. Five years later, I did the wedding decorations for the man I had dated and for his beautiful wife, both of whom are special friends.

I remember being challenged by a disciple in her early twenties. She said that I needed to surrender to the idea that I may never be married. She pointed out the possibility that *perhaps* it is God's will for me to remain single forever. I had to wrestle in prayer over that one! While I absolutely agree that every disciple needs to be willing to utterly surrender her or his will to God's will, I also had to realize that surrender doesn't mean giving up hope. We all have to have those "Garden of Gethsemane" prayers where we wrestle and cry out to God with our faces to the ground. For me, Proverbs 13:12 rings true: "Hope deferred makes the heart sick." I need to hope. It makes me happy to hope. I know I'm not promised a husband and family. But it's important for me to remember and trust God's goodness. He knows the desire of my heart. God willing, it will happen. My God meets all my needs. Plus, having been around the kingdom for fourteen years, I've had the benefit of seeing many of my single friends' dreams come true after seven, ten, thirteen years of waiting for God's perfect plan. Unfortunately, I've also seen the agony of women who didn't wait on God's time.

So for now, while I'm single, I am going to enjoy life to the full. Here are some of the valuable lessons I've learned through the years:

1. Be thankful now or you won't be thankful later.

Luke 2:36-38 tells us of a prophetess named Anna. What strikes me about Anna is that her circumstances didn't dictate her joy. She became a widow after only seven years of marriage, and when she saw Jesus in the temple, she was eighty-four years of age. Yet, she was full of joy and thanksgiving. She was focused on Jesus. She was committed to God's people. Her mind was set on things above (Colossians 3:2). The reason she never grew bitter was because she remained thankful.

In my years as a disciple, I've seen too many women grow bitter because they stopped seeing all of God's blessings. Take time to write a letter to God thanking him for all the ways he's showered his love on you—even through the hard times. You've probably heard it said, "If you're not content as a single, you won't be content if you are married." After years of faithfully worshiping in the temple, Anna received the incredible privilege of seeing the Messiah, the promised Redeemer! If you persevere in joy, what blessings might God hold for you?! Learning to get your joy from God and not from circumstances will be an amazing gift you can someday offer to your spouse.

2. Don't bide time; live life to the full.

I think many of us can think, "When I get married, then I'll be content; then I won't feel lonely." We teach non-Christians the story of Solomon's search for happiness in the book of Ecclesiastes, yet we often fall into the same trap. God designed us so that only a relationship with him will truly satisfy us (Ecclesiastes 3:11). Want to know a secret? Married people feel lonely sometimes too. Only God can satisfy us. A marriage relationship is icing on the cake. The cake is the full life Jesus gives us now.

3. Make memories while you make friends for life.

Love is about what you can give, not about what you get. The cool thing is, God takes care of us—when we're thinking about others. My roommate, Gloria, and I came up with this fun idea of having a "Mary and Martha" home. Mary and Martha were always entertaining Jesus and the disciples in their home. (See Luke 10:38-42.) We've made it a practice to have a couple of brothers over for dinner, not for a date, but for a time to serve our hard-working brothers a home-cooked meal, hang out, talk, maybe watch a movie, just spend time together. This builds unity and healthy friendships with the brothers. It is also a lot of fun!

One of my pet peeves is hearing people complain about how their life should be different, but then doing nothing to change it. My friend Mary once told me, "Take responsibility for your own happiness." This stuck with me. My life will be what I make it. So, make it happen. Throw a party. Plan a road trip. Go for your career dreams. Invest everything in your relationships. Give your heart completely to the lost. Never stop learning. Do something daring. Do something you've never done before. Do *something*! Have fun. Live life passionately. And don't forget to take pictures of all the memories you're making. Through it all, you will be bonded for life with the friends you take along for the ride.

4. Be the best in every role you play.

One night at church I was heading for a parenting class (at the time I was discipling single moms). My friend saw me and said, "Pam, I didn't know you were a mom."

"Oh," I said, "I have many children in the kingdom." As a single, I have more time to give to others' children. I have time to give to the lost. I have time to give to God's family. I have time to disciple "spiritual children."

I have many roles: I am a daughter to my mom (my dad passed away two years ago after almost fifty-one years of marriage!). I am a sister to my four sisters and two brothers. I am an aunt to my precious nieces and nephews. I am a friend. I am a discipling partner. I am a teacher.

Every now and then, I need to reevaluate how I'm doing in each of these roles and make sure I'm giving God my best. I suggest you take time to evaluate your different roles. Of course, we can always do more. And although I am not yet a wife to a godly man, I am a wife to God. And that's my most important role.

So, as you also learn to stay thankful, to make the most of your time, to make memories and to be the best in every role you play, remember to keep it simple. Psalm 119:2 tells us the secret to true happiness:

> Blessed are they who keep his statutes
> and seek him with all their heart.

It's simple. Happiness doesn't come when we feel sorry for ourselves or when we think "the grass is greener on the other side." Happiness comes when we simply trust and obey, when we passionately seek God, when we dare to dream big and when we make the daily choices to see our dreams come true.

Jesus promises life to the full (John 10:10) for those who remain in him and for those who lay down their lives for others. Love God. Love people. Don't live a life of regret. Life is short. Live a little...no, live a lot...live a life so full that it makes a difference in the world!

Pamela Roy
Los Angeles, USA

God's Plan for a Wife

> Submit to one another out of reverence for Christ. Wives, submit to your husbands as to the Lord....Husbands, love your wives, just as Christ loved the church....However, each of you also must love his wife as he loves himself, and the wife must respect her husband.
> Ephesians 5:21-22, 25, 33

I still have the paper. "Why I Don't Want to Be Submissive" was the title. It was written in a flurry of anger and rebellion after my husband's speech at a marriage retreat twenty-six years ago. His speech was entitled "The Role of the Wife." My anger and arrogance poured out on the paper as I listed the reasons why I didn't like the whole idea. I long ago repented of such flagrant rebellion toward God's plan for order in the marriage relationship. But in subtle ways that old attitude can express itself still if I allow my heart to become hardened and self-focused.

As wives we must guard our hearts and keep them soft in order to love God's plan for us in our marriages. God spells out his plan for harmony and effectiveness in marriage in Ephesians 5:21-33. The key is in verse 21—each person should have a submissive, humble attitude toward the other out of respect for Christ and a desire to follow his example. Then out of this attitude each must take on the role God has assigned. The husband is to be the leader and to love his wife. The wife is to be the follower and respect her husband. A simple, straightforward plan. God's plan.

Submission

To help us be the wives we have been called to be, we must focus on the two responsibilities God gives us in Ephesians 5—to submit to and to respect our husbands. In Jesus we see the perfect picture of submission. We see that submission to the plan of God unleashes the power of God. Submission is a decision to trust God—to trust that his plan will work. This is what Jesus did. And the plan did work. In our arrogance and rebellion we thwart the plan of God. Then we stew around and complain about not seeing God's power working in our lives. Is it any wonder?

The cross says that you cannot get to the power without going through the plan. We cannot step over our marriages and expect to be the mothers, sisters or leaders we need to be. God will not allow it. The most basic test of a married woman's heart is in her willingness to be humble, vulnerable, submissive and giving to her husband. If these attitudes are present at the center of her life, concentric circles will ripple the same attitudes into every other relationship. Submission does not mean being spineless or being mindless. It does mean being selfless and being "prideless."

Respect

The Spirit led Paul to tell women they needed to respect their husbands. Why? Because it is more natural and much easier not to! The same rebellious and arrogant attitudes that keep a wife from accepting her role also cause her to attack and criticize her husband as he tries to be faithful to his role. Is he perfect? Is he always right? Is he always selfless? No, but we aren't either. These aren't the questions to be asked. Instead we need to ask, "Am I respecting my husband out of reverence for God?"

We as wives have a tremendous ability to undermine and destroy the confidence and growth of our husbands by not respecting them. We also have the God-given potential to encourage and build them up through our godly respect. Different husbands feel respected in different ways. The key is to want to show respect to your husband and then to find the ways to show him. For example—he may have asked you to balance the checkbook. If after three days you have not done it and have many "reasons" why, then he gets the message that what he asks is not a priority for you. He does not feel respected. You have not put him down in front of others. You have not told him, "I do not respect you." But your actions have told the real truth.

Years ago in our house the ironing board became a symbol of respect. I knew that Tom did not like to come into the bedroom and see the ironing board still up from that morning. Sometimes I was so rushed as I left that I didn't want to take the time to put it away. But I realized that if I respected him, I would take the extra few seconds that were required. Otherwise, I was showing that I respected the people I was rushing to be with more than I respected him.

God's plan is *the* plan—the *only* plan. Anytime I try to rewrite it, things go *bump* in my marriage. The message of this chapter is not that we should tolerate God's plan. It is not even that we should accept God's plan. It is that we should love God's plan. God will bless our lives and our ministries in incredible ways when we have a disciple's heart in our marriages.

Sheila Jones
Boston, USA

Reprinted and adapted from the *Boston Church of Christ Bulletin* (Vol. 10, No. 45, November 12, 1989). For more on being a godly wife, see *Love Your Husband* and *Friends and Lovers*, both published by DPI.

No Longer Two

"Haven't you read," he replied, "that at the beginning the Creator 'made them male and female,' and said, 'For this reason a man will leave his father and mother and be united to his wife, and the two will become one flesh'? So they are no longer two, but one. Therefore what God has joined together, let man not separate."

Matthew 19:4-6

Jesus teaches that God made husband and wife to be an inseparable unit. Their union supercedes their relationship to their parents. This commitment and loyalty are to be for life. They are to be *"no longer two, but one."* Jesus is referring to an intimate sharing of the whole of two people's lives, including the past, present and future. Consider the implications of such oneness in marriage.

The Past

Sharing in the Consequences of Past Sin

She committed sexual sin before they were married. He accepts her child as his. He made some greedy business decisions before he became a Christian. She is careful to budget as they dig out of a deep financial hole. When two people become one, they share the consequence of each other's past sins. Jesus' message would not support an attitude that says, "This is your fault. Why should I have to suffer for what you did?" Instead, it leads to an attitude that says: "We are both forgiven. As Jesus loved me enough to accept the consequences of my sin, so I will love you enough to share the consequences of your sin."

Sharing in the Consequences of Mistakes

We all forget to do important things. We all make mistakes in judgment. What my husband forgot to do today, I could just as easily forget tomorrow. We need to extend grace immediately because we have committed ourselves to be one. He forgets to pay a bill, and she gets an angry phone call from the bill collector. She forgets to turn the oven on, and he eats a peanut butter sandwich. But no matter what happens, oneness leaves no room for blaming and being self-righteous. As a wife, I need to freely own up to my mistakes, while never withholding respect from my husband because of his.

The Present

Not Making Selfish Decisions

In a marriage, we should never live like two singles, but we should accept the responsibility of living an intertwined life. If we did not want this, we should not have ever married. We cannot have "the best of both worlds." We chose marriage—therefore we must consider each other. When either partner lives and thinks independently, oneness is destroyed. When this pattern continues, "emotional divorce" is the result. When I feel insecure and helpless, I want to be a unit. I desperately need that acceptance and support. But when I feel confident and on top of things, sometimes I feel that being a unit curbs me. This is not only the sin of independence, but of tremendous self-centeredness. I want my husband to meet my emotional needs, and I do not care if his are met. This is not the oneness that Jesus talks about.

Encouraging Each Other's Ministry

If in my marriage I begin to feel competitive, think that my ministry is more important, or feel that my husband's success diminishes my ministry, I have violated the oneness of life that Jesus expects. The result is that neither ministry will be all it can be. I will not grow because of competitive, self-centered thoughts, and he will not be as effective because of my lack of support. Oneness, however, will enrich our ministries, even as it enriches our marriage. At a recent picnic, we divided into teams and ran relays. One thing we learned during the three-legged race was that it did not matter how agile one partner might be, she had to adapt to the other one. If they did not synchronize movements, neither of them would go anywhere. How true that is in a Christian marriage as we try to go forward in our ministries.

The Future

Committing Ourselves No Matter What

Life will bring some tough moments. Inevitably, we will have health problems and we will age. Oneness means saying to each other, "I am committed to you if you have a breast removed, or if you lose your hair; if your face becomes wrinkled or if you get cancer." Oneness brings a self-discipline and commitment that trains the eye and heart not to wander lustfully in search of a younger, more attractive body or face. My sister Emily and I saw the deep commitment our parents had to each other until death parted them. They faced poor health and trying times, but they stayed together for forty-eight years. They knew what Jesus meant by oneness.

Committing Ourselves to Do God's Will Together

If half of the unit says, "Let's go," and the other half says, "Let's stay," the net result is inertia or stagnation. The norm in the Christian marriage should be a oneness that says, "We trust God." The norm in a Christian wife's life should be a submission that says, "I trust my husband because I trust God."

The worst mistake any married person can make is to try to maintain independence. In the effort to be "yourself" and "do your own thing," you lose the oneness that is the essence and joy of marriage.

Sheila Jones
Boston, USA

Reprinted and adapted from the *Boston Church of Christ Bulletin* (Vol. 9, No. 44, November 6, 1988). For more on being a godly wife, see *Love Your Husband* and *Friends and Lovers*, both published by DPI.

A Godly Atmosphere in Your Home

The moment we walk into a home, we receive some kind of impression. What we see, what we hear, what we smell puts the experience together and gives us a feeling about that home. The atmosphere of our homes is a reflection of our hearts for the people who come to share that home with us.

After having had the opportunity to be in homes all over the world, from the wealthiest to the poorest in the kingdom, I have found this proverb to be true:

> By wisdom a house is built,
>   and through understanding it is established;
> through knowledge its rooms are filled
>   with rare and beautiful treasures. (Proverbs 24:3)

By Wisdom a House Is Built

According to this proverb, we build our homes through the wisdom that comes from God, and it comes with the highest standard of expectation for our lives. James' description of that wisdom gives us a good idea of the atmosphere that should permeate our homes:

> But the wisdom that comes from heaven is first of all pure; then peace-loving, considerate, submissive, full of mercy and good fruit, impartial and sincere. (James 3:17)

We can read this passage and test ourselves and our roommates or families to see how we are doing in promoting a godly atmosphere that welcomes and encourages others to join us. Are we reflecting the nature of God and his wisdom? In this chapter we will look at two of the attributes mentioned by James: peace-loving and sincere. Perhaps in your own study times you can consider the other six.

Peace-Loving

Are the people in your home committed to creating a peaceful atmosphere? This requires overlooking the little hurts and loving beyond the moment to treasure unity and forgiveness in our families. There is never a time for destructive language, bitterness, slamming doors, cool silence, or even staying hidden in a room, unwilling to communicate.

Our children were never allowed to speak in an angry tone to each other. Obviously there would be times of disagreement, but they had to find a way to express what they felt without retaliation. Adults, likewise, have not been given special permission from God to be rude and insensitive.

A peace-loving home does not necessarily mean a quiet home, and when our kids were growing up, the Metten family home was far from quiet. At the dinner table it was difficult to follow the flow of the conversation because everyone was excited to share his or her view. It was just so much fun to be together. There were certainly those moments when the atmosphere became tense, but each one of us got involved in bringing the situation to a positive conclusion. If the problem was between my daughter Jennifer and me, my husband Greg and son Matt would both help us to have a godly response to each other by helping us to see our own faults. This kind of honest communication helped each of us to feel loved and secure.

Several years ago I received a phone call from a college student who had lived with us for a short time. He had made some bad choices and basically left the church and his relationship with God. We loved him a lot even though it was a painful time for all of us, especially our kids. But thankfully he had come back to God and was stronger than ever. When he called, one of the things he said was, "I would like to come to your home and have a meal with your family. I miss those times together." A peace-loving home leaves a lasting impression on people.

Sincere

It will never work to put on the pretense of a warm, inviting home. An insincere heart is one of the easiest attitudes to discern; people feel uncomfortable around those who are fake. If we are sincere, people will feel it and be attracted to us. The people in our family will certainly know if we are being insincere because once the door is closed and the friends are gone, we will be different. If that is what happens in your home, then you are teaching that it is okay to say one thing and then do another. If you are self-controlled when others are around and yell at each other when by yourselves, you will destroy your family and your influence on others.

Being sincere means that you have the *heart* of a servant, not just the *skills* of a servant. It means that you want to help, not just that you are expected to help. Sincerity is an attitude of the heart, not just a lifestyle.

When we lived in India, our days were long, tiring and at times very emotionally challenging. But every evening before we all went to sleep, we would sit on the bed and play some card games and talk. It was a bonding time for our family and anyone else who was there with us. We would talk and laugh and sometimes even cry together. The sincerity born in those special times together bonded us and caused our home to be warm and inviting to others who joined us from time to time.

When I'm asked where my favorite place to live has been, my response comes easily...Bombay, India. Although we lived in other Indian cities, Bombay will always be dear to my heart as our first Indian home. There I learned what it means to be sincerely cared for. Rosie Athaide's family made me feel at home. She would spend her last rupee to buy me a bottled drink (because of my health problems). Whenever I was sad, it was to Rosie's house that I headed for encouragement and guidance. Six family members lived in one room, but they always found a place for me.

Rooms Filled with Rare and Beautiful Treasures

Many Indian Christian homes are only one room, but in that one room can be found all of the treasures of God. You will rarely find expensive furniture and fine china, but from the moment you walk into the room you will be served and loved. All of your needs will be met, and you will feel like a dignitary in a wealthy Indian palace. The rare and beautiful treasure of a home is the safe and loving atmosphere created there.

If we are to fill our rooms with the rare and beautiful treasure of a godly atmosphere, we must take time to plan. It will not just spontaneously happen. Chaos communicates a message to others to stay away. The secret to having an orderly home is to be organized. For years I have planned my meals for an entire week. When the children were at home, I took time to think through the needs of each family member and how I could meet those needs. I also considered how I could meet the needs of friends. Our week always included a family night dinner and devotional that we often shared with others.

It is so important to be organized so we can plan to have others into our home and be ready to receive them enthusiastically. Having a plan makes a busy home feel relaxed and inviting. People don't see the planning, but they feel the effects of it.

How would your home be described if someone walked in unannounced today? Would the treasure that fills each room be an atmosphere that is inviting and warm? Would there be a sense of protection and concern for each person as if they were family?

We must build our homes with wisdom and create the rare and beautiful treasure of a godly atmosphere—the same atmosphere Jesus is preparing for us:

"In my Father's house are many rooms;...I am going there to prepare a place for you. And if I go and prepare a place for you, I will come back and take you to be with me that you also may be where I am." (John 14:2-3)

Shelley Metten
Los Angeles, USA

This article is reprinted from the hardback *The Fine Art of Hospitality* (Billerica, Mass.: Discipleship Publications International, 1995), 41-44. (no longer in print)

Friendship with Adult Daughters

God is the giver of "every good and perfect gift" (James 1:17). The relationship we can have with our adult daughters is one of these gifts! If your daughter is a disciple, you will be able to identify with the joys of this gift. If your daughter is not a disciple, the *potential* for an incredible relationship is still there. Either way, we can always be learning how to deepen the bond and enjoy the blessings God has in store for us.

My daughters are twenty-seven and twenty-five. (I also have a thirty-year-old son, who has a two-year-old son and another on the way, but that is another topic.) My girls and I benefit not only from the mother/daughter bond, but also from the joy of close friendship.

Mothers and Daughters

Mothers and daughters usually end up sharing common values and perspectives. Our outlook on life and ways of viewing certain challenges and situations are very similar, because, after all, we have been coping with life together for almost twenty years!

It is so much fun to share common memories and traditions. We often relax in the same ways. (My family likes to eat, watch movies and play board games.) And then there are those silly sayings and phrases that have special meaning to "just us."

As mother and daughter we usually have some personality traits in common and along with that, a common sinful nature! What has helped one be victorious can help the other as well. Not long ago, when I shared my journal *What I Am Learning* with one of my daughters, she was very encouraged because many of the entries applied to her struggles, too.

There is great security in knowing that the mother/daughter relationship is for a lifetime. My girls will always be my daughters, and I will always be their mother. The unconditional love I feel from them is what Naomi must have felt when Ruth said that nothing but death would separate the two of them (Ruth 1:16-18). I know that my daughters will never leave me in thought or closeness of heart. The trust I feel with them helps me in my other relationships, teaching me to give my heart there as well.

Friends

As friends, we are able to talk on a "feelings" level. We share disappointments, frustrations and sadness. We share goals, dreams, victories and joy. We share embarrassing moments, humiliating lessons and life-changing insights. Regular phone calls between us always include requests to pray about some person, situation, goal, challenge or dream.

We can "let out hair down" and truly relax with each other. We can be silly. As friends, we bear with each other's quirks and idiosyncrasies. We don't feel the need to correct every little thing. We give each other the benefit of the doubt that we love God, we're not perfect and we're working on things.

Friends protect each other. Mothers of adults, although not as involved in protecting their children's surroundings and circumstances as before, still protect through prayer, encouraging words and Scripture. At this stage, the daughters become protectors as well. My daughters protect me with concern, encouragement and prayer when they detect the slightest hint of an attack from Satan. For example, one of my daughters recently said, "I prayed for you to have a great holiday, Mom, even though you have no children at home this year." We both knew that the potential was there for me to become depressed and ungrateful! What a blessing to have a friendship where you watch each other's back in the spiritual battle.

How can we nurture this mother/daughter friendship and avoid possible pitfalls? Consider the following suggestions.

Mothers

Transition from Parental Authority to Friend

Parental authority is a necessity when our children are young. During this time we train them to respect and obey us as parents. We teach them our values and our love for God. But from the preteen years to adulthood our children begin to have their own views, opinions and convictions. We want them to develop their *own* hearts for God, love for the Scriptures and Christlike value systems. During this time, it is very important to do a lot of listening, a lot of explaining the "whys" for things and a lot of training in how to think. Our goal is to become a trusted friend and respected counselor. Our authority turns to influence—an influence born out of our unconditional love for our children and their respect for our example of living out what we believe. Perfect example? No. But open, humble, repentant and faithful.

When my daughters were teenagers, disciples helped me to see the value of listening to their feelings and becoming more of a friend. I am so thankful for that input because God blessed those efforts. My daughter Holly writes:

> The most important thing in any relationship is unconditional love. That's what has built such depth and security in my relationship with my mom. I know she loves me no matter what. As a teenager, I went through tumultuous times of rebellion. It was important for me to know that even though I had hurt her, she still loved me anyway. It was important for me

to be able to express to her the insecurity and shame I'd felt because of messing up, and for her to reassure me that she'd forgiven me, that she loved me and believed in me. Because of this foundation of trust, I was able to be real with her and share with her my struggles as I got older and throughout my college years, as well as the challenges of today. She is my greatest confidant. As the teen ministry leader of our region, I work with teens who feel that they can't talk to their moms about how they really think and feel. They feel scared of their reaction or feel like when they do get open, there is no forgiveness.

As a parent, you have the responsibility before God to raise your children in the ways of God. This means restricting and disciplining them as is appropriate. But it is extremely important that they feel listened to, that they feel heard. If you shut them down by your reaction, they won't be open next time. Don't just disciple their behavior, but rather draw out their heart (Proverbs 20:5). Even if they don't want to repent and do what's right, they need to feel unconditionally loved by you—a love that's not based on performance. They need to be secure that no matter how they feel or what they've done, you still love them and believe in them (they will know if it's just words or how you really feel!), even as you rightly discipline them. Express love despite weaknesses and sin. And they will want to come to you for input, advice, and guidance now and especially as they become adults. The people we help the most are the ones who feel secure in our love for them. My mom has been the greatest help and influence in my life and relationship with God, thanks to her undying love for him and for me.

Involved but Not Overbearing

When we try to control our daughters' lives, we've crossed the line! This usually happens when we do the following:

(a) We want to shield our daughters from hurt rather than watch God put them through the hardships and challenges which will strengthen and mature them. Our role is to help them through, not prevent the lesson.

(b) We trust our own opinions over everyone else's. As our daughters become teenagers and then adults, they will be guided and influenced by others. Teen workers, ministry leaders, teachers and eventually husbands will have impact or authority in their lives. We need to trust God with the big picture. Rather than feeling threatened, envious or resentful, we can be thankful for these "many advisers" (Proverbs 15:22).

Involvement is important. The Bible teaches the principle of older women training younger women in all kinds of important areas of life (Titus 2:4,5). Again, we can learn from the relationship between Ruth and Naomi how much the younger woman benefits from the wisdom and experience of the older. (Ruth ends up with a great husband and a blessed life!) I remember going to the extreme in trying to let my daughters live their own lives and not interfere. Finally, the sister discipling me encouraged me to speak up and say what I thought. She reminded me of how much they needed my counsel and guidance and would respect me for it. Sometimes we have to risk ruffling feathers, but God always blesses courageous love. This is what my older daughter Angie says:

> I am twenty-seven years old, have been married for three years, and I will celebrate my thirteenth spiritual birthday in a few days. I thank God for pouring blessings into my life, and I am especially grateful for the parents and family he gave me. Because of God and his perfect ways, I am blessed with the most incredible relationship with my mom. We are not only mother and daughter—we are sisters and best friends. I know that I can tell her anything in the world, and she will love me just the same. I can share my fears, my struggles, my anxieties, my sin, and she does not react or judge or condemn me. She listens, she relates, she shares her own struggles and what helps her to overcome, and then over and over again, she directs me to the truth of God's word.
>
> I tend to feel guilty often (an "accused nature"), and my mom helps me to remember that my struggles are common and normal. Yet at the same time, there have been several occasions when she has lovingly told me the truth even when it was contrary to my desires. I am so thankful for those conversations; I was able to listen to the difficult truth because I knew she cared for me and spoke out of love and concern for me. It is so amazing to get to be in the battle together, strengthening and encouraging each other along the way. We absolutely treasure the moments we get to spend together! And all of this is because of God's abundant love and flawless ways.

Connected Through Thick and Thin

When one of us hurts the other it is tempting to withdraw emotionally. In this way we try to avoid the anger, frustration, hurt, fear or sadness we feel. Or we may try to deal with the hurt of sin through scolding or belittling. This just causes walls to go up, openness and vulnerability to disappear and the close emotional connection to be lost. Prayer, help from an objective friend and then honesty with each other, in love, is always the answer to conflict.

Geographic distance can be another hindrance to emotional closeness. Regular phone conversations (usually once a week) keep my daughters and me feeling close. We pick up from the last phone call and share all the news since then! We are encouraged to see how God is working in our lives and we have an opportunity to be vulnerable and real and giving.

Another way we stay close is through special cards and gifts. I love to find good "deals" that are perfect for my children. These help them know that I think about them all the time.

Of course, visits are the best. I load up the refrigerator and cabinets with far too much food, prepare favorite dishes, and make the bedroom comfy with candles, candy and reading material. We take advantage of every moment we have together: prayer walks and arm-in-arm shopping trips, meals shared with friends so everyone gets to know one another, and a workday schedule that involves my daughter whenever possible.

Daughters

Learning from Anyone in Humility

It may be tempting to turn a deaf ear to your mother, thinking that her input is too clouded by emotion, too slanted by opinion or just too outdated! Take what is helpful, value her experience, and trust her motives. This will keep you from becoming critical, defensive or closed.

Beware of the other extreme—putting your mother on a pedestal, thinking her way is the only way. This will cause problems when it comes to submitting to a husband and other leaders God puts in your life.

Take Time

Any great relationship must be nurtured. In today's fast-paced society, along with the disciple's "life to the full," it can be easy to crowd out time for communication. If mothers are placed on the far back burner, this relationship cannot be kept current, alive and growing.

Many of you may read this chapter and long for closeness with your mother or your daughter. Life situations are varied and complicated, and each requires careful prayer and dedication to repair the relational damage. But I do want to offer some general tips on ways to repair a relationship.

Apologize. Thankfully, as disciples we're always learning and growing. One of my daughters, in her teen years, had to have the help of an aunt to talk to me about some embarrassing events of her life. I realized some of my mistakes in communication. I apologized to her because I had often neglected to ask questions about how she was feeling and what she was thinking. After hearing my apology, she burst into tears and admitted that she'd thought I hadn't cared. What a breakthrough we had in feeling close!

Ask. Open yourself up to input. You might start by saying, "I love you. How can I make you feel my love?" In the area of communication, I discovered that one of my daughters feels love if I just listen to her problems without giving solutions right away. My other daughter feels love if I have a ready Scripture or a new perspective for her to think about.

Act. Put into practice what you learn. Work consistently to meet your daughter's or mother's need, whatever it is: time spent together, patient listening, verbal encouragement, respect, greater vision, etc.

I try to talk on the phone every day to my mom who was widowed six months ago and lives 700 miles away. I listen to all she has done and all she is frustrated or worried about. I try to tell her some good news and make her laugh. She often says, "Thank you for all you do for me"—meaning the phone calls. We are closer than we have ever been in our lives.

As we clear up past hurts, listen and learn how to love, and then make changes, positive results will happen, because love never fails!

God's plan for mothers and daughters is a unique friendship. What a "good and perfect gift"! If we nurture it through unconditional love, respect and humility, it will last forever.

Mary Lou Craig
Columbia, S.C., USA

Choosing Faith over Fear

Like most couples who have been eagerly waiting to start a family, Jeff (my husband) and I were joyfully anticipating the birth of our first child. In November of 2000, however, I woke up around midnight to find that I was bleeding heavily. Horrified and heartbroken, I woke up Jeff. As we waited for a call back from the doctor, we prayed. The doctor said it sounded like I had already lost the baby, but told me to go to the emergency room. As we drove to the hospital, we prayed. Somewhere along the way, it clicked in my mind that I had a decision to make: Would I let faith and surrender dominate in my heart, or would I be controlled by fear?

During my nineteen years as a disciple, the sins that have plagued me the most have been fear and worry—faithlessness. I believe that God decided that my pregnancy would be the crucible in which to refine my character and to help me to make lasting changes in this area. On the way to the hospital, I decided that I was going to trust God—whether we had lost the baby or not—and I was going to believe that he was working and had a plan. We prayed again while we waited at the hospital for the doctor.

A heartbeat! They had found a heartbeat. We were hesitant to get too excited and had such mixed emotions because something was obviously wrong, or I would not be bleeding so heavily. An ultrasound revealed that I had placenta previa, a condition in which the placenta touches or covers the cervix and can easily detach. (I was also given a RhoGAM shot because we found out that I was Rh negative.) Placenta previa happens in less than one percent of pregnancies, and there was nothing I had done to cause it. The placenta was completely covering my cervix. The doctor said that if I limited my activities we could perhaps avoid losing the baby. If we could sustain the pregnancy to twenty-eight weeks, the baby could probably survive if they did an emergency C-section. In any event, I would definitely have to have a C-section because the baby could die and I could hemorrhage if they tried a vaginal delivery. The only hope the doctor offered was that sometimes, as the baby grows and the uterus expands, the placenta "moves" to the side.

I was very afraid about the possibility of having a C-section because we have a family history of being allergic and/or sensitive to painkillers and anesthesia. I was also full of fear about the impact this was going to have on my life. With my activities restricted, how was I going to continue to work and contribute financially? How was I going to be able to get simple things like the vacuuming and the food shopping done? How would I be able to serve other people? I was disappointed that I would not be able to do a lot of things I wanted to do. I felt bad that Jeff was going to have to carry more than his share of the load and that our sexual relationship had to be put on hold. He was only concerned about my safety and that of the baby, but I still felt bad. But we decided to trust God with these issues and we made a plan. We also began earnestly praying that not only would the placenta "move" out of the way, but that I would be able to have a vaginal delivery with no painkillers or anesthesia.

Blessings in Disguise

The amazing thing was that we immediately began to see many good things coming out of this difficult situation, the most striking of which was the improvement in my relationship with my physical family. Walls were broken down that I had not been able to tear down through the last nineteen years. My relationships within my family had been strained ever since I became a disciple and had gotten worse through the years, to the point that I was not invited to my brother's wedding. There was a lot of hurt on both sides. We had begun to communicate and to try to work things through when we went down to Florida to visit them in May of 2000, but much still seemed unresolved in my heart—and I did not know how to "fix" it. When we began experiencing problems with the pregnancy, and especially with my health, my family rallied around me and took the opportunity to reconcile and to rebuild their relationship with me. We are in the process of working through old hurts and miscommunications. It is an amazing blessing to have the hope again of having a great relationship with my family after all of these years.

I also developed a greater sensitivity to the physically challenged and "shut-ins" in our fellowship. My pregnancy challenges were temporary, but those with chronic illnesses may never "get better."

New Challenges

Despite another bleeding episode, we "made it" to twenty-eight weeks. Jeff and I were so happy—it was looking very likely that we would get to have our baby! But our joy was quickly overshadowed by concern when we learned that another problem seemed to have developed. The doctor discovered that I seemed to be leaking amniotic fluid. I was sent to the hospital again. She said that I needed to be ready to have an emergency C-section and that our very premature baby would be born that night if her fears were confirmed. I was very afraid. We prayed some more. The doctor ordered another ultrasound, and it was then that we found out the good news—not only was the amniotic fluid apparently okay, but the placenta was out of the way and there was a good chance that we could have a "normal" delivery! We were ecstatic!

Imagine our disappointment, then, when we found out shortly afterward that I had gestational diabetes. The doctor said that there was a good chance that the baby would become too large for a vaginal delivery and that I would likely need to have a C-section. Additionally, I would have to stick myself four times a day to test my blood sugar, and I would have to follow a special diet to try to keep the baby from becoming too large.

I was crushed. My hopes had been raised that the remainder of my pregnancy would be less problematic. I had only gained ten pounds in the whole pregnancy despite not being able to exercise, and it was very disappointing to have this new issue to deal with. I could not see how anything good could come of it. And, again, I was very afraid. I very carefully followed the diet and continued to pray that despite everything, I would still be able to have the kind of delivery I wanted.

Once again, something good came out of my challenge. I have had difficulty with my weight since seventh grade, but because of the pregnancy I learned that I have a slow metabolism (issues with my thyroid gland) and that my body produces insulin and processes sugar abnormally. Maintaining a healthy weight is challenging for me because of these medical issues. But I realized that by using some of the dietary principles I learned during my pregnancy, I can keep my weight down going forward and also avoid having full-fledged diabetes when I am older.

Blessings from God

Another area in which I had been fearful at the beginning of the pregnancy was our finances. I did not want to become a materialistic mother who was consumed with "things," but I did want my baby to have what he needed. Although Jeff and I both work full-time, and although Jeff is in school and has made a lot of progress recently in his career, we still were not in a position to be able to afford much for the baby. I prayed that God would provide everything that he needed. I prayed specifically that the friends whom we have who are not disciples would be especially generous.

God answered my prayers more than I asked or imagined. We received at least one hundred gifts, some whole basketfuls from friends who are not disciples. Our friends who are disciples have also been incredibly generous. (The disciples in New Hampshire threw an amazing shower for me, and I am very grateful.) We were given everything that we needed—and a lot of "extras" as well. I had wanted a bassinet, but could not justify the expense, as it is something that is only used for a few months. One of our neighbors came over and asked if we wanted a bassinet she had that had never been used!

God had answered so many prayers. My fear was being conquered with faith. A few days after my due date, my doctor wanted to try to induce my labor since she was concerned about the baby's size and since she was going out of town. I felt that inducing was not the best decision, so I prayed that God would block it somehow if my hunch was correct. When I arrived at the hospital to be induced, there was "no room at the inn." Every bed was taken! Many women went into labor that day, and there was simply no room for me! My doctor flew out that night.

The next Sunday morning, April 29, at 5:00 A.M., my membranes ruptured. God had answered another prayer because I had asked for him to help my mother feel a part of things. It was hard for her to be in Florida and not to be here. She had gone into labor with me exactly thirty-seven years before, on April 29, at 5:00 A.M., and my labor progressed almost exactly as hers had, which made her feel a special bond with me. On April 30, my birthday, our beautiful son was born—vaginally, and without the use of any anesthesia or painkillers, just as I had asked in prayer. David Paul was only eight pounds and nine ounces, despite the concerns of having a huge baby because of the gestational diabetes.

Friends had given me the advice to have several scriptures in mind to focus on to help me to remain calm and at peace throughout the delivery, which I was able to do. (See the scriptures at the end of the chapter.) This enabled us to share with the midwife and nurses who delivered him, since they noticed something different about us. And my fears about my doctor being out of town? It turned out that not only did the midwife who replaced her help me tremendously, but she was already being reached out to by two disciples from the church unbeknownst to me—one is her neighbor and the other works for her husband! God was working in all the details.

God truly increased my faith and taught me a great deal about overcoming my fears through specific prayer and claiming and trusting God's promises. I wish that I could say that I have no fear in any of my current challenges, but that is not true. However, my experiences throughout the pregnancy have encouraged me to continue to go to God in specific prayer about the areas in my life right now. More often than not, I am choosing faith over fear.

"For nothing is impossible with God."
"I am the Lord's servant," Mary answered. "May it be to me as you have said." Then the angel left her. (Luke 1:37-38)

Let us fix our eyes on Jesus, the author and perfecter of our faith, who for the joy set before him endured the cross, scorning its shame, and sat down at the right hand of the throne of God. (Hebrews 12:2) [Note: I focused on the fact that if Jesus was willing to go through the pain of the cross to have a relationship with me—"good" pain—I could go through the "good" pain of labor to have a relationship with my son.]

He tends his flock like a shepherd:
He gathers the lambs in his arms
and carries them close to his heart;
he gently leads those that have young. (Isaiah 40:11)

But women will be saved through childbearing—if they continue in faith, love and holiness with propriety. (1 Timothy 2:15) [Note: I focused on spiritual "safety"—and on conducting myself in faith, love and holiness with propriety during the labor and delivery.]

As it is written: "I have made you a father of many nations." He is our father in the sight of God, in whom he believed—the God who gives life to the dead and calls things that are not as though they were.

Against all hope, Abraham in hope believed....Yet he did not waver through unbelief regarding the promise of God, but was strengthened in his faith and gave glory to God, being fully persuaded that God had power to do what he had promised. (Romans 4:17-21)

"I prayed for this child, and the LORD has granted me what I asked of him." (1 Samuel 1:27)

When it was time for Elizabeth to have her baby, she gave birth to a son. Her neighbors and relatives heard that the Lord had shown her great mercy, and they shared her joy. (Luke 1:57-58)

Lisa Morris
Boston, USA

We Can Do It!

> I can do everything through him who gives me strength.
> Philippians 4:13

We *can* do everything through him who gives us strength! Being a single mother is certainly a challenging life. God's ideal plan is for children to be raised by both a mother and a father. Due to sin and tough challenges, though, many women find themselves raising their children all alone. But we are not alone! God is our father and the father of our children.

> A father to the fatherless, a defender of widows,
>   is God in his holy dwelling.
>   God sets the lonely in families... (Psalm 68:5-6a)

If we submit to our heavenly father, we can live a life filled with passion and purpose. We *can* raise our children to be disciples.

My Story

I was met while I was in college, divorced, with a three-year-old son. As a young Christian the first area of my life that had to change was my relationship with my son, Dustin. Up to that point in his life he had not received much discipline. As I repented, he changed so much and so quickly it was amazing. As he became secure, he also became a real joy. God's plan of discipleship is truly the only way. He changed so much that my sister and my brother-in-law, who had been deacons in their denomination, decided to study the Bible and later became true disciples.

I led a Bible Talk in the campus ministry, and then in the singles ministry. After moving to San Diego, I led a ministry almost entirely of single moms. That is when I began to realize that there were a lot of us around! After being single for three years, I met and married my husband, John Rosness. In those three years, I had personally met eight people who became disciples—to God's glory. Three of those were people who were initially impressed with my relationship with Dustin. Now eight years later, John and I are in the ministry, leading the church in Reno, Nevada, and we recently baptized Dustin into Christ. God has been good to me!

I'm not anything special. What I mean is that I'm not some superstar, intellectual giant or some mega-talented woman. I'm just a Puerto Rican ex-party girl from nowhere who realized that the God of the universe was giving me a chance to start my life all over again—and I jumped at the chance. Yes, I've struggled as a disciple over the past eleven years, but I never quit and I clung to God's promises. Dustin is fourteen; he is the starting quarterback on his freshman football team, and a top athlete in all sports he competes in. He is handsome, warm, loving, popular and he has chosen to follow Jesus over the world. God can do anything with our lives if we let him. What will you let him do with yours?

I want to share with you five keys to living life as a powerful single mom.

1. Your Relationship with God

He has showed you, O man, what is good.
And what does the LORD require of you?
To act justly and to love mercy
and to walk humbly with your God. (Micah 6:8)

As a single mother you play many vital roles: disciple, mom, dad, nurse, provider, housekeeper, chef, friend, mechanic, landscaper, tutor and more. You must be filled up with God so you can pour yourself out. Your main goal is to get yourself and your children to heaven. This will never happen without a growing relationship with God. Only he can save you. God is the best father, husband, provider and friend in the universe. (See Jeremiah 3:14.) Have a set time to be with God daily and protect it.

Sharing your faith comes from your relationship with God. Be creative. Take your children to the park; share when you're with them; reach out in your children's classroom and daycare, and as you go. I was engaged, working full time, and in leadership when I invited one of Dustin's friend's mom to church. She became a disciple and helped serve at my wedding. Isn't God amazing?

2. Your Relationship with Your Children

Train a child in the way he should go,
and when he is old he will not turn from it. (Proverbs 22:6)

The rod of correction imparts wisdom,
but a child left to himself disgraces his mother. (Proverbs 29:15)

The greatest thing we can do for our children is to love them, and true love means sacrifice; that is how Jesus loved us. Do not neglect your children. Spend time with them, and in that time direct them to God. You need to walk as a disciple in your own life and then you need to teach them how to apply it to their lives.

Have meaningful time with them daily. Pray every night with them—pray for them, the people you are reaching out to, situations at school, other disciples and more. Be sure you are praying for them in your own time with God. Never, ever give up praying for them. (See Luke 18:1-8.)

Educate yourself! Read books, especially those written by disciples (for example: *Raising Awesome Kids in Troubled Times*[1] and *The Wonder Years*[2] by the Laings). See the list of other recommended books on parenting on page 215.

Don't be afraid to discipline your children. Romans 12:2 tells us not to conform any longer to the pattern of this world. Do not buy into the psychological garbage being taught in our society that kids should not receive discipline. Study it out in Proverbs. (See Proverbs 13:24.) God knows what he is doing. Follow his word. Certainly if counseling is needed, get it.[3] Also be sure to get lots of advice from spiritual leaders (especially if an ex-husband is involved). There may be legal issues you will need to consider.

Repent of all bitterness and resentment you have toward your ex-husband. Not only will it hinder your relationship with God, you could eventually have bitterness toward the children you share with him. (See Romans 12:18-21.)

3. Humility and Gratitude

> Humility and the fear of the LORD
>   bring wealth and honor and life. (Proverbs 22:4)

Deal with sin. (See Proverbs 16:18-20.) Below are a few areas where pride can cause us to fall:

Independence: "I don't need anyone!" (See Romans 12:4-5.) It is most likely you have been hurt in the past. This is true of many single mothers, and as a result, they have decided to never rely on anyone again. As a disciple of Jesus, you need to repent of this attitude and decide to trust those who are helping you grow spiritually.

Self-Pity: "No one understands." "It's so hard." "Where do I fit in?" First of all, God understands, and many wonderful, spiritual people do love you and do want to help. They don't have to be a single parent with your exact situation for you to be able to learn from them.

---

[1]Sam and Geri Laing, *Raising Awesome Kids in Troubled Times* (Billerica, Mass.: Discipleship Publications International, 1994).

[2]Sam and Geri Laing, Elizabeth Laing Thompson, *The Wonder Years,* (Billerica, Mass.: Discipleship Publications International, 2001).

[3]I recommend that you read chapter 12, "Childhood Disorders," in *The Wonder Years* to help you evaluate whether your child needs to have counseling or to go on medication.

Guilt: This one is so important to deal with, or you will be self-focused. Give in to guilt, and life with you will be no fun for your children. Accept God's mercy and grace. You desperately need it. (And your children desperately need you to accept it from God and extend it to them.)

In order to grow spiritually and to be successful as a single mom, you need to have two specific attitudes:

Gratitude: This attitude is the greatest weapon against all the sins listed above. Treasure this time in your life. Focus on the positive. Make special memories. Dustin still talks about "Dustin Days." He and I used to play all his favorite games and eat his favorite foods. (See Proverbs 15:15.)

Teachability: Above all things, have a teachable heart. (See Proverbs 11:14 and 12:15.) You must die to defensiveness and excuse-making, or your children will imitate those negative flaws. Be approachable regarding your children and your parenting skills. Initiate getting input by asking questions like, "What do you see in my son that needs to change," or, "What can I do to help my daughter in that area?" Get close to at least two families who you want to imitate, and get input regularly. Be open to input from anyone. I started off in the campus ministry and lived with young girls who never had kids, but they helped me and gave me plenty of input. Don't ignore correction. (See Proverbs 10:17.)

4. Your Schedule

Make plans by seeking advice;
> if you wage war, obtain guidance. (Proverbs 20:18)

Do you fail to plan? Then you should plan to fail. You must have a schedule to live by. Again, seek advice. The church is full of women who live disciplined lives who can help you. Have a standard schedule as much as possible. For example: get up at the same time every day, eat dinner at the same time every night, put the kids to bed at the same time every night, and so on. This will give your children security and confidence.

Suggestion: Have two families who watch your kids for events such as devotionals and dates. In turn you can serve these families by babysitting for them.

5. Personal Discipline

He who ignores discipline comes to poverty and shame,
> but whoever heeds correction is honored. (Proverbs 13:18)

This one is a challenge. There are times when we are drained and feel overwhelmed. This is when discipline usually goes out the door. Strive for it. Life will be so much more fun if you do!

For example, be disciplined with your finances. Have a budget. Get help from mature financial advisors in the church. This was a tough one for me. A friend had me put together a plan and she held me to it. It was challenging. But to God's glory, when I married John I had only one school loan I was still paying off. John was fired up to marry a woman not loaded down in debt. Discipline didn't seem pleasant at the time, but it made me happy in the long run.

Suggestion: Have a standard menu and shopping list. This helps you shop for only what you need, saves money and helps with knowing what to cook every night. Grocery shop only once a week. Going back and forth to the store wastes time and money.

Another area for discipline is weight and personal hygiene. (See 2 Corinthians 5:20.) God has made us ambassadors of Christ. We need to die to the old image of ourselves and take on the new one. Again, initiate getting help in this area. I believe strongly in the Weigh Down Diet which is Biblically based, and you don't have to go to the gym to lose weight.[4] Many women can help you with your style of dress, make-up and so on. Don't be too prideful to get that help.

Delight yourself in the LORD
   and he will give you the desires of your heart. (Psalm 37:4)

I will never forget when Ali Jackson, the girl who first met me, read this scripture to me. I didn't think I could become a disciple. I was so afraid to trust, believe, hope and step out on faith. When I read this scripture, I believed God put this one in there just for me. I have clung to this scripture for years, and I read it to my son the day my husband and I baptized him. I am still clinging to it. It's a promise and I'm living it. You can too. As single moms, with God's help, we can do it!

Debbie Rosness
Reno, USA

[4]Gwen Shamblin, *The Weigh Down Diet* (New York: Doubleday & Co. Inc., 1997).

Special-Needs Children: FAQs

The following answers to frequently asked questions are a collaborative effort of staff and parents from the Spiritual Resource Ministry, Hope Technology School and Parent Support Group in San Francisco.

1. Why does my child have special needs?

"My thoughts are completely different from yours," says the LORD. "And my ways are far beyond anything you could imagine. For just as the heavens are higher than the earth, so are my ways higher than your ways and my thoughts higher than your thoughts." (Isaiah 55:8-9, New Living Translation)

God's reasons are completely different from ours. It's not our responsibility to always understand. But it *is* our responsibility to always trust. People with differences have been with us from the beginning of time. In the Gospels we find that twenty-six of Jesus' thirty-four recorded miracles involved helping people with some kind of special need or disability.

There are many lessons we can learn from both adults and children with special needs. We need tolerance and acceptance of human differences. The world can learn acceptance and freedom from hate and prejudice through the love seen in God's kingdom towards those with special needs.

It is difficult to see our children suffer because they are different. We suffer with them. But we are being transformed to become like Jesus when we suffer. Suffering helps us to develop perseverance. James 1:4 teaches us we must develop perseverance so that we may be mature and complete in Christ. Here are the fruits of perseverance:

- miracles (2 Corinthians 12:12)
- righteousness (1 Timothy 4:16)
- endurance (Hebrews 12:1)
- harvest (Luke 8:11-15)

There are generally two reasons we struggle to be fruitful and grow—lack of faith and an unwillingness to persevere.

When our child is born with special needs, we can begin to question God. Why, after we have tried to do everything right, would God give us a child with special needs? Often, we have to count the cost again of our devotion to God. In the midst of trials, we must decide if we will hold to the commitment we made to follow Jesus no matter what life would bring us.

As disciples our purpose in life should be the same as Jesus' purpose. He healed and touched the unlovable. The Bible often refers to people with special needs being healed:

• A boy robbed of speech	Mark 9:17-27
• Bartimaeus healed of blindness	Mark 10:46-52
• The centurion's servant healed of an unknown sickness	Luke 7:2-10
• Royal official's son healed of an unknown sickness	John 4:46-53
• An invalid for 38 years healed and able to walk	John 5:5-9
• A man crippled from birth healed and able to walk	Acts 3:2-8
• Aeneas healed after eight years of paralysis	Acts 9:33-35
• A man from Lystra healed of crippled feet he had since birth	Acts 14:8-10

The very heart of God is seen through the compassion of Jesus touching the lives of those with special needs. Let us strive to be imitators of Jesus.

2. How does the NET World Sector affect special-needs children?

One focus of the NET World Sector is "loving the exceptional children." We will accomplish this goal through a variety of ways, including Spiritual Resource Ministries available for every church in the kingdom. These provide support for children with special needs and their families. (See questions 9-11 for specific information regarding the SRM.)

The SRM reaches out to thousands of families around the world who would otherwise have little hope for seeking God due to the intense needs in their families. It has served to strengthen disciples with relationships, appropriate discipling and support, and hope and guidance to help their children become disciples. The ministry also inspires many therapists, educators and related professionals to make a difference in the world.

3. My child was just born with special needs. What do I do?

Discovering your child has special needs will affect you on many levels. You'll need to deal with emotional, spiritual, physical and mental pain, depending on your individual situation. The emotional pain has to do with coming to grips with the fact that the dreams and goals that you have for your child have to be changed. Most parents are already dreaming about what their children are going to become, and the thought of limitations doesn't occur to them. The emotional pain of discovering that your child

SPECIAL-NEEDS CHILDREN   61

has some sort of cognitive or physical challenge can be as real and intense as mourning a death.

When you first discover that your child has special needs, you immediately want to know what to do next, how to get help so your child can have the very best life possible. The type and degree of the challenge will determine the approach to meet his needs. Usually, a social worker is assigned to your family right there in the hospital, and will be ready to begin referrals. *Early intervention is important at this stage in their lives. Many strides can be made in children's development if they start receiving therapy services as soon as possible.* It usually takes a while to figure out what to do next, where to go for help and how to choose the right program for your child. Other parents with special-needs children are a great support and resource at this time.

4. I suspect that my child has a special need. How do I go about finding out if he does and what the diagnosis is?

The answer to this question depends on the age of the child. Some special needs are apparent when the parents notice that the child is not reaching expected developmental milestones. This usually happens around walking age. It begins to become clearer in other children when they are not speaking and putting words together, which is usually older than walking age. Other children can already be in school before any clear signs are noticed.

Depending on the age of the child, you can do many things. The first step is to ask your *pediatrician*. However, many pediatricians are not adequately prepared to diagnose children with special needs. They may refer parents to a specialist such as a *developmental pediatrician*, who is specifically trained to track the development of a child. This is where you can get a diagnosis and/or find a *specialist*. These doctors may refer you to other doctors for more specific testing. Sometimes it is appropriate for the child to see a *speech and language therapist* or an *occupational and/or physical therapist*. Developmental pediatricians often make these referrals.

Older children can sometimes be referred to a *neuropsychologist*, who can test the child for cognitive delays. If the child is in school, the *school psychologist* can do assessments that can help determine where the child needs help.

5. How do I potty train my special-needs child?

This is a difficult and very individual question. There are no easy answers, and much of the advice needs to be based on what kind of special need your child has. There are many special-needs children who have physical issues that make it very difficult to regulate potty training, especially bowel movements. In evaluating your child's situation, first eliminate any *physical problems* that could be contributing to potty issues. Chronic diarrhea and/or constipation should be dealt with after consulting a doctor.

The next thing to consider is the *sensory* issue. The feeling of having to use the bathroom is different for the child. This makes potty training physically painful and fearful. It also creates a desire for control. In general, the parent of a child with special needs has to consider the developmental age of their child, as opposed to the chronological age. This will help parents to be more patient with their child and will help them to have more realistic expectations for him.

Overall, potty training a child with special needs is generally very different from potty training a typical child. Using "pull-ups" during the particularly difficult times can take some of the pressure off of the child and the parent. Some children respond well to reinforcement and reward systems, such as stars or stickers. Some just need to be at a certain developmental stage—that only comes with patience. Finding special books on this topic may also be helpful.

6. How do I discipline my child?

This is such a broad question because discipline has to be determined for each individual. All children are different, and when you consider the vast differences in special needs, they become even more distinct. In spite of these differences, here are some pointers that may be generalized for special-needs children.

It is useful for the people working with children with special needs to know *why* they behave and react the ways they do. Most behaviors come with a reason, ranging from stress and change in environment, to fear, dissatisfaction, frustration and rebellion! Sometimes children are in pain and cannot effectively express it. Imagine how we as adults would behave if we were experiencing some of these things. Adults must learn how to set the child up for success. Sometimes this means not putting children in situations that may pose unwanted problems. Even in our own family, we have to cut our visits short because we are aware of what our child is able to handle socially and emotionally without having a meltdown. Prevention is often the best way to be sure that the child is really being disciplined for rebellion or deliberate disobedience, as opposed to some other problem.

However, the main piece of advice regarding discipline is—do it! Most children need some form of discipline in their lives. It never helps them to have the idea that they can behave in any way they want, wherever they want, whenever they want.

Be consistent! Discipline becomes more powerful when it is consistent and when the lines are clearly drawn for the child...and when the husband and wife agree. Be deliberate! Plan the discipline ahead of time, and then carry it out all the way through to complete change and total acceptance. This helps the child to really learn from his mistakes. Let the child know the consequences of disobedience, and be sure to follow through.

7. What type of school should my special-needs child attend?

You want to find a place that will address all the needs of your child *and* your family. Many schools offer special education programs but often show resistance to giving a child a generous amount of therapy that he might need (e.g., physical, occupational and speech therapy as well as resource specialists). These institutions generally lack support groups, educators and professionals who are working closely as a team. You will want to find a school that encourages your child's growth and socialization. They should provide opportunities through mainstreaming or full inclusion at the same campus. Talking with other parents who have enrolled their child in a school often gives an inside perspective on the excellence of the school and its appropriateness for your child.

8. I heard the NET World Sector was building a school for exceptional children. Can you tell me more about this?

An incredible school is being built in the San Francisco Bay Area. However, it is being built by the Hope Technology Group, not by the NET World Sector. Hope Technology Group is a non-profit, non-religious group that supports various projects for all children and especially those children with special needs. The Hope Technology School offers cutting-edge curriculums and a highly technological learning environment that meets the needs of children with and without special needs. The regular education program uses small group and individual instruction approaches in all curriculum areas. By implementing this approach, we expect to help students become lifelong learners in order to realize their full potential through our education and technology classes. We will offer children with special needs opportunities for both mainstreaming and full inclusion in the same facility. They also benefit from a variety of resources including Handwriting Without Tears; Treatment and Education of Autistic and Communication Handicapped Children (TEACCH); Modified Applied Behavioral Analysis (ABA); Picture Exchange Communication System (PECS); on-site occupational, physical and speech therapy; medical advice and a dynamic sports program.

Hope Technology School is unique in that it offers educational technologies in every classroom, along with special tutorials for each child. A dynamic and close-knit team of professionals focus on a positive educational approach for each child while emphasizing family involvement and support. (Check our Web site at www.hopetech.org.)

9. What is the Spiritual Resource Ministry?

The Spiritual Resource Ministry is a fruitful, dynamic ministry which seeks to meet the needs of children with special needs and their families. There are several basic components within the Spiritual Resource Ministry:

- The Spiritual Resource Class
  This is a specialized class that offers a student-teacher ratio of 1:1 with reversed mainstreaming of typical peers. The children are taught using the Kingdom Kids Curriculum in conjunction with special activity centers that offer children opportunities to capitalize on their strengths.
- Parent Support Groups
  If the Spiritual Resource Class could be described as the heart of the Spiritual Resource Ministry, then the Parent Support Group is the soul. There is no one who can understand the pain and joy of raising a child with special needs like another parent who shares in the experience. The support groups provide parents with incredible opportunities to learn from, share with and strengthen one another. Parents and professionals alike have become disciples as a direct result of the parent support groups.
- Special Education Exposition (SEE)
  The Special Education Expositions are yearly conferences which allow parents and professionals to collaborate and learn about the latest approaches, research findings, therapies and treatments in the field of special education. The local leader of the SRM is responsible for inviting various professionals to speak on relevant topics.
- Sports Program
  The Spiritual Resource Ministry is able to offer a fabulous sports program to help special needs children expand their athletic and gross motor abilities alongside their typical peers. Not only does the sports program encourage athletic development and healthy competition, but it also provides venues for children to build relationships and grow in their self-esteem.

10. How do I know if my child needs to be in the Spiritual Resource Ministry?

SPECIAL-NEEDS CHILDREN 65

Ask yourself the following questions to determine whether or not your child needs to be in Spiritual Resource Class as opposed to the regular children's ministry classes:

- How is my child doing in regular children's ministry? Is he consistently unhappy? Does he need continued help? Does he seem to be disciplined more than would usually be expected without improvement? Do behavioral issues keep him from really learning the Biblical lessons?
- Does my child have an IEP and require special services in the school system? (See question 12 for a definition of IEP.)
- Is the child experiencing the same difficulties in children's ministry as he is in school? Do his teachers express the same concerns as the volunteers in children's ministry?
- Does my child seem to have difficulty focusing or completing particular tasks?
- How are my child's relationships? Does he seem to have a hard time building relationships even in church?
- Is my child reaching his developmental milestones (such as gross motor, fine motor, socio-emotional, academic learning, etc.)?
- Does my child need more one-on-one attention to be able to succeed in class? Does he react strongly to large groups of children and prefer quieter, less chaotic settings?
- Does my child's learning style make it more difficult for him to understand Bible lessons? Does he have a hard time grasping intended concepts?
- Does my child have difficulty with transitions, moving from one activity to another? Does he have strong negative reactions to change?
- Does my child have physical challenges that make it difficult for him to participate in the regular children's ministry classes?

11. There is no Spiritual Resource Ministry at my church. What can I do?

Ask the leaders of the children's ministry to make accommodations to meet the needs of the child/children and their families. Work to provide them with additional help within the classes. Find out if there are any people in your church who have experience in working with children with special needs (e.g., teachers, therapists, doctors, etc.). Enlist their services on some level.

Be proactive and start the Spiritual Resource Ministry in your church! Contact the San Francisco Church of Christ for more information 650-259-0550 or e-mail us at ekids@upcyberdown.org.

12. What is an IEP/IFSP?

An IEP is an Individualized Education Program for children three years of age and older, which sets forth in writing the educational program for the student. The IEP is developed at an IEP meeting by a team of people, which must include the parents, a special education teacher, a regular education teacher (if appropriate), a district representative or school administrator and the student (if appropriate). If the IEP meeting is being held following an assessment, a member of the assessment team must participate. Other people who may participate are a therapist, a nurse and anyone else selected by either the parent or the district if they have knowledge or special expertise regarding the child.

IEPs include a variety of information, including the following:

- The child's present levels of educational performance, including how the child's disability affects the child's involvement and progress in the general curriculum. For preschoolers, present levels must include how the disability affects the child's participation in appropriate activities.
- Measurable annual goals related to meeting the child's educational needs.
- A statement of specific education and related services that the school district will agree to provide (e.g., class size, teacher qualifications, instructional aides, physical therapy).

An IFSP is an Individualized Family Service Plan for children under the age of three who have special needs. It includes measurable annual goals and statements of specific developmental services which will be provided for the child just as the IEP does. However, the IFSP includes services the family may need for support. For example, the child with communication difficulties may be provided with speech therapy and the family that is caring for the child may need counseling services. All this would be provided within the IFSP. The IFSP differs from the IEP in that it is "family focused."

13. Is there a glossary of terms (ADD/PDD/ADHD, Cerebral Palsy, Down Syndrome, Autistic Spectrum Disorders, etc.)?

There are a number of resources that provide glossaries of various disabilities. The Internet is an excellent resource. The Special Education Forum by KidSource.com is geared towards parents of children with special needs. The address is www5.kidsource.com/forums.

14. Is there a glossary of legal special education related terms (CAPE, LRE, IDEA, etc.)?

The field of Special Education is riddled with terms and acronyms that can leave parents and professionals feeling like they need to learn a whole new language! A San Francisco Bay Area based group called Community Alliance for Special Education (CASE) published an excellent book entitled, *The Rights and Responsibilities Handbook*.[1] Legal terms and issues are defined in an easy Q & A format. Another book entitled *The Complete IEP Guide*[2] has an extensive glossary of special education law terms.

If these books are not easily accessible, the Internet is an excellent resource. A glossary of legal special education terms specifically made for parents of children with special needs can be found at www.disabilityrights.org/glossary.htm.

15. How can I find other parents who have children with special needs like mine?

On our Web site (www.upcyberdown.org/eKids). Most disorders have foundations and/or organizations that can connect people to other parents. You can start by contacting your social worker or school psychologist and asking for these Web sites. Sometimes magazines such as *Exceptional Parent* will have lists of Web sites and organizations.

The world feels the impact of people with special needs and the statistics are overwhelming. We have overlooked this population for far too long. As disciples our mission should include reaching out to these families and becoming like Jesus in our love and compassion.

Gail Ewell
San Francisco, USA

---

[1] *The Rights and Responsibilities Handbook* (San Francisco: CASE, 2000). To order call 415-928-2273.
[2] Lawrence M. Siegel, *The Complete IEP Guide: How to Advocate for Your Special Ed Child* (Berkeley, Calif.: Nolo Press, 2001).

Hospitality for 'Working Women'

> Share with God's people who are in need. Practice hospitality.
> Romans 12:13

> Offer hospitality to one another without grumbling.
> 1 Peter 4:9

"What is the most difficult challenge you face as a result of working outside the home?" This is a question I asked a group of about twenty working women, mostly married. The overwhelming majority responded not with a specific problem at work, but with the frustration of meeting their family's needs while being responsible at their jobs. They did not feel good about the way they were keeping their homes—cleaning and washing and cooking. Most of all, they wanted to better meet the emotional and spiritual needs of their children and their husbands.

When we feel torn and guilty all the time, we are not much good to anybody. Our limited energy reserves leak out of guilt-ridden holes, rendering us even less able to meet the emotional and spiritual needs surrounding us. To think of offering hospitality to people on a consistent basis becomes overwhelming when we are feeling exhausted, frustrated and guilty. How can we plug up those holes and focus our energy in positive, faithful ways?

Jesus gives a clear answer, as he always does: "Seek first the kingdom of God and his righteousness" (Matthew 6:33). The truth of Jesus' statement is reflected in Dr. Seuss's story about Bartholomew Cubbins and his many hats. Each time he removed one hat to show respect for the king, another one sat on his head. After removing 499 hats, he finally got to the bottom of it all—a magnificent, jewel-studded, purple-plumed hat of all hats.

As working women, we must wear many hats. In fact, I asked a group of working women to take two minutes to write down some of the hats they wear. One woman, gifted with a quick-thinking cap, wrote down twenty-five! But the point is, no matter how many hats we wear (including the hat of the hospitable hostess), we will not wear them well unless we wear the hat of all hats underneath them—the hat of seeking first to please God. We cannot balance the 499 without first carefully placing on our heads the foundational one.

Prayer and Planning

We hear so much about the need to plan, and rightly so. The working woman, especially one who is married with children, simply will not be able to function well in all her different roles if she does not take time every week to plan. But even weekly planning will not enable us to wear all the hats...only prayer will bring the peace and steadiness to maintain our spiritual lives day in and day out. And if there is anything the working woman needs, it is a sense of peace in her fast-paced life.

For years I posted a weekly menu on the refrigerator. My middle daughter was the type who always planned ahead, even when she was a child. When I would finally get all three girls in bed and was almost ready to pass out in a state of exhaustion, Bethany would look at me and ask the inevitable question, "What are we having for breakfast?" I would maintain my composure, take a deep breath and say, "I don't know." It was to the advantage of my mental health at that point to have a menu posted so she could know what was happening the next morning. Naturally speaking, I never gave too much thought to the next day in my life. I totally experienced today and gave it my all, but tomorrow hardly ever entered my mind.

It seems that people are either *born planners* or *born let-it-happeners*; I naturally am a let-it-happener. But through the years I have had to learn to think ahead, to plan, to be organized. Since I started working a 9-to-5 job four days a week, I have had to learn even more. Somewhere along the way I stopped posting my menu. I don't think it was just because Bethany stopped asking, grew up and went off to college. I think I got too busy, and my life was running me rather than the other way around. I sometimes did a menu and sometimes didn't. When I didn't do one, I hated that feeling that came over me at four o'clock in the afternoon when I thought, *What are we going to have for dinner?*

I spent some effort (and time) reevaluating my priorities and goals. More than ever I am learning to plan ahead and budget my time according to the most important needs.

When I have done the best at being organized, I have sat down at a specific time to plan and pray through all the different aspects of my week, to set specific goals in different relationships and areas of responsibility. During this time, I would make up my weekly menu, and to the side, would make an accompanying list of all the ingredients needed to produce each meal (even down to eggs and milk). Then I would make a grocery list of needed items, and make notes throughout my daily planner reminding me what I need to do to prepare ahead of time for the next day's meal. (For example, cut vegetables for stir-fry on Wednesday while talking to Barb on Tuesday night.) I would make promises to myself and evaluate at the end of the week how I have done in following through with those promises. (For example, get up as soon as the alarm goes off.)

In order to have people over and feel good about it, I must have a sense of organization in my home and in my life. Although I tend to think I work well under pressure, I am sure that I work better, calmer and more joyfully when I plan ahead.

Ask Others to Help

Children. I came from a home where my mother graciously fixed many meals for people all by herself. I'm ashamed to say that my sister and I did not help very much during those times. Mother should have expected more of us, to be sure, but I have seen the pattern repeat itself....When we have had company through the years, I have tended to get meals ready and serve them all by myself, too. If I had it to do over, I would expect more out of my girls during their younger years. Since I did not work outside the home then, I *could* do it all, and I did. But to the extent that we do this, we rob our children of an understanding of their responsibilities in serving others.

Friends. We also need to ask for help from others more often. When we invite people for dinner and they ask to bring something, we usually should let them. When I fix the meal, but someone else brings a tossed salad, I am so encouraged to see it arrive. They are happy because their contribution was not time consuming, but they are still about to enjoy a full meal with friends.

My prideful tendency is not to ask people to do something because it may not be done the way I want it done. Instead of taking the time to explain how I would like it, I just do it myself. When time and energy are limited, as they both are for me at this point in my life, I need to explain, assign and trust others to do it excellently.

Working has caused me to have to rely on others more. One morning I left an egg boiling on the stove. I realized this when I was already at work (30 minutes away). I was on my way out of the office to go back home to turn it off, thus wasting an hour of prime work time, when my husband asked, "Isn't there someone you could call to go in the basement door and turn it off?" The truth was that the seldom-used entrance had cobwebs, and the storage area and hallway were in a mess. My pride hated for anyone to see that area of my house (and my life!). I died to my pride and called a friend to go over, and to this day she *still* loves and respects me!

Groups. When we lived in a larger home, it was used often for group activities both during the week and the weekend. I talked with the "regulars" about their responsibility to help with clean-up. Instead of getting attitudes, I got honest and told them that when we as a group use any home, we as individuals are responsible for cleaning and straightening it afterwards. Most people are willing to help; they simply have not been taught or shown what to do. But in order to have help, we must be willing to have other people opening our refrigerators and cabinets and drawers. The more we keep order in our homes, the easier it is for others to help us put things away.

Working women leave for work early the morning after an evening activity and cannot afford to say, "Don't worry. Just leave it. I'll get it later." But I'm afraid that sometimes people say just that, and then inform someone several weeks later, "It's just too hard on me to have group meetings in my home. Someone else will have to do it for a while." Since hospitality certainly includes offering our homes for group activities, we must learn to communicate to others how they can help us be able to do it.

'Another Saturday Night'

For working women, perhaps the best night to invite people for dinner is Saturday (or whichever day you have off). But it is tempting to be selfish with your day off since it is your only day to do this and that and everything else. Good planning is needed because if we put everything off until Saturday, we will usually be frustrated and even tense on that all-important day. If we do a few well-planned errands during the week, we will not be so overwhelmed on Saturday.

But busy day or not, we can still have people over. We simply need to plan carefully, put something on to cook while we are doing other jobs in the house or yard. If we find that several weekends have passed and we have not even thought about inviting friends, either disciples or non-disciples, to have dinner or even just to have coffee and dessert, then we are letting our busy lives run us and squeeze out the time to practice hospitality. The truth is, we need it as much as the people we invite!

As disciples, we must decide that it is God's will for us to open our homes to others, to share our food with others, to take time and energy to serve others. If we are not doing this and are excusing our lack of hospitality by saying, "I'm just too busy," we need to reevaluate, repent and resolve to get the help we need. We must learn all over again that to serve others is to be truly refreshed ourselves.

> A generous man will prosper;
>   he who refreshes others will himself be refreshed.
>   Proverbs 11:25

Sheila Jones
Boston, USA

Housekeeping and Housegiving Tips for the Working Woman

- Decide what jobs need to be done and how often, whether daily, twice a week, weekly, twice a month, monthly, semi-annually or annually. Work out a plan to get these jobs done.
- When you have a plan, you can take advantage of small amounts of time to do small jobs (like scouring the sink). When you do not have a plan, you might wander the house for five minutes and get discouraged at the work you do not have time to do.
- If you can afford it, hire some help from time to time to do cleaning or ask a friend for help.
- Buy meat in large quantities and store in the freezer; keep a supply of items you use often.
- Fix some or all of a meal in the morning before you leave for work. It is encouraging to come home to an already prepared meal.
- Have on hand the ingredients for a meal that can be fixed quickly if unexpected guests arrive.
- If you have a small child, fill the sink with a few inches of water and let him or her sit in it and play while you are working next to him to fix a meal. (As the supermarket carriage says though, "Do not leave child unattended.") Or place a large pan with a small amount of water on the floor. Give your child a toothbrush and plastic animals. Tell him or her to give them a bath. Then the sink is free if you need to use it.
- If you have a kitchen at work, some food can be prepared during your lunch break (if the kitchen is not too full of people and if your boss doesn't mind).
- Have theme dinners and assign each person a dish or item to bring.
- Make double portions of casseroles and freeze one for later.

Chasing After the Wind

We live in a culture obsessed with being thin. People today are deceived by society's message that thinness is beautiful and beauty equals happiness. The media's preoccupation with these issues places an enormous burden on women in our society (especially adolescents). This pressure, combined with other biological, psychological and familial factors, can lead to eating disorders. According to researchers, "The standard of female beauty has become more narrowly defined and restrictive, making it nearly impossible to be thin enough, fit enough and young enough. Society keeps moving back the finish line, ensuring that most will never attain the unrealistic ideal."[1]

Solomon stated in Ecclesiastes 1:14, "I have seen all the things that are done under the sun; all of them are meaningless, a chasing after the wind." Is it possible to catch the wind? Of course not! Is it possible to be the "ideal woman" by worldly standards? Absolutely not! A runner would never run a race that didn't have a finish line. The finish line represents winning the prize, accomplishing a task and completing the work. Are we running toward a finish line that "society keeps moving back"? The person with an eating disorder will never attain the unrealistic goals to be thin enough, good enough and happy enough. She will be "chasing after the wind."

This chapter deals with some of the eating disorders that stem from society's influence, family dynamics and the internal messages of the heart. God has a plan and can provide a way out of this common but potentially dangerous challenge.

Definition of Eating Disorders

Hannah is an example of a woman in the Old Testament who let her emotions affect her eating. In 1 Samuel 1:1-20 we read of her being heartbroken because of her barrenness. To make matters worse, Hannah was provoked and irritated by Peninnah, Elkanah's fruitful wife. In this time of history to be barren was a disgrace. Society looked down upon a woman who could not have children; she was unacceptable.

Although Hannah received special attention from her husband, nothing would take away the pain of her disgrace. Hannah was so troubled that it affected her appetite. She wept and would not eat. The Bible describes her as being "downhearted," weeping "in bitterness of soul" and

---

[1]Information from a speech I gave in 1995 at the Melpomone Institute for Women's Health Research in St. Paul, Minn. The exact source for the quote is no longer in my files.

"deeply troubled." This went on year after year. Elkanah may have observed Hannah slowly losing weight, as she could not eat during times of emotional distress. Double portions of meat seemed to make things worse. Her husband simply wanted her to eat and be happy. Easier said than done!

This story parallels so many of my clients who struggle with eating disorders. The feelings of insecurity and disgrace are very common with young women who hate their bodies and who feel like they are not fitting into the "acceptable norm" of today. They compare themselves to others and frequently feel that they do not measure up to the standard of beauty, weight and image. The provoking may start at home or school—comments come from family members, friends or coaches. Irritated by the constant struggle within their thoughts, they start to feel worn down.

Not eating will eventually result in a loss of appetite. Not feeling hunger goes hand in hand with not feeling other emotions. Emotions that are hard to handle include guilt, fear, anger, resentment and loneliness. By numbing their emotions, they are able to dull the pain.

Of the eating disorders prevalent in our society today, anorexia nervosa and bulimia nervosa are the most common.

Anorexia Nervosa

Anorexia nervosa is an eater's attempt to control something in his or her environment by controlling food. Often anorexics have an intense and irrational fear of gaining weight or becoming fat. Food intake is often limited and restricted and may drop to a few hundred calories each day. Their fasting will eventually dull the normal hunger cues in their body and anesthetize the pain. Clinically, anorexia nervosa must meet DSM IV diagnostic criteria as stated below:[2]

- Refusal to maintain a normal body weight (less than or equal to eighty-five percent of normal)
- Intense fear of gaining weight or becoming fat, even though underweight
- Body image distortion and excessive reliance on weight or shape for self-esteem[3]
- Amenorrhea—the absence of three or more consecutive menstrual cycles

Bulimia Nervosa

Bulimia nervosa is compulsive overeating followed by purging the food. The purging is done with self-induced vomiting, laxatives or exercise. The first binge of bulimia nervosa may be triggered by diet-induced hunger, a

---

[2]Task Force, *Diagnostic and Statistical Manual of Mental Disorders, Fourth Edition,* DSM-IV, (Washington DC: American Psychiatric Association, 1994), 539-545.

[3]Philip Mehler, Arnold Andersen, *Eating Disorders: A Guide to Medical Care and Complications* (Baltimore: John Hopkins University Press, 1999), 5-9.

normal response of deprivation. That is, they deprive their bodies of food, and then overeat to compensate. Over a short period of time bulimia generalizes to become a way to deal with any distressed mood, including depression, anxiety, feeling stuck or feeling bored.[4] Bulimics feel empty, so they binge again; then they feel guilty, so they purge again. It is a no-win, cyclical pattern.

Women with bulimia are addicted to their eating behavior and not to food itself. Wanting desperately to be free from this addiction, they despise their voracious hunger and loathe their imperfect bodies. Because they misinterpret their hunger as physical (an empty stomach), they gorge on food. Then they see food as the enemy (it will make them gain weight) and their bodies as traitors (it digests the food and makes them fat). Caught up in the denial that is ever present in all addictions, they fail to recognize the starvation of their spirits. They do not recognize that the emptiness is spiritual or emotional, not physical. Eating disorders are about feelings—not about food.

Below are the DSM IV criteria for bulimia nervosa:[5]

- Eating, in a discrete period of time (within any two-hour period), an amount of food that is definitely larger than most people would eat in a similar period of time
- Compensation after binges by purging (vomiting, laxatives, diuretics), exercise or fasting
- Regularly engaging in self-induced vomiting, the use of laxatives or compulsive exercise in order to prevent weight gain
- A minimum average of two binge-eating episodes a week for at least three months
- Fear of fatness and distortion of body image—letting weight or shape determine self-esteem[6]

Other Eating Disorders

A significant number of women suffer with other eating disorders which do not fit the criteria mentioned above. Some of these women may have a normal weight and some may be obese.

Eating disorders not otherwise specified may be atypical eating disorders that do not meet diagnostic criteria but are no less serious. They all have their physical dangers and complications and may present themselves in different types of eating patterns.[7]

---

[4]Anita Johnston, Ph.D., *Eating in the Light of the Moon* (Carlsbad, Calif.: Gurse Books, 1996), 31.

[5]*DSM IV,* 545-550.

[6]Mehler, 8.

[7]Michael Levine, Ph.D., Margo Maine, Ph.D., *Resource Catalog* (Seattle, Wash.: Eating Disorders Awareness and Prevention, Inc., 1998).

1. All of the criteria for anorexia nervosa are met except the individual has regular menses.
2. All of the criteria for bulimia nervosa are met except binges occur at a frequency of less than twice a week for a duration of less than three months.
3. A binge-eating disorder (compulsive overeating) is characterized by a lack of control resulting in overeating within a discrete period of time. The individual often feels she cannot stop eating or choose how much she eats. The main difference from bulimia is that binge eaters do not purge.

Eating disorders, like the ones mentioned here, become solutions to a problem, a means of survival from the constant pain and deep-rooted trouble that may seem overpowering. Imagine being swept through rapid waters and about to drown—some might grab on to a log of comfort...and overeat. Others might grab on to a log of control...and stop eating. The problem is, in either scenario, the log is on its way over the falls with its occupant in tow. Neither extreme is God's way to deal with the challenges that come our way.

Food That Satisfies

We must follow Hannah's example of pouring out her heart to the Lord. Praying in great anguish and grief was the way she got through the challenge of being barren and a "disgrace" to society (and the challenge of her body not being what she wanted it to be). She surrendered to God her situation and her pain, and she made a decision to trust the counsel of Eli. He understood her and told her that her request for a child would be granted. At that point she ate something and her face was no longer downcast.

God's word is our spiritual food. Our relationship with him fills us up spiritually and emotionally. We should search our hearts and lifestyles to see if they reflect a deep desire for this food that truly satisfies:

"I have treasured the words of his mouth more than my daily bread." (Job 23:12b)

How sweet are your words to my taste,
    sweeter than honey to my mouth! (Psalm 119:103)

"My food," said Jesus, "is to do the will of him who sent me and to finish his work." (John 4:34)

Warning Signs

Below are some general warning signs of unhealthy eating patterns:

EATING DISORDERS   77

- A marked increase or decrease in weight not related to a medical condition
- The development of abnormal eating habits such as severe dieting, preference for strange foods, withdrawn or ritualized behaviors at mealtime, or secretive bingeing
- An intense preoccupation with weight and body image
- Compulsive or excessive exercising
- Self-induced vomiting; periods of fasting; laxative, diet pill or diuretic abuse
- Feelings of isolation, depression or irritability[8]

Distorting God's Message

Although eating disorders may be defined as psychological, there are influences from our culture, our families and ourselves that contribute to the problem.

Culture

Society's notion of how a person should look can toss us back and forth and blow us here and there. (See Ephesians 4:14.) The norm of the culture that dictates what is acceptable forever changes. We can never find our security in conforming to that norm.

Body image is how you see yourself when you look in the mirror or when you picture yourself in your mind. Body image is shaped early in life and is influenced by the culture we live in. The Barbie doll we played with, if life-size, would be six-feet nine-inches tall and have a nineteen-inch waist. Many of the female Disney characters are communicating images and messages of unrealistic thinness to our young girls.

However, thin was not always considered beautiful. A seventeenth century artist, Peter Paul Rubens, painted full-figured women who were revered for their beauty. More than 150 years later, artists like Dante Gabriel Rossetti and Edouard Manet painted pictures of women who were "rounded." This represented status and high class. If you were wealthy you could afford to eat and did not have to work. The Roaring '20s brought the flappers, women renowned for their bold freedom from conventional conduct and dress. A famous World War II pin-up girl was Betty Grable, a new ideal for women.

In the 1960s Twiggy was one of our earlier examples of the look that led up to the increase of eating disorders. The 1970s brought a quest for physical perfection with an emphasis on fitness and the athletic look. Since the 1990s we have seen the waif look hitting the magazine ads. The media has glorified thinness and malnutrition. These

---

[8]Kathryn Zerbe, *The Body Betrayed: A Deeper Understanding of Women, Eating Disorders, and Treatment* (Washington DC: American Psychiatric Press, 1993), chapters 3 and 4.

messages have contributed to the rise of eating disorders and created a culture that values people on the basis of their physical appearance and not their inner qualities and strengths.

Family

Family dynamics can often contribute to disordered eating patterns. Below are a few of the scenarios that I have observed in my practice:

- Mothers who emotionally smother their adolescent or hinder the process of separation when moving on to college[9]
- Fathers who are distant and unavailable—separated by physical distance or time or lack of emotional connection—and therefore unable to foster a daughter's development of self[10]
- Parents who are not resolved with their own issues of low self-esteem and insecurity
- Mothers who focus too much on their own body weight, image and appearance
- Conflict or divorce within the parents' marriage

Self

Satan is the father of lies, and he constantly sends messages that are negative and detrimental to our self-worth. Satan does not want us to understand or connect with God's intimate love. What messages do you hear about yourself every day? Are they similar to the following? "I feel fat." "I hate my stomach." "I hate my thighs."

Many women do not go through a day without thinking negative messages about their bodies. These internal messages will lead us to unhealthy behaviors. These negative messages must be brought under the control of spiritual thinking. To put it bluntly, Satan tempts us to hate ourselves. One of the sins described in Galatians 5:19-21 is hatred. When asked if we hate anyone, most of us will quickly say, "No!" But how many of us consider whether we hate *ourselves* before we answer? Do you hate yourself? Self-hatred stems from many things, the most common being one or more of the following:

- Limited or poor nurturing as a child that leads to a negative message that you don't deserve to be treated right and that your needs are not worth anything
- Sexual abuse that triggers guilt, resulting in feelings of shame and unworthiness that may create a subconscious desire to hurt yourself
- Numerous negative comments from family, friends or peers resulting in forgetting the truth of the Bible and how God views you

[9]Zerbe, chapters 3 and 4.
[10]Zerbe, chapters 3 and 4.

EATING DISORDERS   79

- The media's message about beauty, thinness and fitness portraying a perfect look and body shape that makes you feel insecure in comparison

Self-esteem destroyers such as guilt, anxiety, fear and criticism wage war and imprison us with the sin of self-hatred. Satan is also using worldly influences to make us feel bad about ourselves. Somehow we think we need to be perfect in order to be loved, but God reassures us that his love in unconditional.

"Let the beloved of the LORD rest secure in him,
    for he shields [her] all day long,
    and the one the LORD loves rests between his shoulders."
(Deuteronomy 33:12)

If we don't understand God's heart, reading scriptures that encourage us to "be perfect" as God is perfect (Matthew 5:48), can become overwhelming. God is well aware that we are not perfect (Psalm 103:13-14). Although God wants us to give our whole heart, he gives us the forgiveness of Jesus and the power of the Spirit to help us mature and grow. The Greek word used in Matthew 5 (*telios*) conveys the idea of "reaching the point of full growth or maturity."[11] God's desire is for us to grow and mature—and he will grant us the security we need for that to happen:

Therefore my heart is glad and my tongue rejoices;
    my body also will rest secure. (Psalm 16:9)

Perfectionists will not accept anything short of perfection. Those who strive for perfection are often challenged with "black and white" thinking: "I am perfect" or "I am awful." If left unchecked, this desire for perfection may cause them to turn to eating disorders to cope with their feelings.

Recovery

Growing in your walk with God and becoming a godly woman is the way out of this destructive sin of self-hatred. To overcome this crippling negativity we must make a decision to believe the truth. It is time to meditate on the scriptures that build you up. Below are some meditations and affirmations from God's heart to yours:

I am a new creation.   2 Corinthians 5:17

I am made in the image of God.   Genesis 1:26

I am God's child.   1 John 3:1

[11] J.D. Douglas, Merrill Tenney, eds., *New International Bible Dictionary* (Grand Rapids, Mich.: Zondervan Publishing 1987), 766.

I am wonderfully made.	Psalm 139:14
I am not condemned because I'm in Christ.	Romans 8:1
I am the apple of God's eye.	Deuteronomy 32:10
I am precious and honored.	Isaiah 43:4
I am God's treasured possession.	Exodus 19:5

Making peace with the body that God gave you requires that you see yourself as God sees you. However, healing deep wounds will take time and the work of God's Spirit.

1. Admit you need help and have a problem. (1 John 1:5-10)
2. Pray and ask God to reveal the roots of your sin and pain and ask for wisdom and healing. (Psalm 139:23-24)
3. Expect the Holy Spirit to lead and guide you into all truth. (John 14:16-17)
4. Speak the truth in love to yourself. (Ephesians 4:15)
5. Take responsibility for getting the help that you need. Prepare your mind for action. (1 Peter 1:13)

As we attempt to improve our health and take good care of our bodies, we need to be careful to avoid extremes. Common but sometimes detrimental behaviors, such as restricting calories or being obsessed with fat grams, severely limiting some foods, using diet pills, laxatives, constantly dieting or being preoccupied with food, will take its toll.

God has a plan and a way out of every physical and emotional challenge we face. (See 1 Corinthians 10:13.) We need to be open with God and with the spiritual people in our lives so that we can get the help we need. Also, eating disorders need to be treated professionally. Early diagnosis and intervention will enhance recovery. A "team" approach is necessary to address and untangle the multi-faceted roots that these disorders can have:

- A medical doctor especially trained in working with eating disorders will be able to identify the symptoms, which are sometimes not so obvious. For example, the teenager who sees a pediatrician who may say that everything is normal. Unhealthy behaviors are not easily detected. Blood work typically comes back normal because the body has an incredible ability to adapt. Missed menstrual cycles are sometimes easily dismissed and eating patterns may not be addressed. "She is just a typical teenager."

- Psychological counseling by licensed health professionals is just as vital. Individual and family therapy will serve to surface the real function of the eating disorder. This may be difficult for a family to accept because teens and adults may label counseling as something weird or shameful. But it is the wise person who gets help and counsel.
- A dietitian trained to work with eating disorders coordinates with the other members of the team. For example, my role is to educate the patient about normal eating, metabolism and hunger patterns and guide them to develop a healthy relationship with food. Meal plans often serve as the initial guide to help the patient follow through on healthy eating habits that provide caloric requirements for weight gain or food intakes that decrease the binge–purge cycle.

Many people with eating disorders respond to outpatient therapy; however, inpatient and residential treatment is available when the physical problems become life-threatening.

Other Helpful Web Sites and Books

- www.edap.org (Eating Disorders Awareness and Prevention,Inc., a non-profit organization devoted to the awareness and prevention of eating disorders.)
- www. somethingfishy.org (A Web site about eating disorders that includes news articles, professionally run discussions and resources.)
- www.anred.com (Anorexia Nervosa and Related Eating Disorders, Inc., a non-profit organization that helps answer questions about eating disorders for the lay person.)
- www.nutritional-therapy.com/proto.html (my own Web site)
- Abigail Natenshon, *When Your Child Has an Eating Disorder* (San Francisco, Calif.: Jossey-Bass, Inc., 1999.) A step by step workbook for parents and caregivers.

If this chapter spoke to you personally, it may comfort you to know that God is using this disorder to get your attention that something is not right. Are you moving down the wrong path? Do you need to evaluate the messages that you have been influenced by? How much does society affect you? Does the media give you an unrealistic standard of thinness? Are you running after a moving finish line? How are things with your mother or father? What internal messages are you listening to? Do you hear and believe God's voice or do you listen to Satan's voice? Is your pain too much to bear alone? Do you stop eating in order to lose your hunger and therefore dull other emotions you cannot handle? Do your emotions affect your appetite? Do you pour out your heart to God in prayer?

Make a decision to pour out your heart to God. Seek godly counsel or possibly professional advice. Make a decision to entrust your troubles to God and seek counsel from godly friends. Don't let disordered eating undermine your physical health, spiritual growth and true identity as a child of God.

Melanie Breitenbach, R.D.
Detroit, USA

Abortion and Forgiveness

> The king of Egypt said to the Hebrew midwives, whose names were Shiphrah and Puah, "When you help the Hebrew women in childbirth and observe them on the delivery stool, if it is a boy, kill him; but if it is a girl, let her live."
> Then Pharaoh gave this order to all his people: "Every boy that is born you must throw into the Nile, but let every girl live."
> Exodus 1:15-16, 22

How could anyone be so heartless towards innocent babies? When I read these verses, I am struck by their callous hearts. This inhumane attitude caused countless lives to be lost. How could they take human life so lightly?

Just as quickly as I ask these questions, I am pained by the memory of something that I did many years ago. I, a decent person who would never dream of causing harm to anyone, was heartless toward an innocent baby. I had an abortion.

Even as I write these words, the pain about what I did returns. I remember that I destroyed a child, but I also remember the cavalier attitude I had in doing so. I took lightly the abortion itself, but I also took lightly the sin that led to that event. In fact, so many things in my life were chosen flippantly, foolishly. But I will never take lightly the grace that God has given me in forgiving those foolish acts.

Up until the time that I found myself pregnant, I had been opposed to abortion. As a young girl I had read much on the subject and was convinced that a fetus was indeed a human life. I knew that the fertilized egg became a real person with a unique genetic make-up. I understood that as early as a few weeks after conception, the skeleton was formed, the sex was determined, and the heart began to beat. My convictions had nothing to do with how God felt about abortion; in my mind, abortion was morally and ethically wrong.

But there I was—a nineteen-year-old college student with no heart to marry the father of the child and no desire to be a single mother. What was I to do? It was 1972, and abortion was not even legal in the state of Florida where I lived. But I had a friend with connections to an abortion clinic in New York, where abortions were legal. With no thought for this child and all my thoughts on "my predicament," I made arrangements to travel to New York City for the procedure.

Only my boyfriend and a few others knew of my plans. I flew to New York by myself and was transported in a bus with other women who had flown in from all around the United States. Some of us began conversations, explaining how and why we got into the situations we were in. There was the girl who said, "I only did it once." There was the woman who had enough children already and did not want any more. Another woman was a repeater—she had visited the clinic before. We were pleasant with one another, encouraging, as if we were all on a trip to the dentist.

Upon our arrival at the clinic, all of us were herded into waiting rooms where we filled out forms and had our blood tested. A nurse instructed us, in mass, about what the operation would involve. We chatted as we waited for our turn. One by one names were called, and women would put down their magazines and walk out of the room. When it was my name that was called, I went into a dressing room, removed all my clothing and jewelry, and put on a hospital gown. I walked barefoot into the operating room where the nurse instructed me to lie down on the table. She put my feet in the stirrups as the doctor entered, a surgeon's mask covering his face. A gas mask was placed over my mouth and nose, and I was told to count backward. The last thing I heard was a loud whirring sound, and then I fell asleep.

The next thing I remember was being in a recovery ward with dozens of other women. Some were moaning, some were crying, some were vomiting. I awoke with no pain, no discomfort except for some slight cramping. There was a slight ache in my heart, but only slight. I was relieved. It was over. My "problem" was over.

The rest of the trip was uneventful. I returned home, went to classes, and life was normal. I continued to see my boyfriend, but eventually had other boyfriends as well. I was more careful than before. I certainly did not want to go through that ordeal again. There was an occasional twinge of guilt, but I quickly pushed it out of my mind. I had done what I had to do. And that was that.

A New Understanding

A few years later I finally gave in to my friend Mary and went with her to a Bible study group. After much arguing, doubting and questioning, I was convinced that there was a God who cared about me. I was delighted to become a Christian, to have faith and to have my sins forgiven. I would never take sin lightly again.

As much as I recognize the horror of my sin in the taking of a human life, what always strikes me the most is the fact that I could do certain things so easily. I was quick to give in, even to things I did not believe in or agree with, if the need arose. The overwhelming theme of my life was, "It's all about me." Therefore, abortion wasn't my "big" sin, nor was it the promiscuity that got me there. Rather, my big sin was my selfishness. Even as I look back at the events surrounding the abortion, my thoughts were not on the baby whose life was being snuffed out. My thoughts were on me.

I do not often feel guilty for the sins of my past. This is not because I am out of touch with them, nor do I excuse them by saying, "I was young and irresponsible." I accept the fact that I did wrong, but I also accept the fact that God has promised me that he has forgiven me:

> As far as the east is from the west,
> so far has he removed our transgressions from us. (Psalm 103:12)

> But you were washed, you were sanctified, you were justified in the name of the Lord Jesus Christ and by the Spirit of our God.
> (1 Corinthians 6:11)

Because of these promises in God's word, I have promised that I will take any and every sin in my life seriously. Because of these promises I can thank God daily for his mercy and love.

Several years ago, my daughter and I were in a discussion about certain types of sins. I had been very open with both of my children about the wrong choices I had made in the past, and the grace God has shown me. I had vowed that I would never lie to my children, but would always tell them the truth. When the subject of murder came up, my daughter innocently said, "Well, you've done a lot of bad things, but at least you have never committed murder. Right, Mom?" As hard as it was, I explained to my daughter, that yes, I had committed murder. I had an abortion. Abortion is killing an unborn child. I had been guilty of the most grievous sin. This conversation led to a very significant time with my daughter, and I do not regret our frank discussion. Through it all, with her and with others, I have reminded people that no matter how bad a sin is, God's love and mercy are big enough to take it all away.

Perhaps there are some women reading this who have struggled with the guilt of an abortion. Or there are others who have never actually aborted a child, but were lucky; they sinned sexually but did not get pregnant. Other readers may even be thinking, "I was never immoral." But I say to any of you: Any time you take sin lightly, you are becoming just like the king of Egypt. You are taking a human life casually. It may be a baby's life, or it may be your life.

Remember that every life is sacred, even your own. Treat it as a treasure, for that is how God treats it. Never forget that God knit you together in your mother's womb (Psalm 139:13). He formed you—*he made you*—so that you could live with him forever. That is our glory and joy.

Kay Summers McKean
Boston, USA

Facing Reality

My mother is seventy-six years old and has congestive heart failure. She has already had two open heart surgeries and cannot survive another one. Gordon's mom is alive physically, but for all practical purposes, she left us five years ago. These two moms are precious to me and have given more to me than I could ever express. I constantly rely on God to give me the strength, wisdom and compassion to be the daughter they need in their twilight years. Only with God can I face the reality of their aging and death...and be at peace.

The Reality of the Aging Process

> Therefore we do not lose heart. Though outwardly we are wasting away, yet inwardly we are being renewed day by day.
> (2 Corinthians 4:16)

This verse reminds us that our bodies are aging with wrinkles, weakening muscles, energy loss, deterioration of the inner organs and growing health challenges in general. Facing the truth about this description from God is so hard when it applies to our aging parents. I have cried many tears and have grown in my compassion as I have seen this process with my mother and mother-in-law.

My mother will continue to degenerate in her heart condition because nothing really can be done for her at this point. So it is just a matter of time until she dies, which could be very soon. In the meantime she is as active as she can be, considering her limitations. With every ounce of energy she can muster, she is still driving her car, serving people, working in the yard, reading her Bible, attending church services, studying the Bible and praying over the phone with my brother or me, and talking on the phone to others. She is outwardly focused, a most gratifying quality for the family and me. My mother and I have enjoyed a deep relationship all of my life, and in some ways she has been more like a sister and friend than simply a mother.

My mother-in-law is also like a true mother to me. I have known her since I was a young teen, which is now over forty years! We "chose" each other when Gordon and I were first dating, but we didn't tell Gordon, since he was a rebellious teen at the time and not ready to abide by our choice! She loved me and was a special friend to me during those early dating years and also during our thirty-six years of marriage. The past five years, however, she has not been physically, emotionally or spiritually who she had been. The deterioration of her body has brought many of her weaknesses to the surface, and these weaknesses have hurt most of the family. It is almost as if the first person is already gone, and we are grieving her loss. We are even left wondering if the former person had such a protective wall built up that perhaps we didn't know her as well as we thought we did. This is both a confusing and hurtful discernment to make.

She has been in an assisted-living environment for several years, and more recently, in a nursing home. She is in poor health, confined to a wheelchair. Due to both her emotional and physical state, she has not been able to live with her daughter or us. When she is able to come and visit us, I make the sacrifices that are needed, including changing her diaper, bathing her and caring for her basic needs. I rub her head, which once was filled with beautiful blonde hair, but now is covered with thin white hair and large knots under the scalp. I also massage her now deformed feet that once were busy serving our family and me. I listen to her and reminisce about all of the fun times and about the countless ways she has served all of us. When she has felt embarrassed about my changing her diapers, I remind her of the ways she took care of me after my two miscarriages and other surgeries. I tell her how I cherish every minute that I have with her.

At this point in her life she says mean and hurtful things to all of us, but we have purposed not to allow her actions or reactions to affect our love for her. Whenever she treats me in a hurtful way, I do not take it personally, but I realize that she is going through her own struggles. I apologize when I do not respond well.

On the other hand, I refuse to be manipulated by her unkind words and actions. I continue to call her, serve her and meet all the needs that I am able to meet from a distance. When we are together, I really listen to her and empathize with her about her aches, pains and unhappiness. I realize that she is now in her own world, remembering mostly the bad things and the ways that I haven't measured up to her expectations. I pray to treat her as if she were Jesus, regardless of her actions and words. I have to pray a lot when I am with her, and before I call her, I prepare by thinking of the good things that she has done for us in the past. I made a list of over thirty things that she has done for me and have written cards mentioning these things as I express my continuing gratitude.

The Reality of Death and Judgment

Facing the reality of a parent's aging is much the same emotionally as facing a death, and you go through the same stages of grief. First comes shock and denial, as you grapple with the fact that the old days are gone and there is no going back. It is simply hard to believe that this is happening or has happened. Second, the stage of anger may come in as we grow to resent the changes. We are tempted to be angry at the person, at the aging process and maybe at God himself. Third, the feelings of guilt and depression come as we think back to what we should or could have done, and to what we are doing or failing to do now. Fourth, the stage of acceptance must finally be reached as we work through the earlier stages. Wherever our parents may be in the aging process, we know that death is destined to be the ultimate outcome of it.

I have experienced all of these stages personally in a deep way through facing the aging and death of close relatives: my favorite aunt (who was like a grandmother to me), my cherished grandmother, my wonderful father, and my dependable and noble father-in-law. Reaching closure has not always been easy or quick. I wrote each of them a long letter after their death in which I evaluated our relationship and worked through my feelings about them. I faced the truth about their spiritual destinies and my own regrets about how I didn't help them spiritually. This helped me to plan and carry out my good intentions with those who are still alive. (See chapter 15 in which a disciple shares a letter written to her mother, who died several years ago.) I am dealing with my aging parents and close relatives in a much better way, as to leave *no regrets*. I have determined to give flowers to the living in the forms of letters of appreciation, acts of service, gifts and many hugs and kisses. In this way, I can make the most of their last days with me.

Recently, I was able to help my mother face her own death and judgment before God. It began as one of my greatest challenges but ended as one of my greatest joys. I will cherish the memories of that experience forever. I expressed to her that one of my deepest regrets was that she wasn't going to be with me in heaven. This led to our studying the Bible, and now I'm thrilled to say that she is going to be with me in heaven!

When I was a child, she was the one who first taught me to love God; now as an adult, I was blessed to teach her more accurately what the Bible teaches about loving God. My brother Curt, his wife, Janet, their son Ian and I were able to baptize her into Christ in February of this year. When she does die, the grief will be lessened greatly by the knowledge that she will have met God prepared and will be with me forever in heaven. Even if our parents do not respond to our outreach positively as she did, we must never give up trying to reach them until they take their last breath.

The Reality of the Blessings Left Behind

Don't let the blessings of the past be diminished by the challenges of the present. I have purposed to hold on to the good qualities, skills and experiences that my mother and mother-in-law have been blessed with.

I want these blessings to live on through my life. I share with them now how much those things have meant to me, and I promise to not let them die. I mention such things as learning to cook certain dishes and entertaining large groups. I tell Gordon's mother that I learned how to be a good mother-in-law from her. I tell my mother that I learned how to teach my children Bible stories and songs about God; and I learned perseverance, patience and sacrifice from the way she dealt with my father's alcoholism and other challenges in her life.

Even though my mothers may feel useless in their weakened conditions, I want to make sure they know how much I appreciate all that I learned from them and experienced with them. I want them to know that the blessing they have been to me will live on as long as I live…and then through my children and grandchildren after I'm gone. I tell my children what I learned from their grandmothers, and I ask them to pass these things on to their children. I also ask my children to share with their grandmothers those things that I said I learned from them. I want my mothers to understand clearly that these ways of giving love trace back to them. The children also express appreciation to their grandmothers for those things.

I can do nothing to stop the natural process of aging and dying, but through God's power I can make the process a positive one. Praise God that we don't "grieve like the rest of men, who have no hope" (1 Thessalonians 4:13), whether it is the grief that comes through the aging process or through death itself!

My prayer is that by sharing with you my experiences, I can help you look to God and deal with this life-passage spiritually. We have to face the pain involved and allow the tears to flow as we let it out. We need to take advantage of all who have faced these times before us, and to surrender our parents to God, knowing that he loves them much more than we do. He will work through us as we, together with our parents, face the realities of aging and death. It is comforting to know that God is feeling with us in these ultimate realities and has promised to reward our faith as we cling to him. I urge you to meditate on two passages that have helped me most through these trying times:

> Therefore, since we have a great high priest who has gone through the heavens, Jesus the Son of God, let us hold firmly to the faith we profess. For we do not have a high priest who is unable to sympathize with our weaknesses, but we have one who has been tempted in every way, just as we are—yet was without sin. Let us then approach the throne of grace with confidence, so that we may receive mercy and find grace to help us in our time of need. (Hebrews 4:14-16)

Praise be to the God and Father of our Lord Jesus Christ, the Father of compassion and the God of all comfort, who comforts us in all our troubles, so that we can comfort those in any trouble with the comfort we ourselves have received from God. For just as the sufferings of Christ flow over into our lives, so also through Christ our comfort overflows. (2 Corinthians 1:3-5)

I thank God for his presence, his love and his help during a difficult, but unavoidable, part of life. I am grateful that his reality gives meaning to all other realities that I have to face.

Theresa Ferguson
Boston, USA

As Our Parents Age

The dilemma is real. It is heartbreaking. It is confusing. Our parents are the ones who gave us birth and who have cared for us through the years—from changing our smelly diapers to sending us to college—and now they need us to take care of them. It just doesn't seem right the first time you help your father dress or your mother sit on the toilet. Those are things they are supposed to do for us, aren't they? This role reversal turns our worlds upside down emotionally.

How do we respect our parents' right to make their own choices and yet make sure they are in safe situations? How do we get them to stop driving when it is no longer safe for them or for others? Is there a point at which we have to take over the reins of their lives when they do not want us to? Are we willing to deal with the guilt we feel when we allow them to make life decisions that are not in their best interest? And what about when they live hundreds of miles away from us...should someone move?

In her excellent book about supporting aging parents, *Another Country*, Mary Pipher makes the following statement:

> Adults have always worried about aging parents but our current situation is unique. Never before have so many people lived so far away from the old people they love. And never have old people lived to be so old.[1]

As disciples of Christ, how do we face the aging of our parents? The specific questions we could ask are as varied as the parents we want to help. Thankfully the Scriptures give us some basic guidelines that will help us with those specific situations.

Biblical Basis

Honor and Respect Our Parents

> "Honor your father and mother"—which is the first commandment with a promise—"that it may go well with you and that you may enjoy long life on the earth." (Ephesians 6:2-3, Exodus 20:12)

> Listen to your father, who gave you life,
>   and do not despise your mother when she is old. (Proverbs 23:22)

---

[1] Mary Pipher, Ph.D., *Another Country* (New York, New York: Riverhead Books, 1999), 5.

Rise in the presence of the aged, show respect for the elderly and revere your God. I am the LORD. (Leviticus 19:32)

From the time we are small children, God commands us to honor and to respect our parents. Not because they are perfect. Not because they always "deserve" it. Not even because it is the right thing to do. We honor and respect our parents because in so doing we honor and respect our Heavenly Father. (See also Proverbs 17:6, Proverbs 23:22, Malachi 1:6, Matthew 19:9.)

In our era, the idea of rising in the presence of the aged is far gone. Older people are not held in the high esteem that they should be. They have a boatload of experience that we can learn from, and they deserve to receive the honor they are due. Alex Haley said "The death of an old person is like the burning of a library."[2] To what extent are we "avid readers" of our parents? We need to listen to them. Learn from them. Give them focused attention.

Many years ago I interviewed my grandmother. She lived during times that I only see on TV and in the movies. She was a contemporary of Laura Ingalls Wilder from *Little House on the Prairie.* I loved hearing her stories, discovering new revelations about her life, finding out whether she got any input before her wedding night (she didn't), and sharing her joys and pains through the years. Those tapes are special to me, and I look forward to passing them on to my girls.

Having this kind of interest in our parents' and grandparents' lives shows honor to them. They know we are busy, and they appreciate our slowing down and focusing on them and wanting to know them better.

Bring Our Parents Joy

The father of a righteous man has great joy;
    he who has a wise son delights in him. (Proverbs 23:24)

A wise son brings joy to his father,
    but a foolish son grief to his mother. (Proverbs 10:1)

In bringing joy to our parents, we bring joy to ourselves. The closer we are to God, the better equipped we will be to bring joy to our parents. I lost my own mom fourteen years ago this month. Yesterday I was looking for some information to use in this chapter, and I came across a letter Mom wrote me less than a year before she died. It filled my heart with joy to know that I was a joy to her. She wrote,

[2]Pipher, 11.

I've been cleaning a little, and everywhere I look there are so many things in this house that remind me of your thoughtfulness and love—the little mailbox with Dad's picture, the beautiful picture of the girls and all the snapshots, etc. you keep us up to date on, the frame for our "centennial" picture, yours and Tom's tapes, the tape and notes you want us to use to tell of our life together, the beautiful rose blouse I wore yesterday with my grey skirt and vest. The concern you have about our health and habits—so many, many things you do that remind us that no matter how busy you are with your life, there is always room for loving thoughts and acts of kindness toward your mom and dad. We are so grateful to God for giving us two such lovely, caring daughters and two wonderful, caring sons-in-law.

My mom was a grateful and forgiving woman. I wish I could have done more to show my love, but I am thankful that she felt it anyway.

Certainly there are times when, try as we might, we are unable to bring joy to our parents. Because of their own problems or bitterness, some parents will simply not allow themselves to be pleased. And they regularly attempt to send their children on guilt trips. In this type of relationship, we have to find our peace in knowing that we are obeying Paul's injunction in Romans 12:18: "If it is possible, as far as it depends on you, live at peace with everyone." If our hearts seek to bring joy to our parents, we must realize that God "credits it to [us] as righteousness" (Romans 4:3). In the Lord lies our peace, not in our ability to please our parents.

There were times I could not bring joy to my dad. The reason was that he was suffering from Alzheimer's disease, which brought along with it tormenting hallucinations. Figures in dark-hooded robes came in and out of the walls of his room. One time they stretched him on the bed and tortured him. These experiences were as real to him as any of my experiences were real to me. I could not take them away and give him the comfort and joy I so much wanted to give him. But I kept doing everything I could to bring him joy: consistent visits, rides in his wheelchair outside, a tape recorder and a tape of Christian hymns, close supervision of his medical needs, his grandchildren coming to see him and hug him and kiss him. My heart was set on bringing him joy even if his heart could not receive it.

Meet Our Parents' Needs

Give proper recognition to those widows who are really in need. But if a widow has children or grandchildren, these should learn first of all to put their religion into practice by caring for their own family and so repaying their parents and grandparents, for this is pleasing to God. (1Timothy 5:3-4)

If anyone does not provide for his relatives, and especially for his immediate family, he has denied the faith and is worse than an unbeliever. (1Timothy 5:8)

If any woman who is a believer has widows in her family, she should help them and not let the church be burdened with them, so that the church can help those widows who are really in need. (1 Timothy 5:16)

Religion that God our Father accepts as pure and faultless is this: to look after orphans and widows in their distress and to keep oneself from being polluted by the world. (James 1:27)

The Scriptures could not be any clearer about our responsibility to care for our parents. Jesus spoke with blistering clarity: Do not use your commitment to God as an excuse for not supporting your parents in their old age (Matthew 15:1-9). In twenty-first century vernacular he said, "Do not give your missions contribution and then tell your parents, 'Sorry, you'll have to get food stamps. I don't have any money to support you.'" Or "I'm sorry I haven't written you. I have been spending so much time reading the Bible."

The challenge for disciples is to take care of our parents' needs and continue to seek the kingdom of God as our first priority. Jesus is a great example in this area, as he is in all other areas. In the midst of excruciating pain, he charged his best friend, John, to take care of his mother, Mary. He took to heart God's heart about caring for our parents as they age.

But this same Jesus did not allow his family to distract him from his commitment to God or to his mission:

While Jesus was still talking to the crowd, his mother and brothers stood outside, wanting to speak to him. Someone told him, "Your mother and brothers are standing outside, wanting to speak to you."

He replied to him, "Who is my mother, and who are my brothers?" Pointing to his disciples, he said, "Here are my mother and my brothers. For whoever does the will of my Father in heaven is my brother and sister and mother." (Matthew 12:46-50)

Jesus would never have allowed his loyalty to his family, even an aging, widowed mother, to keep him from doing God's will. It devastated his mother that he was being tortured to death on a cross. How her heart would have soared if he had come down off the cross and gone home with her. And yet, he could not grant her that desire. He could, however, make sure her needs were met even as he sought to obey his God. Thus, he was true to his statements about the radical nature of following him:

> As Jesus was walking beside the Sea of Galilee, he saw two brothers, Simon called Peter and his brother Andrew. They were casting a net into the lake, for they were fishermen.
> At once they left their nets and followed him.
> Going on from there, he saw two other brothers, James son of Zebedee and his brother John. They were in a boat with their father Zebedee, preparing their nets. Jesus called them, and immediately they left the boat and their father and followed him. (Matthew 4:18-22)

> "Anyone who loves his father or mother more than me is not worthy of me; anyone who loves his son or daughter more than me is not worthy of me." (Matthew 10:37)

> "And everyone who has left houses or brothers or sisters or father or mother or children or fields for my sake will receive a hundred times as much and will inherit eternal life." (Matthew 19:29)

> He said to another man, "Follow me."
> But the man replied, "Lord, first let me go and bury my father."
> Jesus said to him, "Let the dead bury their own dead, but you go and proclaim the kingdom of God." (Luke 9:59-60)

Jesus, who did all things well, had the perfect balance as he sought first the kingdom of God. We must trust that he will help us find that balance through honest struggle, prayer and advice. We, too, can seek first the kingdom and also take responsibility for our parents' care.

Application to Our Lives

We all have to come to the stark realization that our parents are aging and that we have a journey to take with them. Bonnie Raitt sang about this realization in her song "Nick of Time":

> I see my folks, they're getting old, I watch their bodies change...
> I know they see the same in me, And it makes us both feel strange...[3]

On this journey through aging, we will "feel strange." We've never been here before. We will have decisions to make...many of them will be confusing, unsatisfying, heartbreaking and unthinkable. We will make decisions such as whether

---

[3]Bonnie Raitt, *Nick of Time*, sound recording (Hollywood, Calif.: Capitol, 1989).

- to move across country, taking our children out of schools and away from friends, because our parents will not move to live in our area;
- to stay with our parents during a crisis while our children are hundreds of miles away back home, needing us;
- to secure power of attorney while our parents still have their "faculties," or at least *some* of them;
- to put our parents in a nursing home because we cannot give the degree of medical care that they need;
- to authorize a protocol of no resuscitation.

My Decisions

My mother died of gastro-intestinal bleeding…the doctors never could find where it was coming from so they could not stop it. The month before she died we had moved just two-and-a-half hours away from my folks. Up until that point, we had been several states apart. Mom's death left us with many decisions. My only sister, Emily, lived in another state and helped me make the major decisions. But she was obviously not able to be as involved in the day-to-day decision making.

Neither my sister nor I realized how far our dad's Alzheimer's disease had progressed. When Mom died, Dad lost his moorings and became even more disoriented. Because of our house situation, family challenges and my husband's MS and deep depression, I did not see how I could also have Dad there. I had to watch him at all times or he might have gotten up in the middle of the night, looking for some non-existent item, and then falling down the stairs.

We tried an assisted living situation, but Dad was much too confused and disoriented. Eventually, we had to move him into the nursing part of the facility. I stayed in constant touch, visiting him, talking to doctors and other personnel. I said to my dad, "You have always taken such good care of me. Now I will take good care of you." I meant it and I gave my very best.

We made a move to another town to be in a ministry situation that would offer some healing to our lives. Not only did we have situations in our family that needed healing, but I was facing the possibility of major surgery. I moved Dad to a facility in the new town, but I was not at all satisfied with the place. I checked out another one and moved him there.

I became friends with the head nurse, and she loved my dad. Unfortunately, she lost her job. Fortunately, she was hired to be the head nurse at a beautiful new facility across town. Dad and I followed her there. He was the first patient, and they all doted on him. God had blessed us with an incredible partnership in caring for my dad's needs.

It became apparent for various reasons that we needed to make another move...this time to Boston. Dad no longer knew who I was. His beautiful blue eyes stared at me vacantly...my dad was no longer there. I simply did not have the heart to move him from this place that was familiar to him...if anything was. I realized that to move him would be more for me than for him. It would have been to salve my conscience so I could say I was being a good daughter. Dad was much better off where he was. Being with me in a new facility in Boston would not really have been a comfort. In fact, the trip itself would have been traumatic to him in his current condition.

I stayed in consistent communication with the head nurse; I flew down to see Dad after we moved. I simply couldn't do anything else. My family had to move and I had to move with them.

Emily and I made the difficult decision to request that no feeding tube be placed in our dad when he was no longer able to eat. At that point we wanted the nurses to hydrate him and make him as comfortable as possible. Four months after our family moved to Boston, Emily and I were with him when his body finally gave in to the disease. He mercifully breathed his last. The end was bittersweet. We had actually lost our dad months earlier. His body had just stayed around, reminding us of who he was and how much we loved him. We said our final good-byes to this gentle, loving man who had taught us to love God and other people, and to have integrity in every situation. He was so much bigger than the shriveled little body he lived in. He was a hero. He was our dad.

I thank God for seeing me through this very difficult time with my mom and with my dad. Even when I was not consciously relying upon him, he was graciously there with me. And he saw me through to the end.

The Cycle of Life

As I was expending time, energy and love to meet my dad's needs, it occurred to me that I was teaching my children how to someday meet my needs. Time will march relentlessly on until I will be the aging parent, and my kids will be making the difficult decisions about how to deal with Mom.

One thing I want to do is to write them a letter, letting them know my wishes. Tom and I already have a living will that says we do not want to be kept alive on a respirator. We have made this decision, and we trust that our children will love and respect us, and yes, obey us, and abide by our wishes. This frees them up not to feel torn and guilty at a very emotional and confusing time.

Another thing I want to let my kids know is that if I ever have Alzheimer's disease as my dad did, it is okay to laugh if I say something funny. They know I would laugh too if I knew it was funny. I don't want them to feel guilty for having some comic relief in a tense time. My dad said some really funny things. Emily and I did not laugh *at* him, but we enjoyed him. We were relieved to get to laugh because so much of the time we saw absolutely nothing humorous about the situation. Many experiences were much more painful than humorous.

The story of Noah and his sons in Genesis 9 teaches us about protecting the privacy of our parents and showing them respect when they are in a vulnerable situation. Noah had drunk wine made from his vineyard and had passed out naked in his tent. Ham came upon him, and instead of covering him and showing respect, he went and told his two brothers. They took a cloak and backed into the tent and covered up their father. We may come to a point in life that we have to help our parents with daily hygiene. They may do bizarre things that would have horrified and embarrassed them when they were well. These are the times that we must protect them. We should not speak lightly or casually of them in their vulnerability. They deserve our respect until the day they die. If we treat our parents this way, our children will learn to treat us the same way. And so goes the cycle of life.

Sheila Jones
Boston, USA

Other Stories and Input

In the remainder of this chapter, several other women will give brief glimpses into their lives. They, too, are coming to grips with the realities of the aging process in their parents. Some will share about their frustration, their exasperation and their desperation. They will also share how their faith gives them perspective in a dark and difficult time. And some will offer practical suggestions to help you through this time.

Mom has lived with Ron and me for the last fourteen years. Last July we found her frantically searching through her address book for a "Linda Lee" as a clue as to whether she had any children. I am Linda Lee. It was the first time she had forgotten who I was. There had been many other warning signs that she was losing her memory, but this was the shocking one. A doctor's examination the next day confirmed a diagnosis of Alzheimer's disease.[4]

I started asking questions, reading books and attending an Alzheimer's support group. I couldn't seem to catch up emotionally or practically with

Mom's changing needs as her deterioration over the ensuing months outpaced my adjustment. Hardest for me was the emotional hit of losing my place in my mom's life. For her I only exist as a small child. The rest of my life is erased. She introduces me or refers to me alternately as her sister, her cousin or her niece. She knows I'm familiar. She knows I'm related. But she never knows I'm her daughter anymore.

Every expert source I read taught that I should not try to reorient her, but instead I should enter her reality. As one woman told me, "She is not able to come back into your world. You must go with her into hers." That sounded easy, but as her reality shifted, the mental gymnastics required for me to be her sister, Dottie, one minute and her cousin, Loreen, the next were agonizing for me. But hardest of all is dealing with the anxiety, paranoia and delusions that almost inevitably accompany the disease.

I used to think, "Alzheimer's—what could be so terrible about losing your memory?" But it truly is a cruel disease and the memory loss is the easy part! I am the closest person in my mom's life, and I often feel helpless to comfort and reassure her (I'm her only child, and my dad is dead). It is so painful. Whatever her current delusion (e.g., the police are coming to arrest me; I've just been raped; the children I'm responsible for are in life-threatening danger and I can't get to them), I am unable to reassure her that it is okay, it's only a trick of her imagination, or that I will take care of it. She is inconsolable. This is hardest for me. Unlike comforting a child, who has total trust in a reassuring parent, an Alzheimer's patient can only grasp his or her own reality. So emotionally, I struggle with the frustration of helplessness.

The greatest challenge for me is to disassociate myself emotionally, so that the problem can be about her and not about me. In every way, it reveals my selfishness, my lack of patience and my own anxiety level. But this disassociation has its own emotional barb, because it can feel like you've stopped caring about the relationship. I'm trying to practice (and having some success with) the "best friend" approach to caregiving. It helps me feel involved and caring without clinging to my role as daughter. If Jesus did not grasp at equality with God, but let it go for my sake, I can for Mom's sake not grasp at my role as daughter, but accept a role that better meets her needs.

I've been very grateful for the support of my husband, Ron, and other disciples, whose love for Mom has been unfailing. Their example of still being able to enjoy her, instead of plummeting emotionally, has been a great visual for me to imitate. It has made me better understand Romans

---

[4]Although a clinical diagnosis is only possible by examining brain tissue posthumously, doctors can, by charting patterns of progressive memory loss and a process of elimination, accurately distinguish Alzheimer's from other forms of dementia. The biggest problem with this is that the diagnosis can sometimes come too late to receive the best effect from drugs.

12:6-8, where Paul admonishes those who have been given the gift of "showing mercy" to "do it cheerfully." With his help I will do just that!

Linda Brumley
Seattle, USA

My parents are living out the nightmare of seniors. Mother has been scammed three times by credit card phone frauds (over $3000). My dad has been in and out of the hospital for high blood pressure and chest pains. Mother's appetite has diminished to practically starvation level and yet she has the nervous energy of a child. It is unbelievable! As the grown kids we are trying to allow them personal dignity of making their own decisions but it is getting more apparent that we may have to "manage them" soon.

Another challenge we face is that our parents understandably do not want to give up their independent living. Uprooting from their home to move across town or country away from their doctors and familiar places is frightening to them. We tried to persuade them to make some of these changes much earlier in their lives but to no avail. After moving them into a smaller but lovely nearby condo, mother now says, "You kids should have tried harder to get us to move back then! This is a nice place, but now there is nothing to do, it's boring." I have to tell myself not to own the guilt I am tempted to accept.

The following is a excerpt from a letter I wrote to my brother. It expresses how I am working through the heartache and frustrations of my parents' aging:

To my brother,

You are a messenger from God! I know that you surrendered to his side a long time ago, and even though it is a battle, the war will be won. I love and respect you and am praying for you!

I am convicted by how faithless I have become through these trials with the folks. I could feel it all wearing me down, and I was frustrated about feeling so helpless. I realize that I really do not like feeling powerless, and that is an understatement!!! But I have not gone to the power source enough, not with the right spirit anyway. I pray that God will use each of us in the unique way that he can.

This all reminds me of the days that we had to pull through for one another when Dad was in the hospital and we were just little kids. We played "orphans stranded on a deserted island" a lot back then. Maybe some of those same feelings are what I am fearing now, but even as kids we learned to pull together and be "heroes" for one another. Mom and

Dad could not be there for us then, but we were there for each other. We knew that each one of us was hurting about the situation but still needing each other. Mom and Dad cannot supply the strength we need to get through this. We have to be their strength, but we each have got to draw our strength from God. He is the only source that doesn't run out!! That is a source that we barely knew back then. But he is making himself known to us today! I love you all and pray for your strength. Please pray for mine.

It seems as if all the key issues and challenges go back to keeping God our number one source for undying love and strength. With God as our Eternal Father, a painful passage of life is made less painful and even transformed to a beautiful passage by the opportunity to lovingly serve and honor our parents.

Love,
me

A Disciple
USA

It seems to me that this is one of the hardest stages of life. There are so many variables and so many aspects that are unpredictable. From my experiences I would offer the following suggestions:

- After losing three of our four parents, I am sure of one thing: you do not regret time spent with them. I don't think I have ever heard anyone express regret about spending too much time with their parents. Defining how and when to spend time with them is difficult given our active lives and many responsibilities. We are so grateful for the input and advice we were given at those times. Thank God for discipling!

- If at all possible, it is best to have heart-to-heart talks with your parents about their wishes for this stage of their lives. It is wise to write those desires and plans down in order to follow them as closely as possible. Shortly before my mom died, she and my dad talked about what he would do after her death; then they shared their thoughts with us children to discuss. It helped so much to know that we had all agreed ahead of time that my dad would come to California to stay with both my brother and his wife and with us.

- One of the most important aspects of caring for your parents in the latter years of their lives is to work closely with any siblings you have. It helps to share the load of the various decisions that must be made as well as to share in the actual care of your parents if possible. The communication between siblings and their spouses is very important—especially drawing out and being open about the feelings each has. The more you cooperate and can be on the same page, the better things will go.

- If you are married, realize that your spouse will probably not have the same emotional bond with your parents that you have. But you will need to work together as a team to make decisions and to care for your parents. Do not "pull into yourself" and shut your spouse out as you deal with aging parents. You need each other. My love and admiration for Al grew as I saw him serving my dad so unselfishly.

Gloria Baird
Los Angeles, USA

After consulting with our family, I made the decision first to move to Michigan to be with my parents as my dad fought Alzheimer's disease. After he died, Mom moved back to Boston with me where we bought a house together. Now we live in Pennsylvania, closer to other family members, whose support I very much need as my mom is going down emotionally, mentally and physically.

I want to offer some practical suggestions from things I have learned through working with Mom's situation over the past few years:

- Have a talk with your parents about how they view their future. Include all siblings if possible so that you can all hear it once and discuss it. What to do if one parent is left is often dictated by financial restraints. Start investigating options before they are needed...it's a real education.

- Get the advice of a few estate lawyers that are up to speed with the elder law in your parents' state. Laws change state to state dramatically as do the opinions of lawyers. Get your "ducks in a row" early—as Medicaid, for example, has a "look-back" of three to seven years. (That is, in making decisions about whether to give aid, the government and other agencies will look at your parents' net worth. If funds are transferred to family members far enough back, your parents will be eligible for more help.)

- If one parent dies, allow the remaining parent to maintain independence at some level, but remember that there will be a need for you to help in many areas: physically, emotionally, medically and financially.

- Keep in mind that the frequency of doctors' visits will increase, not decrease with age. Don't rely on your parents to advocate their own care. You will need to listen with them and for them.

- Count the cost socially. If your decision is to have a parent live with you, realize that their health may decline and you may not be able to maintain the lifestyle that you are used to. Be willing to ask for advice and for help. Friends can help you by sitting with your parent while you get out of the house.

- A most common error is to assume that insurance pays for care in or out of the home. *It does not.* After each hospital admission if rehab is required, Medicare will pay for twenty-one days in a facility. An assessment will be done to see what services are needed after discharge. If you are told you will get a nurse and an aide for a couple weeks, don't overestimate their contribution as the nurse visits will be brief and the aide typically stays an hour…not all day like you might have hoped.

- I have found that in our area the average cost for a "companion" (a person who keeps your parent safe and fed) is twelve to fifteen dollars per hour. Keeping someone at home requires a lot of juggling to get the best care for the least money.

- Type a medical history sheet that lists surgeries, medical conditions, prescriptions including doses and even a social history. Keep this sheet copied and updated and in your purse and in key places in the house so if or when an ambulance is called it can be handed to the driver and the ER personnel. It should have all insurance numbers on it. Accuracy at the time of admission is important because the bills will be a nightmare if initial information is incorrect. They will need insurance cards to copy as well. *This list is extremely useful.* It helps the medical staff "cut to the chase," and after being asked the same history over and over, you will definitely appreciate this little piece of paper!

- Don't rely on hospital staff to be there to cover all the needs. Hospitals are extremely short-staffed typically, and one-to-one nurse to patient care no longer exists. Family members need to be present to pick up on needs and help the communication between the staff and the patient. The staff appreciates a helpful—not bossy—family.

- If you are at work, don't hesitate to call the hospital during the day and ask for the doctor to be paged if you have an urgent matter.

You will probably not access the doctor after you get there in the evening—since their rounds are generally done very early, it can be difficult to catch them.

- Realize that caring for a parent is an emotional and physical drain. Go to caregiver support groups. Ask for coverage at work or at home and get out regularly. There are many resources available right now for the caregiver as more and more people are trying to do at-home care. The big issue is money. This usually determines the path to take. Be realistic with your siblings in the initial discussion, and make sure they are willing to change with the needs and contribute also. Time and distance may be issues, but there are still ways to be supportive. I could write a whole chapter on "support your local caregiver" but I won't. Suffice it to say that cards, calls, flowers, visits, coverage of care...just plain acknowledgment...encourages them as they are trying to help their parent.

- As people come in to help, you have a natural base of people to share your faith with. (For example: I am so happy because this past week we studied with the aide whom I have come to cherish. She should be at church today.) In a situation in which your parent is homebound, "outreach" will likely shift to becoming more "in-reach."

- In 1 Timothy 5:8 it says, "If anyone does not provide for his relatives, and especially for his immediate family, he has denied the faith and is worse than an unbeliever." In today's society we are taught to live for ourselves. The world thinks that giving up your wants for someone else is not a legitimate expectation. I feel there is a balance and each person needs to know their limits—but I also know that God expects a sacrificial, caring heart. Lifestyle changes will probably need to happen, and God will bless a wise, informed and unselfish decision.

Donna Western
Philadelphia, USA

Our parents are pioneering the way through aging. We are not there yet, and it is very difficult for us to know what they are thinking and feeling. Perhaps it is good to give them the chance to verbalize their thoughts and fears if they are still able. Caged up, those inner tenants can terrorize and depress them. Opening the cages and letting them out will give our parents and us a sense of freedom. When they speak of their fear, its hold on their hearts will be loosened.

One senior expresses some of her feelings in a little book titled *Prayers of an Omega*. Katie Funk Wiebe writes the following:

I Sure Liked to Drive My Car

Lord, this morning I turned in my license to drive. I put it in an envelope and wrote a note saying I wasn't going to drive any more. The kids patted me on the back and said, "Great, [Mom]. Good decision. We're all for you." Then they drove the car away.

I think I felt relieved. At ease.

No more worrying whether I'd make the left turn onto the highway before another car zoomed by. No more worrying whether I'd see the little girl on the bicycle behind me. No more worrying whether the elusive shadows at night were pedestrians enjoying the evening air.

But I miss the feel of a ring of hard keys in my pocket. I reach for them, just to give them a caress. But they're not there. I want to go out and start the car. For no reason. Then I remember. The car is gone. I will never back it out of the garage onto the road again. I will never again experience the power of the engine with me at the wheel.

We always had a quiet life. Not much traveling. Others talked about Disneyland and Yosemite, but we like it here. At home. We had a car to dash to the store to get milk for breakfast. To go to church. And to visit the children. And to check on the waving wheat fields in early summer with [car] windows open....

The children say they will take me anywhere I need to go. Just phone and they'll come. But my longing to see that lilac tree disappears when I have to squeeze a passing look at it between a dentist's appointment and a quick trip to the post office.... Middle-aged children haven't got time for nature's all-out shout of welcome in spring just yet.

Lord, I desperately want to know if the redbuds bloomed this spring on the street where we used to live. I want to know what color Jim and Helen painted their house. I want to spend the afternoon driving—for no reason.

Reach out your hand, my Lord, and place it here in the warm hollow of my hand where I used to hold the keys.[5]

Aging and its companions—loneliness, disease, hurt and death—are a sad group. We cry when we read prayers like this. We hurt when we see those we love lose strength and mental awareness. But we have to remind ourselves that this is God's plan. We are not here to live forever. We live in an earthly tent that wears out with age. But with Paul we can affirm our faith and fix our eyes on eternity:

Therefore we do not lose heart. Though outwardly we are wasting away, yet inwardly we are being renewed day by day. For our light

---

[5]Katie Fink Wiebe, *Prayers of an Omega* (Scottdale, Pennsylvania: Herald Press, 1994), 57-58.

and momentary troubles are achieving for us an eternal glory that far outweighs them all. So we fix our eyes not on what is seen, but on what is unseen. For what is seen is temporary, but what is unseen is eternal. (2 Corinthians 4:16-18)

With our parents we walk the way of all mankind. Let's trust the one who is the Way and who gives meaning to our way...every day.

Sheila Jones
Boston, USA

Letter to Momma

The following is a letter written by a disciple to her mother, who died several years ago. After writing the letter, she read it aloud to trusted and loving friends. The freedom she felt afterwards was comforting and encouraging. Reading this may help you write a similar letter to someone who has died and with whom you have "unsettled business." It may also encourage you to communicate with someone who is still alive.

Dear Momma,

Wow, this brings back memories and emotions right away—the memories of writing to you once a week for about 27 years. I feel a tremendous amount of emotion welling up in me now. I miss you so much! I just wanted to take this time to talk to you. I have been going to CR with a friend and am learning a lot. I have been thinking about the past and how I wish things could have been done differently. I am thinking a lot about Daddy and his being drunk and what you must have had to go through. I just want to say some things to you that I wish I had known how to say when you were still alive and here with me.

First of all, I am so thankful for all the things you did for me from the time I was born until you died. You were always there for me in every way you knew how to be. You made all my clothes and nice ones for which I wasn't as thankful as I should have been. You always provided me with what I needed for school. That was always fun and special to get to go to town and buy our school supplies. You always cooked great meals for me. You taught me how to clean house. You taught me how to love my children and take care of them by the way you took care of me. You taught me how to be disciplined. You took me to church so I could learn to love God. Momma, I want to thank you for all that you did for me. I wish I had thanked you more when you were still with me. I'm sorry I didn't express to you more of my feelings. I know that wasn't the way our relationship was. I regret I didn't try harder to do that after I learned how to. I know that was something no one ever taught you. I don't blame you at all. I'm just grateful for all that you did give me. You were always there for me in whatever way you knew how to be. I always felt loved by you.

The thing I feel most regret about is not being there more for you after I grew up. I'm really sorry and wish I could go back and redo things. We didn't have the money to go see you a lot, but I wish we would have borrowed money or sacrificed something else to have seen you more over the years. I know moving here was the best thing that ever happened to me and my family spiritually and I would do that over again. I know it hurt you a lot and I am really sorry I wasn't more sensitive to that. I now know how much it hurts for my kids to be away—my heart was ripped out. You never showed it, but I know now it must have ripped your heart out each time I moved further away. Please forgive me for not being as sensitive to you as I should have been in each of those moves.

I want to thank you for holding the family together when I wanted so much for you to leave Daddy when he seemed to always be drunk and in a bad mood. I know you never left him even through all the grief you took from him—being verbally abusive to his actually physically harming you. I now know what you did was probably because you loved him so much. I respect the love and commitment you had for him. I really want to thank you for the sense of family you tried to have in our home even in the midst of all that Daddy was doing. I learned so much from you. You really did do a great job of protecting us kids and trying to make sure we didn't suffer because of Daddy's drinking. You gave so much of yourself to us. I now can look back and see that. Thank you so much.

I know I have been feeling a lot of things since you died. First of all, I miss you very much. I guess I just never thought the day would come when I wouldn't have you. You just kinda think you'll always have your mom. I'm grateful God gave you to me for as long as he did. But I miss you now! You'll be glad to know [my brother] and I are staying in contact every week or every other week. He isn't working as hard at it, but I call him here and there. I'm really sorry we didn't do more of this while you could know it. I know you always wished this for us. I understand it more now because I know how much I want my kids to stay close to each other. I feel a lot of guilt because I didn't go see you more and help out more when you were sick. I want to say I'm really, really sorry for that. I want to say I wish I could go back and live it over. I'd make a way to go visit you and help out with taking care of you more. There is not really any way to live it over, but I want to ask you to forgive me and please know my heart. My heart was to be with you at the time, but mainly because I let finances hold me back I didn't go visit you enough. I am so thankful I got to go be with you that last week in the hospital. I want to think you knew I was there and heard me talking to you and praying and quoting scriptures to you. I am thankful I got to visit you before you died. I am just sorry I didn't do more of that earlier on.

Momma, I know we tried many times to get you to fly up to see us and we were going to pay for you to do that but you always thought you couldn't because of responsibilities at home and later in life, of course, you couldn't because of your health. I need to tell you that it hurt me that you would not come see us. It hurt me because it made me feel as if you didn't care enough about seeing us to let someone else see to the responsibilities at home, which [my brother] would volunteer to do each time. We tried to get you to visit here. I know when you flew here after we moved, you loved flying. I wish I had expressed my hurt to you while you were still here to hear me. Please forgive me for not doing that. I am really sorry I didn't.

There's one other thing I need to talk to you about. This is really hard because I know you didn't know how to deal with this situation. I just need to say how it made me feel. When you and Daddy were making love in the same bed with me or in the bed next to mine it really was scary to me. I thought he was hurting you. It also left me with the feeling that it was happening to me. I felt dirty and embarrassed. I appreciate the one time you assured me verbally he wasn't hurting you. This has caused me to be overly sensitive in that area to protect our kids. I guess I'm feeling a lack of protection from you in that area. I don't know how you could have protected me because you were probably trying to keep peace with Daddy and not get him upset with you. Maybe you just didn't know any better, but whatever the case it made me feel unprotected. It has made me resent you and have unkind feelings toward you about that. Again, I wish I had talked to you about this in person. Please forgive me for not doing that and for resenting you and having unkind feelings toward you.

I also know there were times when I felt stupid because of the things you said to me—specifically about my thinking I had started my period when I hadn't, about not knowing how to cook, about not liking the farm life—outdoors, animals, etc., generally anytime I thought differently than you on something (which was most of the time) or when I didn't know how to do something. However, I learned to keep my thoughts inside me growing up and just do things as near your way as possible so there wouldn't be conflict. I remember when I began to disagree out loud with you after I went away to college.

I want to again apologize for not telling you about these things because I know you didn't mean to do any of them to hurt me. You didn't know any better. Nevertheless, they did hurt me and that's what I need to say to you by writing this letter. I don't write these things to hurt you or give you a bad name but only to try to help myself. Please forgive me for all the ways I hurt you over the years, and know how much I appreciate all you did for me and how much I miss you.

Momma, I do forgive you for the way you hurt me. I know you never intentionally meant to hurt me in any way. I know you love me very much.

Love,
Me

A Disciple
USA

NOTE: This disciple is currently in the process of writing a letter to her deceased father. She is finding that much more anger and hurt are pouring out as she opens her heart in this writing. The process is painful, but needed. For years she has blocked the pain that her alcoholic father inflicted upon her and her family. In order to break through to healing, peace and forgiveness, she must face the facts in this relationship. The reason her letter to her mom did not bring such anger is because she knew her mom really loved her...but never once did she think her dad really loved her.

We add this note simply to make clear that writing a letter like this is a very personal thing. No one's experience will be like anyone else's in content or tone. Each person must write her own feelings and experiences, and pray that God will work to bring peace and closure.

Temptations and Opportunities of the Physically Challenged

Those of us who are physically challenged go through trials and emotional turbulence. God is with us every minute, working to bring us closer to him—while Satan is scheming to wrench us away. Being chronically ill is one of the greatest challenges a disciple can face. Sometimes we wish our illnesses were of an acute nature so we could go through them, die and go be with God. Living in constant pain or sickness without knowing when it will end, yet trusting that God truly loves us, summons every bit of faith we have…one day at a time.

I have been ill off and on most of my married life, twenty-two years now. For the past eleven years I have experienced debilitating fatigue and headaches. After many trips to various doctors with no diagnosis, I figured I was crazy or just needed to have more faith. My life as I knew it came to a grinding halt when Ryan and I got out of the ministry ten years ago. It was at this point, after moving to San Diego, that I received a diagnosis of Chronic Fatigue Syndrome. In an open-minded effort to get well, I tried many treatments: traditional therapies consisting of countless prescription drugs; physical therapy; unconventional and natural treatments such as diets, purges, chelation, herbal remedies, vitamins, colonics; a headache clinic; a muscular pain clinic; fibromyalgia treatment; yoga and psychotherapy. I didn't want to close any door to something that God might use to heal me. In fact, God *is* using some of these things to help me, yet, the spiritual lessons that I have learned have brought far more healing than any drug or treatment—a therapy that goes beyond the physical to the deepest part of my soul. Here are a few things God is teaching me.

Temptations of the Physically Challenged

Bitterness Toward God

> A man's own folly ruins his life,
>   yet his heart rages against the LORD. (Proverbs 19:3)

"Woe to the man who fights with his Creator. Does the pot argue with its maker? Does the clay dispute with him who forms it, saying, 'Stop, you're doing it wrong!' or the pot exclaim, 'How clumsy can you be!'?" (Isaiah 45:9, TLB)

As I began dealing with the fact that I was legitimately ill and probably not going to get better, my prayer life disintegrated and my outreach virtually stopped. I was barely even giving to my family. My energies, such as they were, were focused on myself and finding that silver bullet, that right treatment that would heal me. Becoming more and more miserable, I realized that I was very angry with God. A faithful sister, Ramona Garnier, told me to go outside, pray and express my feelings to God. I resisted, stuffed my emotions and attempted to deal with it on a rational level. Trying to find why it was happening, I reasoned, "Well, he allowed me to get sick because he wanted to teach me this or that, or I had to get sick for certain changes to happen." I was desperate to understand.

When I finally got down to what I was really feeling, it was like lancing an ugly sore. The words came out like putrid pus. *What terrible thing have I done that you are punishing me like this? Is it that you don't need leaders any more that you decided to make me sick?! Is this your idea of blessing a disciple's life? I've given everything I am and have to you since I was twenty-two years old, and this is what you give me in return?* The bitterness was overflowing.

After an intensive study of Job and lots of reading and counsel, I realized that *God doesn't owe me an explanation.* I do not have to know why he allows things to happen. If he wanted me to know, he would give me a revelation. My job is to trust him. His love cannot be measured in how healthy or prosperous I am. God's devotion to me is clear in his giving Jesus to die for me and forgiving me when I was a rebellious, immoral, self-serving, blaspheming girl intent on fulfilling my life as I saw fit. The proof of his caring for me doesn't get any more potent than that. He has continued to nurture and guide me for twenty-three years as a disciple even though at times I have treated him shabbily.

I remember when Bob Ricker of the San Diego church was dying. He kept repeating over and over to everyone he spoke with how much God loves him. There must have been many painful questions and temptations in his heart, such as why would God take him at thirty-seven, leaving Jayne a widow, two small children without a dad, a thriving ministry he had built, and a huge curriculum-writing responsibility without an editor and leader. But he didn't let those questions and temptations cause him to lose his trust in God. There will always be unanswered questions. We will die with unanswered questions, but we cannot allow those questions to erode our faith in God. (See chapter 21 in which Jayne tells their story.)

Questions

1. If you had bad feelings toward God, would it be righteous to tell him? Why or why not? Are your prayers open and honest?

2. Have you asked the "Why...?" questions? What did you come up with? Are these answers your speculations or are they Scripture?
3. How do you feel toward God?
4. What would it take for you to leave God?

Additional Scriptures: Job 1-2, 40:1-8, 41:11; Jeremiah 18:1-6; Lamentations 3:31-33

Depression

A man's spirit sustains him in sickness,
  but a crushed spirit who can bear? (Proverbs 18:14)

"The eye is the lamp of the body. If your eyes are good, your whole body will be full of light. But if your eyes are bad, your whole body will be full of darkness. If then the light within you is darkness, how great is that darkness!" (Matthew 6:22-23)

Depression is a multi-faced demon. It can have physiological, psychological and spiritual roots. In fact prolonged pain and depression, not surprisingly, seem to go hand in hand. Many psychological experts say that depression can also be anger turned inward. I was angry with God and other people in my life, but didn't feel it was safe or "Christian" to express it. This brought about a crushing sense of hopelessness. Although it is at times belittled, even in the kingdom, depression is very real and often debilitating.

To a person who is experiencing depression, the glass is not just half empty...

- It is never going to be full again.
- It is my fault that it happened.
- I don't have any way to stop the water that's in it now from evaporating so it's just a matter of time before the whole thing goes dry.
- I should be able to fill it up but I can't; this is just one example of how bad I really am.
- People would be better off without me, and my life is not worth living.

Some of these thoughts may sound humorous, but a person who is seriously depressed sees no humor in these thoughts at all; it is how they really think. Satan's greatest victory is to get someone so warped in her thinking that she would take her life. I've considered this more than once. He turns right into wrong and wrong into right. He makes life seem like slow torture and death like relief. Sometimes the pain of depression is so excruciating that you can almost feel your heart breaking inside your chest. We want to blame ourselves, our illness, God, our family, the medical profession or uncompassionate disciples. The enemy is Satan—and Satan wants me to believe that God has lost my file somewhere and doesn't really care if he finds it. He wants me to believe his lie and separate myself from God.

Some of us don't go so far as to think of killing ourselves, but instead we are the walking dead, going through the motions yet being faithless and hopeless. Satan's purpose is to get us to lose hope to whatever degree he can. The best therapy for depression is to change your mind, change how you think. Most of the time we need help with this because our perceptions can get so distorted and are often deeply rooted. We need each other for reality checks. Even in the best of times, there will always be sin, sadness and negative things vying for our focus. Proverbs 11:27 reminds us that we will find what we are looking for, so we need to choose to look for the good:

He who seeks good finds goodwill,
but evil comes to him who searches for it.

Some people want to know when to seek help from a professional. Hopefully the number of disciples who are professionally trained counselors will be growing in the future, but in some places this service is not available. If your depression significantly affects your relationships, job or other important areas of your life; causes you considerable distress over a period of time; or brings recurring thoughts of suicide, then it is time to get professional help. Enlist the help of friends and pray for God to lead you to suitable counseling.

Along with the depression often comes a deep sense of shame. We feel somehow it is our fault, that we deserve to be sick because of things we have done or just because we are "bad" people. Satan often uses experiences in our childhood to wound us and establish a shame-based perception of ourselves. All the more reason to let the cross touch our hearts and see the truth: God loves us and wants to bless us in ways we never dreamed possible. He wants to heal the past and give us a fresh start. Let God change the "eyes of your heart" to see his love and his caring ways every day of your life.

What about medication? Having been on and off antidepressants for many years, my opinion is this: It is not a sin to take medicine for depression if you need it, and you should do what God leads you to do through your doctor (and through prayer and advice!). Of course, it is important to have a doctor that you trust is not "pill happy." I believe prayer is a vital part of choosing a doctor.

Having said that, here is the bottom line for me: Medication, if it is doing its job, is merely going to emotionally bring you up from the ocean floor to the surface so that you can learn to swim. To use another analogy, it can bring you to the starting line, but it cannot run the race for you. Nobody can run the race but *you*, and you cannot run it without God. Taking a pill will not change the way you think—and thinking is the chief component of depression.

One of the hardest things for a depressed person to accept is that the Spirit of God will enable them to have control over their thoughts. You are more than what you think. You are more than what you feel (1 John 3:19-20). The Spirit of God in you has all the power (and sanity) of God himself. Colossians 2:9-10 says that Jesus has all the power and character of God (his fullness), and we have Jesus in us! It is like sitting in a cold, dark house with no electricity, no way to get warm, cook or wash. What a miserable life. If someone said you should make yourself something to eat, you would say, "I can't." If they said, bring in some light, you would say, "I can't. There is a little candle but it is going to burn up soon, it's hopeless." You could see no way to function. What if someone said the electricity has been on all along, you just *thought* it was out. The reality for a Christian is that we are full of power and wired for maximum wattage "24/7." We have everything we need for life and godliness. The power is on all the time. The lights work, the heater runs, the stove is ready to use. Our challenge is to realize this and fight against the way Satan deceives us with an impotent mindset.

> The weapons we fight with are not the weapons of the world. On the contrary, they have divine power to demolish strongholds. We demolish arguments and every pretension that sets itself up against the knowledge of God, and we take captive every thought to make it obedient to Christ. (2 Corinthians 10:4-5)

The cognitive aspect of overcoming depression is important. Allowing God to reshape the patterns of your mind through the Scriptures is the key. I believe he uses people to help us with this because so many times we cannot see how skewed our thinking has become. God can help you learn to change the way you think, and when your thinking changes to be more spiritually accurate, you will be better able to overcome the schemes of Satan.

Questions

1. How does this section apply to you?
2. On a scale of one to ten, how hopeful do you feel right now? Why?
3. Are you ever tempted to give up? To what extent?

4. Who are your real enemies? (shame, fear, feelings of powerlessness, hopelessness, etc.)
5. Think of a person who can help you change your thinking, and share these feelings with her.

Additional Scriptures: Psalm 112:4, Lamentations 3:19-23, Habakkuk 3:17-19, 2 Corinthians 5:16-17

Self-Pity

> When Jesus saw him lying there and learned that he had been in this condition for a long time, he asked him, "Do you want to get well?"
>
> "Sir," the invalid replied, "I have no one to help me into the pool when the water is stirred. While I am trying to get in, someone else goes down ahead of me." (John 5:6-7)

> If the foot should say, "Because I am not a hand, I do not belong to the body," it would not for that reason cease to be part of the body. (1 Corinthians 12:15)

Nobody understands what I'm going through. "Each heart knows its own bitterness, and no one else can share its joy" (Proverbs 14:10). *Nobody really knows how I feel and the intensity of the pain I deal with.* This is very true. Nobody, that is, but God. I don't like to think of myself as self-pitying, but when the cataloging of my afflictions and the recounting of how people have misunderstood or hurt me keeps going through my mind, I know I'm busted. (See how Elijah, after a bout with fatigue and hopelessness, repeatedly journals his woes in 1 Kings 19:10, 14.) Self-pity focuses on the bad, the weak, the sin, the hurts, everything opposite of Philippians 4:8. Self-pity causes you to be defined by what you cannot do, how much you hurt or how much you have been abused instead of letting yourself see the good that God is doing all around you.

I went through a time of feeling very guilty about being sick and the effect I was having on my family. I regretted that I was restricting our family life by my limitations and giving my kids a sick mom as a role model. Once after coming home from the park where I had watched parents and kids play soccer, Joe, my then young son, said, "I wish you could play soccer like the other moms." Instead of letting him express his feelings, I jumped in and scolded, "Be thankful you have a mother and we're not digging up roots for dinner somewhere in Africa!" I angrily reacted out of my guilt of not being the athletic mom I thought I should be. Sometimes self-pity leads us to envy those who are healthy. Comparing our life to others is a trap of Satan to keep us from finding peace.

God knows what he is doing, and he works all things together for good. If I had not gotten ill, I might not have spent the time with my kids that they needed when they were young. If we were to see all he is doing to help us in our lives, we would probably be in shock! Illness changes our lives and dreams, but it doesn't have to destroy us! True, I cannot do the things I used to do, but there are things I can do now that I couldn't do before—like helping people who are really hurting. I am a better mom because I am more able to prepare my kids for adulthood now that I am in touch with some of the deeper issues of life. I knew a lot of appropriate scriptures about suffering, but they had no personal meaning. Through the weakening of my body, God has strengthened my spirit, and there is nothing more valuable than that.

Questions

1. Have you experienced self-pity lately? How?
2. How do you feel about the effect of your physical challenge on those around you?
3. Do you truly believe God understands what you are going through, hurts with you and wants to help you? Is that enough?
4. Do you find yourself envying healthy people? Do you confess it as a sin?
5. How has God strengthened your spirit in the last few months?
6. What is the best thing spiritually that has come out of your physical challenge?

Additional Scriptures: Proverbs 14:30, Philippians 4:11-12, James 3:14

Entitlement

> "Who has ever given to God,
> that God should repay him?" (Romans 11:35)

> You, my brothers, were called to be free. But do not use your freedom to indulge the sinful nature; rather, serve one another in love. (Galatians 5:13)

As physically challenged disciples, we want people to be compassionate and to trust us when we say we can or cannot do something—after all, "Love always trusts" (1 Corinthians 13:7). That is true and right. But we must never take advantage of someone's trust in order to get out of doing something that we decided we really aren't obligated to do. Sometimes we feel that because we are physically challenged, we are already carrying a cross heavier than anyone should have to bear so we don't have to really be a team player. We reason that our role is to be a long-suffering, yet stoically persevering, disciple—a paragon of martyrdom. We are "the special case," the loophole that states that if you are physically challenged then God doesn't require you to be a full disciple. We expect the boundaries of discipleship to be moved for us because we are afflicted. When we feel too much is being asked of us, are we open and do we go to God; or do we play our trump, the "victim card" that "wins" the hand and justifies our rebellion?

Paul says in 1 Corinthians 10:13 that there is nothing happening to you that has not happened to someone else before. Sometimes in our minds we think we are being targeted by the "Demon of Ongoing Hardship." We think we could win a "Who's Got the Worst Problems?" contest (or at least make the finals). But the scripture says that our problems (even though legitimate) are not unique. Other people have experienced them and overcome. God is faithful. He will not let things go on to the extent that you will be crushed. He always provides an escape so you can stand up under Satan's pressure.

What about Jesus? If anyone was entitled, he was. In Philippians 2:6-7 it says that Jesus did not cling to his rights or privileges. He had the power of heaven and earth. He did not have to die, experience temptations of the flesh (sexual, pride, greed, etc.) or ever be separated from his Father. Yet, he gave it all up to come down into the trenches of humanity, daily giving up his freedom to redeem a thankless people and show them a picture of what God is like.

The stipulations of following Jesus are no different for us than for a healthy person. We simply need to implement them more creatively. It is not *if* I'm going to be a disciple but *how*. By the power of the Spirit, we can still reach out, still love our brothers and sisters, still be an involved part of the church in ways that God will make clear, even if we don't make all the activities. Even with my physical challenge and its accompanying temptations and the demands of having teenagers, by God's grace I am more fruitful now than I have ever been in my Christian life.

Questions

1. Do you ever find yourself feeling like "Martha Martyr"? "Wendy Whiner"? "Sally Stoic"? Explain.
2. How did Jesus deal with his entitlement? (Philippians 2:5-11)
3. What "loopholes" have you written into your life? In what ways do you feel exempt from participating because of your physical challenge?
4. What is God trying to say to you about entitlement?

Additional Scriptures: Proverbs 16:18, 29:23

Fear and Anxiety

I sought the LORD, and he answered me;
    he delivered me from all my fears. (Psalm 34:4)

"In repentance and rest is your salvation,
    in quietness and trust is your strength." (Isaiah 30:15)

Anxiety is as debilitating as a physical illness. It is a spiritual panic, a faithless response to a challenging situation. There is nothing more miserable than being in the grip of fear. Sometimes we are like King Asa: "Though his disease was severe, even in his illness he did not seek help from the LORD, but only from physicians" (2 Chronicles 16:12). At times I have put more faith in doctors and therapeutic regimens than in God. Oh, I would pray for guidance and blessing, but my hopes were more in the process than the Provider. "Unless the LORD builds the house, its builders labor in vain" (Psalm 127:1a). God is the great healer. He uses treatments to help us. Too often we "run after all these things" like pagans (Matthew 6:32) and then wonder why the storm demolishes our house. Medical treatments, as good as they are, do not provide the peace that passes understanding.

At times we get down on our knees to pray, and we get up with the heart of an atheist! It is like we never prayed—our faith is so low. Faith is believing that after you ask God for help, he *will indeed* help you. Faith is not, "Maybe he will," or "Wouldn't it be nice if he..." Realize that it may not be the way you had planned or the answer you wanted, but he will always give you the fruit of the Spirit when you pray for that fruit with a humble heart. At times I have caught myself thinking, *I'm forty-seven now; how can I face thirty more years of fatigue? What is going to happen to me if Ryan dies? How can I support the family? How can I raise the kids by myself with this illness?* Worries and fears not given over to God will only make our health worse and destroy us spiritually.

In 1999, I went through severe trials with my family and health, yet I experienced peace like I have never before felt. Even while waves crash into the boat, God longs to calm the storm of fear in our hearts. He will always give us the ability to handle whatever comes. He wants to give us peace and joy. I have filled so many prayer journals giving my cares over to him. He wants to help us "overcome evil with good" by calling on him in faith. "If you then, though you are evil, know how to give good gifts to your children, how much more will your Father in heaven give the Holy Spirit to those who ask him!" (Luke 11:13).

Consider Jesus in the garden of Gethsemane. He was so stressed that he was literally sweating blood. He was overwhelmed with sadness to the point of dying from it (severe depression?). What did he do? He could have freaked out and run away. He could have gotten angry and gone into a tirade or lashed out at his unsupportive friends. Instead, he decided to pray, even protectively encouraging his buddies to pray for themselves as he walked away. After he prayed once, it says an angel appeared and strengthened him. Wow! What would that feel like—to be strengthened by an angel? Did he jump up, high-five the angel and say, "I'm healed! It's going to be all right"? No, the strength he received was to enable him to go back and pray again "more earnestly," to persevere through the anguish (Luke 22:39-44). God gave Jesus the staying power he needed—and he will do the same for us.

Questions

1. What is your first response when you receive bad news about your health? Then what do you do?
2. Do you find yourself worrying? About what?
3. Read Philippians 4:4-7. How does God guard your heart?
4. How do you rate your prayer life? Where is your faith *after* you pray?
5. Which fruit of the Spirit (Galatians 5:22-23) do you most want to grow in?

Additional Scriptures: Psalm 46:1-2, 94:17-19, 112:7-8; Proverbs 3:21-26; Isaiah 41:10, 43:1-2; 1 Peter 5:7

Deceitfulness

Surely you desire truth in the inner parts;
    you teach me wisdom in the inmost place. (Psalm 51:6)

If we claim to be without sin, we deceive ourselves and the truth is not in us. (1 John 1:8)

There are different ways of being deceitful. Sometimes we deceive ourselves by denying that we have a physical problem or by denying the severity of it. We don't want to face the possibility of cancer or something life altering, so we pretend that nothing is wrong. At one point I had an elder's wife, our regional leaders and my husband all telling me I should take the medication recommended to me by four different doctors. Why did they have to come at me in force? Because I didn't think I needed it. I was afraid taking drugs would mean I was weak. I could handle things myself. My pride and denial were making me deceive myself. Also, as the illness progresses, we sometimes feel that we cannot cope with another loss, so we ignore the symptoms and do not act responsibly with our health. Denial is self-deception, a fear of the truth. With God's help we can face the unacceptable.

Sometimes we hide behind the illness and use it as an excuse not to do the things we really don't want to do anyway. Our hearts become divided. Do I protect myself and stay "safe" or trust God and his people to lead me? Sometimes we don't express our feelings because we don't want to complain or we don't want people to think we are whining. But then we end up with festering attitudes. The truth is that those of us who are physically challenged have sin just like everyone else, and we need to have the spiritual integrity to confess it. Sometimes our minds and hearts get in a big confusing muddle of pain, disillusionment, fear and self-protection. The best way to get things sorted out is to share how we feel and start confessing sin. Satan always works the night shift. He hides in the dark crevices of our closed mouths.

Many years ago, Ryan talked with someone who was very depressed. He spent several hours trying to help him and never heard back about his progress. Much later it became known that this person had loads of hidden sin that eventually caused him to lose his marriage and family. Unconfessed sin will affect your mind, emotions, body and spirit.

The life of a physically challenged disciple naturally provides many potential crevices of darkness with the isolation, pain and disappointments we experience. Fight back. Tell the truth. Own up to your sin. Psalm 32 says that having unconfessed sin affects your health; it saps your strength and makes you feel as if you are wasting away. I think one reason that I am able to do more now than in the past is that I am dealing with the sin in my heart, and that is giving me more energy through the Spirit.

Questions

1. In what ways have you been in denial? Deceitful?
2. What is the hardest thing for you to face about your life or future?
3. Do you ever protect yourself in wrong ways or for wrong reasons? How?
4. What would God say to you right now about your heart?
5. Do you regularly confess your sins? Are there sins in your life that you have been afraid to confess?

Additional Scriptures: Psalm 15:1-2, 86:11; James 3:14; 1 John 1:5-7

Unrighteous Escapes

"Come to me, all you who are weary and burdened, and I will give you rest." (Matthew 11:28)

"Everything is permissible for me"—but not everything is beneficial. "Everything is permissible for me"—but I will not be mastered by anything. (1 Corinthians 6:12)

The proper use of medication is an ever-present issue in the life of many physically challenged disciples. One of the hardest areas for the physically challenged, especially those with chronic pain and sleep problems, is to learn how to manage their prescription drugs without becoming addicted or psychologically dependent. I could not begin to tell you how many different prescription drugs I have tried over the years. One thing I know is that you have to ask yourself, "Why am I taking this? Am I taking this because there is legitimate pain that I can no longer handle, or am I taking this because I am weary of fighting and I want to escape? Is this a spiritual anesthetic?" Only God can fill the deep needs of our souls. Using a drug to fill a spiritual void is a sin and will only prolong the pain because now you have added guilt and a possible addiction. Do you go to the medicine cabinet before you go to God? Do you thank God for the technology that he allowed to be discovered so you could have this great treatment? Do you ask him to guide you in the righteous use of this gift?

What about food? Many of us go to food for comfort and end up hurting ourselves by what we eat. We aggravate our illness or create new ones by not being self-controlled in our diets. A few days of poor dietary choices can set me back significantly. At times in the past I've resented having to add such a restricted lifestyle to all my other challenges; I felt like God had me on a short leash. Technically everyone is on a short leash. We can do nothing without God. Maybe those of us making constant health choices are more fortunate because we are consciously and absolutely unable to function without calling out to God for his strength.

At times, in an effort to avoid pain pills, I would lose myself in a novel. After awhile, the "losing myself" (from the emotional pain of my life) became as attractive as the alleviation of physical pain. In fact, losing myself would numb me in many ways. I had found a refuge but it was not God. Consequently, my life was not blessed like it could have been (Psalm 34:8). One day I was reading Jonah 2:8: "Those who cling to worthless idols forfeit the grace that could be theirs." I became convicted that I was trading the grace of God for my escapes, which is a really poor exchange.

Many of us who are physically challenged have a problem with insomnia. What do you do when you are up at night, all alone? It is very easy to slip into entertaining ourselves by watching or reading things we shouldn't or ruminating about our sorry plight. Even benign things can take the place of using the time to draw closer to God. I've made a commitment to not get into worldly things if I can't sleep. I can write cards to people, brainstorm ways to encourage others, pray or read my Bible or some good spiritual books. Let's not give Satan an appointment with us after bedtime.

God wants to be involved in our every need. He wants to give us discipline to say no to unrighteous ways of coping. Reach out for him.

When we shut God out of the process or use sinful ways to deal with our pain, we grieve the Spirit and keep God from giving us true peace, even in our distress.

Questions

1. What are the issues you are facing with medications?
2. Do you thank God for these medications and ask for guidance in using them properly? Why or why not?
3. Are there areas of your life that are out of control? In what ways would God have you draw more self-control from his Spirit?
4. Where do you usually go for comfort? Does it work?
5. How could prayer be more a part of your "therapy"?

Additional Scriptures: Psalm 31, 121; 2 Corinthians 1:3; 1 Timothy 5:23

The Opportunities of the Physically Challenged

Being physically challenged has brought many opportunities for spiritual growth into my life, many of which I did not consider a blessing. They have, however, turned out to be some of the most precious treasures in my life. This growth was well worth the grief it took to acquire it. Consider the following opportunities that your physical challenge offers you.

Experience Grace

> For in the gospel a righteousness from God is revealed, a righteousness that is by faith from first to last, just as it is written: "The righteous will live by faith." (Romans 1:17)

> If, in fact, Abraham was justified by works, he had something to boast about—but not before God. What does the Scripture say? "Abraham believed God, and it was credited to him as righteousness." (Romans 4:2-3)

There was a time when I was very grateful for God's grace but was not desperately dependent on it. I could function in every aspect as a disciple, lead people and raise my family. As my illness grew more debilitating, I could no longer "perform" as I had before. I felt worthless, and finally came to see that I got my self-esteem from what I could do. Since I could no longer do the things I once did, then what use was I? This propelled me into a study of grace and a complete reevaluation of my perception of my worth to God. I began to see that God wants my heart, my faith, my trust. He will work out all the other details.

Seven years ago, Suzanne Atkins, a thirty-two year old disciple with two small boys, became ill. She was hospitalized, and three and a half weeks later died of cancer. I remember going to see her in the hospital. She was discouraged and very concerned about her relationship with God because she could not "do" anything. (Suzanne had always been very active in the ministry.) I asked her if, when she was baptized, she had repented and given her whole life over to God.

"Yes, I did," she replied.

"Then you were forgiven, and that's what you've got to hold on to now, by faith."

We read some scriptures, and from that point on she was at peace, trusting God to keep his promise of taking her to be with him forever. In fact, even though she was bald and bloated, she became radiantly beautiful (Psalm 34:5) because she accepted that the shame of her sin was taken away on the cross. I'll never forget the glow on her face and the brilliance of her blue eyes. She arranged a party for one of her friends in her hospital room. She called old friends, trying to get them to church up until the time she died. Once she trusted that she could not earn her salvation with her "works," she was able to see the things she *could* do—and she did them in joy and gratitude. The words of the psalmist show us clearly that God does not delight in what we do; he delights in who we are:

His pleasure is not in the strength of the horse,
    nor his delight in the legs of a [woman];
the LORD delights in those who fear him,
    who put their hope in his unfailing love.
(Psalm 147:10-11, emphasis added)

As physically challenged disciples, we have the opportunity to extend grace to others. Sometimes we react to each other, yes, even our own physically challenged sisters, with an attitude of "Well, I'm being tough, why aren't you? Just pull it together!" Sometimes it is easy to feel this way toward healthy people who have the flu or an obviously short-term illness. We have many opportunities to show grace to those who are insensitive or who simply do not understand what we are going through. When I am not letting God's grace permeate my heart, I do not extend it to others. It is a sign that I'm spiritually grinding it out at the salt mines, not letting God lead me to the oasis.

Righteousness comes from God. By faith I believe that he makes me righteous. In all the times during my day when I am faced with reacting out of my sinful nature, I can choose to obey, choose to believe because of all that he has done for me. What freedom! I am secure in his love for me. I have already won the spiritual lottery. Can I share my winnings with you?

Questions

1. How would you describe grace?
2. In what ways has God shown you his grace?
3. Does Suzanne's example call you higher? How?
4. Do you really believe you are forgiven? Why or why not?
5. If not, who could you talk with about it? When will you?

Additional Scriptures: Romans 4:18-25, 11:5-6; Galatians 2:21, 3:10-11

Recognize Sin

> A rebuke impresses a man of discernment
>   more than a hundred lashes a fool. (Proverbs 17:10)

> Hate what is evil; cling to what is good. (Romans 12:9b)

As we in California know, when the internal pressure inside the earth reaches a certain point, an earthquake will occur along a weak crack—a fault line. Physical illness is like that increasing pressure in your life. Pretty soon, you will be able to map out your fault lines because that is the first place you will blow. The San Andreas Fault is no comparison to the faults that have erupted in my life as I have reacted sinfully during my illness. I have seen the shallowness of my faith—how it could not support an open-ended illness. I've seen how I can become irritable, withdrawn and self-protective. At times I have robbed my husband of a loving wife and my kids of a happy, involved mom. I have seen how easy it is for me to put myself in God's place by deciding what my future should hold. It is a blessing that he has shown me my faults because those are the things that could keep me from being happy, and more than anything, keep me from getting to heaven.

God brought our beloved sister, Irene Gurganus, back from the doors of death last year. She says that it is extremely difficult for her to have therapists come every day to her house and teach her again how to walk, cook and take care of herself. Being eighty, she wanted to stay in bed and rest. She found herself questioning God as to why he would save her life and then give her a debilitating handicap requiring a grueling daily rehabilitation regimen for months. Wouldn't it have been easier to let her die when she was unconscious anyway? Then she realized her sin of ungratefulness. She prayed a lot and began to count her blessings. Now the worst is over and she is mobile again. More importantly, she is thankful.

Irene also has had to deal with the process of aging. For example, she can no longer drive. At first she fought the dependency of having to ask for rides, but now she has come to accept that aging is part of God's

PHYSICALLY CHALLENGED   127

plan. As she says, if she fights this—she is fighting God. Again, she counts her blessings.

Where are your fault lines? Mine are laid open before you and I challenge you as a fellow physically challenged disciple to pray to see your sinful reactions (you know you have them) and to repent daily. We fight a lot of things—insurance companies, our limitations and the fast pace of life—but our primary battle should be against our sin, against the things that steal our joy, sap our strength and weaken our impact on the lost.

Questions

1. In what ways has having a physical challenge put pressure on you? On your family?
2. How does Satan usually come after you?
3. What are the cracks you have seen as a result of the pressure? (i.e., your sinful nature)
4. Are you fighting God? How?
5. Are you grateful to have your sin exposed so you can repent and grow?

Additional Scriptures: Exodus 17:1-3, Matthew 7:24-27, Mark 4:18-19

Live in a Miracle

> But God chose the foolish things of the world to shame the wise; God chose the weak things of the world to shame the strong. (1 Corinthians 1:27)

> But he said to me, "My grace is sufficient for you, for my power is made perfect in weakness." Therefore I will boast all the more gladly about my weaknesses, so that Christ's power may rest on me. For when I am weak, then I am strong. (2 Corinthians 12:9, 10b)

There are many paradoxes in the Bible. God seems to delight in them. An uneducated, manual laborer changing the course of history. A shameful, criminal execution bringing resurrection to all mankind. When I have no strength or ability, God uses me most powerfully. I consider myself one of the Biblically "weak." I am weak physically (definitely) and emotionally (at times). Since I have stopped trying to be "super disciple" and have let God be my strength, he has made miraculous changes in my heart and life. I am doing things that I could not have imagined before. Why? Not because I have been healed, but because I have finally acknowledged what God has always known to be true—I have no power, no talent, no strength apart from him.

A miracle we can experience any day is having the Holy Spirit pray for us when we are disturbed and unable to pray:

> In the same way, the Spirit helps us in our weakness. We do not know what we ought to pray for, but the Spirit himself intercedes for us with groans that words cannot express. And he who searches our hearts knows the mind of the Spirit, because the Spirit intercedes for the saints in accordance with God's will. (Romans 8:26-27)

When we don't know the words to say, the Spirit acts like an interpreter of the deep emotions of our hearts and presents them to God as an advocate.

I have a small part-time business supervising parents who are ordered by the court to be monitored when they visit their children. One day while driving to a visit, I wished I could turn around and go home. I felt extremely tired and confused, definitely not up to the constant attentiveness and activity of following around a small boy and his parent. I was fearful that I would do a poor job, missing some important interactions or just not be able to keep up with their pace. Since these visits are court ordered and highly structured, there was no way I could cancel. I was in too much of a muddle in my mind to pray a long prayer, so I just said, "Help me, God" and put on some Christian music. As it played, I forced myself to sing along. After about ten minutes, I began to feel stronger. By the time I arrived at Chuckie Cheese, God had filled me with the Spirit and given me a joy and energy that was miraculous. I was a different person, still tired but now with a faithful and happy attitude that God was right there helping me, and it would be okay.

How many times have I felt impotent, tired and unable to face something imminent in my day—a meeting, a job, another doctor's appointment, a discipling time, a study, whatever? And then, when I have called out to God (sometimes with a long prayer, sometimes just a "Help!") and either sung songs of praise or put on Christian music to be filled with the Spirit (Ephesians 5:18-19), he always resurrects my faith and gives me a new, courageous heart.

God can change your weariness to worship. What miracle does he have in store for you today?

Questions

1. Why might you doubt that God's grace is sufficient for you? What does it mean to you that it is sufficient?
2. In what ways has God shown you that in your weakness you are strong?
3. Why does God want us to sing?
4. What miracle (apart from being healed) would you like to see God do in your life today? This week? This year?

Additional Scriptures: Jeremiah 29:11, Psalm 40:5, 1 Corinthians 2:9

Discover New Gifts

But in fact God has arranged the parts in the body, every one of them, just as he wanted them to be. (1 Corinthians 12:18)

For if the willingness is there, the gift is acceptable according to what one has, not according to what he does not have. (2 Corinthians 8:12)

Many of us grieve the loss of what we can no longer do, the death of the dreams and expectations we had for our lives. This often becomes depression (anger turned inward) and we feel useless. Our God is the King of Resurrection, the Mighty Recycler. He can raise our physically challenged lives from the dead and give us new roles, tapping gifts we never realized we had. Before I got sick, I was not a person to sit around for very long. I liked to stay busy with the ministry and countless household projects and renovations, not to mention gardening, crafts and thrift shopping. Becoming ill has drastically changed my life, and I discovered gifts that I would have never noticed living that busy lifestyle. For example, I love to read and write. I have also been able to clear out the "fun but not eternal" things that used to keep me so busy. Would the whole kingdom (and those generations to come) be so incredibly blessed with the wisdom from our DPI books had Tom Jones not gotten Multiple Sclerosis and had to "slow down"?

Diane Goff was an interpreter and co-leader of the deaf ministry in the church for many years before her physical challenge forced her to stop. This was extremely disappointing. For a while, she felt adrift and useless. Battling depression and fighting to keep her faith she thought, "I can't do anything so why bother even trying?" As she learned to trust that God knows what he is doing, she began to look for other ways to serve. Diane had always been good at crafts, and someone asked her to make some things for the children's ministry. Through this she and her husband, Dana, got involved with the Kingdom Kid's Curriculum helping with supplies, organization and distribution—very important behind-the-scene responsibilities. They are invaluable in the running of our children's program. Diane says, "I'm amazed at what I can do when my heart is right. When my heart is focused on the teachers and the kids, I have much more energy. It is not that I *have* to do this, but I'm happy that I *can* do something to serve."

God always has a plan to prosper you and meet the needs of the kingdom. *You cannot be happy without a place and a way to serve.* Prayer warriors are just as important as those on the front lines. In fact, there could be some debate about where the "front lines" really are. We are all one body. God wants to reveal his plan for you because he wants you to be happy and useful. Let God reinvent you.

Questions

1. Have you grieved over losses as a result of your physical challenge? How did you come to accept the changes?
2. What are the essential things in your life now?
3. What gifts have you discovered since you have been sick or injured?
4. What would you like to do to serve in the kingdom?

Additional Scriptures: Romans 12:3-8, 1 Corinthians 12:4-6, 1 Peter 4:10

Develop Compassion

When Jesus landed and saw a large crowd, he had compassion on them and healed their sick. (Matthew 14:14)

We have different gifts, according to the grace given us. If a man's gift is...showing mercy, let him do it cheerfully. (Romans 12:6-8)

Before I got sick, I thought if you were ill you went to the doctor, got some medicine and then you got well. I had no real concept of chronic illness, except a vague suspicion of hypochondria. When I was growing up, complaining about ailments was mocked, and malingering was considered a cardinal sin. Being physically challenged has opened the doors of my heart in so many ways. I was accustomed to running on a fast track with little time for prolonged interruptions. In many ways I was skimming along the surface of life, trying to avoid the deeper issues. I remember when I was newly pregnant with Joe, an older brother, Harold, came to dinner at our house. He had cerebral palsy. He was in a wheelchair, drooled constantly, had hands that trembled and made a big mess when he ate, and he smelled bad. I tried to eat at the same table but got nauseous and had to vomit. I remember struggling with the situation and thought, *What if that were you, Linda? Would you want people being grossed out by you when you were doing the best you could? Would you want people to avoid you? He didn't ask to be that way.* I decided that I just needed to grow up, throw up and go on, asking God to change my heart.

Glen Kirkpatrick, a former law enforcement officer, became a disciple after being diagnosed with Hodgkin's Disease. Because of how God had worked in his life and illness, he was able to help Andy Hicks, seventy-eight, (also formerly in law enforcement) become a disciple. Andy was blind and paralyzed from the waist down. Glen said that he was able to learn compassion for Andy as he gave him shots, fed him, listened to him and gave him

PHYSICALLY CHALLENGED

rides to church in his special van. He was then able to bring in other brothers to help Andy, discipling them in how to have compassion.

Consider Jesus having been awake for two days—bleeding, beaten to within an inch of his life and abandoned by all his friends. He was about as physically challenged as you can get, almost dead, hanging on nails. Instead of pulling inward to survive as most of us would do, he sees his mother and remembers that she will need a protector in her old age and tells John to take care of her. The criminal hanging next to him who had belittled him earlier has a change of heart and defends him to his fellow thief. Then he asks Jesus to remember him when he goes into heaven. Jesus jumps on that last minute contrition and forgives the man, comforting him with the assurance of being with him in paradise that very day. What a great model of compassion during physical struggles! What a great model of unconditional love.

Pain and struggle are part of the lives of so many. Jesus always responded with compassion to sick or handicapped people. He was never disgusted—even with nasty, contagious skin conditions. He was never insensitive or contemptuous—even when people were ungrateful for their healing. I believe that he "comforts us in all our troubles, so that we can comfort those in any trouble with the comfort we ourselves have received from God" (2 Corinthians 1:4). When we feel Jesus' compassion for us, we can pass it on to others.

Questions

1. Before you got ill (or before you were a disciple), what was your concept of people with chronic illness?
2. How has being physically challenged opened the doors of your heart?
3. Is there someone who is physically challenged that you find it hard to treat compassionately?
4. How could your compassion be a blessing to others?

Additional Scriptures: Psalm 116:5, 145:9; Isaiah 49:15; Matthew 20:34

Be Part of God's Special Forces

If one falls down,
  his friend can help him up.
But pity the man who falls
  and has no one to help him up! (Ecclesiastes 4:10)

The Sovereign LORD has given me an instructed tongue,
  to know the word that sustains the weary. (Isaiah 50:4)

My cousin, Mike, is a high ranking officer in the Army. His job is to take a special unit into foreign countries who have experienced a natural disaster, famine or devastation from war. They help rebuild cities, transport food, bring medical support and generally assist the people in getting their country back together. His units are trained to meet all kinds of needs in all kinds of situations. In many war-torn countries, they go in and train the civilians how to spot and disarm landmines. They show them how, but do not do it for them.

Those of us who have been dealing with physical challenges have a special calling. We are specially trained to recognize the needs of our fellow strugglers. We know what it is like to experience the losses, pain, fears, anger and all the ups and downs of a physically challenged life. Like the special forces, we comfort, love, support and train, but it is up to each physically challenged person to, with God's help, remove their own landmines. Each one of us in our hearts has to come to faith in God in our distinctive situation, while drawing encouragement from and sometimes being carried by each other.

> Praise be to the God and Father of our Lord Jesus Christ, the father of compassion and the God of all comfort, who comforts us in all our troubles, so that we can comfort those in any trouble with the comfort we have received from God. For just as the sufferings of Christ flow over into our lives, so also through Christ our comfort overflows. (2 Corinthians 1:3-5)

Two fellow special-team members have gone on to be with God, but they taught us by the way they handled their physical challenge and death. Nidia Feast became a Christian as she was dying of cancer. She was able to attend one Women's Day and one service before she was incapacitated. Her husband persecuted her faith and was a bitter man. The disciples served her family (she had two sons) with meals. Staying strong in her faith, she died five months later. Three months after her death, her husband agreed to study the Bible and became a disciple—and then one of her sons also became a disciple!

Amy Calkins lived with cancer off and on for five years. She went through chemo and radiation yet was always cheerful. She hardly ever missed a service. I remember at our last marriage retreat, she was in her wheelchair with the oxygen tank strapped on and the tube in her nose, her denim hat on with a big flower (she had lost her hair), out on the dance floor with her husband, Will. She was dancing with her upper body, Will was dancing while spinning her around and popping wheelies with her chair. Those of us looking on held our breath that she would survive the stunts, but they were having a blast. She went home to be with God a year ago and left her joyful legacy with her two girls, who are very active in the youth ministry.

Recently a long time friend and disciple called me very distraught, mildly hysterical. She had just found put that her Hepatitis C had progressed to the point that the doctor prescribed debilitating chemotherapy (Interferon) for a year. The same day she was told that because of the degenerative arthritis in her knees she would have to permanently go into a wheelchair and use arm brace crutches for short treks. The doctors said a knee replacement would help, but that she was too young, refusing to think about it until another ten to fifteen years. How do you think she was feeling? What would you have said if you were me? She was grieving, angry and emotional. How could she continue to work in the children's ministry, which she loves so dearly? How can she face giving herself shots that produce nausea and fatigue for a whole year? Why is God letting this happen now? Since I didn't (and probably will never) know the answer to those questions, I decided to just listen while conveying my love and support. Knowing how it feels when you are in an emotional crisis, I refrained from rushing over with a copy of this article or giving her an exegetical lesson on faith or insisting she pray with me. She knows all this anyway and it was not the time.

Later she said reading Tom Jones' book *Mind Change* put it all into perspective.

> We need to change our minds about life. Life is a gift. It comes from someone else, and it comes to accomplish his purposes, not ours. When you change your mind about this, it changes the way you look at a lot of things.[1]

I remember the first time I read that book. What an encouragement! Tom was willing to open up and help us understand the games Satan is trying to play between our ears (and in our hearts). As Tom shared about his life and the lives of others, God's Spirit was able to minister to me. Again, when I listened to his tapes, *Finding God in Pain and Problems*, my heart was discipled.[2] He is a great example of using what he has learned to help others. Satan wants us to be self-centered and to isolate ourselves, but true joy is found in openly giving and taking care of others.

Questions

1.   In what ways are you uniquely qualified to help others?
2.   Name a specific defeat and a victory that you could share to help someone.

[1]Thomas A. Jones, *Mind Change: The Overcomer's Handbook, Second Edition* (Billerica, Mass.: Discipleship Publications International, 1997), 73.

[2]Thomas A. Jones, *Finding God in Pain and Problems, Audio Tape Series* (Billerica, Mass.: Discipleship Publications International, 1999).

3. Do you feel a bond with your fellow physically challenged disciples? In what ways could you help "rescue" other physically challenged disciples? In what ways could you encourage them to help each other?

Additional Scriptures: Romans 13:8, 2 Corinthians 1:8-11, Colossians 3:16, 1 Thessalonians 5:11

Bear Fruit

Then Jesus came to them and said, "All authority in heaven and on earth has been given to me. Therefore go and make disciples of all nations, baptizing them in the name of the Father and of the Son and of the Holy Spirit, and teaching them to obey everything I have commanded you. And surely I am with you always, to the very end of the age." (Matthew 28:18-20)

"Neither this man nor his parents sinned," said Jesus, "but this happened so that the work of God might be displayed in his life." (John 9:3)

Everything God does is to "bring all things in heaven and on earth together under one head, even Christ" (Ephesians 1:10). God truly wants all men and women to be saved. He wants us to have the attitude of Paul when he says, "What has happened to me has really served to advance the gospel" (Philippians 1:12). Too often we let our challenges isolate us or make us self-absorbed. Then we end up too stifled by doubts to share our faith.

I remember being in an emergency room with my friend Angie while she was experiencing a debilitating migraine. In between throwing up, getting shots and taking medication, she managed to share her faith with someone. I felt so convicted about the times I let my fatigue and moods keep me from speaking about my God.

Bob Ricker, although with God for two years now, is still bearing fruit. The last Sunday he was able to come to services he had six guests with him. From his deathbed, he was adamant about Jayne, his wife, following up with his barber. After Bob died, the man and his wife were baptized. They are now in the full-time ministry as interns, bearing fruit themselves.

A few months ago, Ryan and I decided to go and meet some people since we had moved into a new neighborhood. When the time came to go out, I was exhausted. I asked my daughter, Rachel, to go with him and, as I was praying, they met a family pulling in with their moving van. My husband and daughter were able to help unload the van and watch their two small girls (things I would not have been able to physically do). Later we planned to go back and invite them again to church. I was feeling really bad

PHYSICALLY CHALLENGED

and struggled with going but I went anyway. She became our sister in Christ. God worked in spite of my weakness. He is always at work.

God keeps reminding me that it is his power and not mine. He has the people he wants to be invited to church and loved. I look back over the last few years at the women I have been able to help become Christians. There was no time during their studies when I felt "able" to lead them. On a physical level I had to deny myself to make every study, every appointment. It isn't how good I feel, how I look, how sharp my mind is, or even the abundance of faith I have. But God has open people for me to reach out to, and if I make myself available, sick or well, he will lead me in helping them.

Questions

1. How is your outreach? How is it affected by your physical challenge?
2. Who would you like to see saved because of your efforts?
3. How can the work of God be shown in your life?
4. How much of your prayer time is given to the lost?

Additional Scriptures: Luke 23:38-43; Acts 16:22-25, 17:26-27

To Friends of the Physically Challenged

Some people don't look sick. This can compound your efforts to understand what they are going through. Some people do look ill, and it makes you nervous or uncomfortable. Being around the physically challenged may bring up fears and questions in your mind. Are they contagious? What if this were to happen to me? How would I deal with it? Becoming close to someone physically challenged can cause you to question your own faith and the character of God. If you find yourself resistant to getting close to your physically challenged friend, it may be that it is bringing up fears in you about your future and mortality.

Paul says in Galatians 4:14, "Even though my illness was a trial to you, you did not treat me with contempt or scorn. Instead you welcomed me as if I were an angel of God, as if I were Christ Jesus himself." Being ill is a trial for the person—and for those around her. Sometimes we react with contempt like, "They're probably making it up," or "It couldn't be *that* bad," or "You manage to do the things you want to do." We must be careful to guard our hearts against suspicion and mistrust.

Earlier, I mentioned a physically challenged man named Harold. As I watched him be lifted from chair to couch to car, watched his trembling gnarled hands unsuccessfully attempt to wipe the drool from his face and food from his clothes, watched him struggle to form the words to ask people to take him home with them, watched those lonely eyes look to see if someone would stop and take the time and effort to talk and listen to him, I began to struggle with my own faith. One day I blurted out to Ryan, "If I were Harold, I just don't know what I would do!" He adeptly replied, "If you were Harold, you would have to come to faith." I'll never forget that. There are so many things we can't explain and cause us consternation, but the call is to be a disciple in whatever situation we find ourselves. "Whatever happens, conduct yourselves in a manner worthy of the gospel of Christ" (Philippians 1:27a).

I believe the book of Job has much to say to a person experiencing physical challenges and trials as well as to the people surrounding them. In fact, it is the most comprehensive piece that God has given us to understand suffering and how the sufferer and friends should deal with it. Here is my personal thumbnail version of its message and how it could apply to us today.

- Satan wanted to destroy Job. After massacring all his livestock, servants, and children (notice he didn't take his wife...it seems she was more of a weapon alive than dead), Job still trusted God and maintained his faith. Satan was stumped and probably frustrated (note the exclamation point in the scripture below). He decided to pull out his biggest gun, his ace in the hole, and attack Job's health.

"Skin for skin!" Satan replied. "A man will give all he has for his own life. But stretch out your hand and strike his flesh and bones, and he will surely curse you to your face." (Job 2: 4-5)

Job was afflicted with "painful sores from the soles of his feet to the top of his head" (Job 2:7).

- Satan continues his attack using the person closest to Job, his wife, to entice him to sin. "Are you still holding on to your integrity? Curse God and die!" (Job 2:9). Maybe Job wondered why she could not have been visiting the children when the tornado struck, such help that she was! Then again, she had just lost all her children, servants and income as well—but she handled it faithlessly, tempting her husband to give up.
- Then Satan moves on to Job's friends. At first they were sympathetic and showed compassionate understanding by quietly being by Job's side. Then after a week, Job begins to express his sorrow.

"Why is light given to those in misery,
    and life to the bitter of soul,
to those who long for death that does not come,
    who search for it more than hidden treasure,

PHYSICALLY CHALLENGED

who are filled with gladness
and rejoice when they reach the grave?" (Job 3:20-22)

How many times have we been in pain and have wished that we could go on to heaven and be done with it? We know we are going there, so why can't we go now? Job's friends had heard enough of this depressing talk and they wanted to "fix" him. It is very hard to stand by and watch someone suffer. It evokes all kinds of emotions within us. They wanted to make sense of this devastation. They couldn't handle it. There had to be a way to get this resolved. It is very frustrating to be around someone who is suffering and not be able to *do* anything about it. But God was using the situation to convict them of their pride in presuming to explain why God allowed Job to suffer.

- Eliphaz contemptuously twists the truth in an attempt to shame Job.

"Your words have supported those who stumbled;
　　you have strengthened faltering knees.
But now trouble comes to you, and you are discouraged;
　　it strikes you, and you are dismayed.
Should not your piety be your confidence
　　and your blameless ways your hope?" (Job 4:4-6)

In effect, he says, "What's your problem? You can do all this good to help others when they are suffering, but let it happen to you and you fall apart." This is abusive, with Satan intending to undermine Job's confidence in himself and God. Job is a righteous man; he does not tout his goodness, but neither does he admit doing anything that would warrant this kind of pain. He is confident of his relationship with God. He refers to his friends as "unreliable" and "of no help."

- Job continues to express his agony and bitterness, honestly expressing his emotions, while holding on to the goodness of God.

"Therefore I will not keep silent;
　　I will speak out in the anguish of my spirit,
　　I will complain in the bitterness of my soul." (Job 7:11)

"Oh, that I might have my request,
that God would grant me what I hope for,
that God would be willing to crush me,
　　to loose his hand and cut me off!
Then I would still have this consolation—

my joy in unrelenting pain—
that I had not denied the words of the Holy One." (Job 6:8-10)

One thing I have learned from Job is that God wants us to express our feelings no matter how ugly or seemingly unfaithful. Just think what might have happened to Job had he stuffed all this! Asaph and David are also great examples of expressing their doubts. "Has God forgotten to be merciful?" (Psalm 77:9). Then they move on to the fact of God's love. God wants us to express our innermost doubts and fears outloud and then follow this by expressing confidence in his love—even if we don't feel like we understand anything.

Job's friends used scriptures and spiritual common sense, but they did not use them in the right way. Remember Satan tempting Jesus in the wilderness? Satan used scriptures and the truths of God but did not apply them properly to the situation. We have to be really careful in counseling each other during trials. We need to use the truth to help and heal in the way God intends. Don't give in to the urge to put everything in a box with a nice neat explanation, "This happened because...."

- In the end, God answers none of the questions posed in the previous chapters, but highlights the power and magnificence of creation. Job repented of speaking about things he did not understand. He repented not of secret sins, but of questioning God's authority to do what he thinks is best. God would not hear the prayers of Job's friends; he was so angry with them. Job shows his soft heart by forgiving their false accusations and praying for God to forgive them for their haughtiness and pride. I wonder about Job's wife—did she repent? Did she ever see how Satan tried to use her to spiritually destroy her husband?

- When we go through spiritual trials, Satan wants to destroy our faith by making us question whether we are really righteous, really loved by God. Actually, most of us do not need a trial to question our righteousness! The very first temptation assault on Jesus (when he was obviously challenged from a forty-day fast) was Satan proposing, "*If you really are the Son of God.*" When we suffer, Satan tries to get us to question our salvation and if God really cares, and to doubt our righteousness that was a gift at our baptism.

- Having a physical challenge (or being close to someone who does), will refine your faith and make you stronger if you hold on to your confidence in Jesus' blood and his forgiveness. Sin does not necessarily *cause* illness, but we can easily sin in how we *deal* with it. Job had to repent of his lack of faith. Do you express your feelings to God? Do you then confess your faith in him?

PHYSICALLY CHALLENGED

- Even if you are not materially blessed or healed, you will be blessed spiritually and, eventually, go to heaven. Job's life was blessed afterward, but I am sure he always grieved his lost children. He bore the sadness of all his servants losing their lives and probably carried the marks of disease on his body until he died. The happily-ever-after ending comes only when we meet Jesus face to face. Until then, we learn to be content in any situation because God is all we need.

Someone going through a physical challenge needs a friend who will listen to her, who is concerned about the details of what is going on, who will tell her the truth in love when she needs to hear it. Whatever the case, God will use your relationship with a physically challenged person to refine you, to strengthen your faith, to bring you to a deeper understanding of Jesus' compassionate heart and to see the reality of suffering and death...and eternity.

Questions

1. How do you feel around someone who is physically challenged? What uncomfortable emotions do you feel? Name them specifically.
2. In what ways are you like Jesus in your attitude regarding the sick? In what ways are you not?
3. What are some ways you can encourage your physically challenged friend? Have you ever been like Job's friends? What could you change?
4. Exercise: Ask your physically challenged friend to verbally walk through her day with you, including how she feels physically and emotionally. Offer very little input...just listen and try to feel what it is like to be in her shoes.

Additional Scriptures: Job 13:15; Proverbs 20:5; Matthew 4:23-25, 12:22; Mark 2:1-5, 8:22; Galatians 4:14

Linda Howard
San Diego, USA

Sexually Transmitted Diseases

Many of us who are now disciples of Jesus were in immoral relationships in the past. As a result, many of us also deal with the consequences of sexually transmitted diseases. As a family physician who has been a disciple for eight years, I find that people often ask me for advice on a variety of health issues. But one topic that is rarely mentioned is STDs. Obviously, sexual matters are uncomfortable for most people to discuss. Yet, of all topics, this one should be mentioned frequently. As disciples of Jesus Christ, we need to

- know the facts about STDs;
- learn how to support people who have STDs;
- learn how to view ourselves if we are infected.

Understanding the Facts

As disciples, we need to make sure our heads are "out of the sand" and that we understand about the symptoms and types of sexually transmitted diseases. This next section provides some scenarios and important facts about STDs. The scenarios are completely fictional as are the names, but the situations are quite real and common.

Oral Herpes

Tammy has been a disciple for one year and she is part of a flourishing teen ministry. She goes out on group dates a lot and prays for a boyfriend every night. Her mom isn't aware of the origin of oral herpes and is uncomfortable bringing the subject up to Tammy.

The facts: Herpes on the lips and in the mouth (orolabial herpes) is extremely common. In fact the Herpes Simplex Virus (HSV-1) affects one third of the world's population. Between 35 and 60 percent of white persons in the United States have antibodies in their blood showing they have had HSV-1. People from low socioeconomic backgrounds tend to be infected earlier in life, probably due to closer living quarters. The most common age for the first infection is preschool age (under five years). Usually a parent will notice painful red bumps on the lips, tongue or inner cheek. The child will often have a fever and feel sick. Unfortunately there is no cure for herpes, only medicines to shorten the course and to help with pain and fever (e.g., Tylenol). There can be recurrences two to three times a year. Excessive exposure to sunlight can often trigger an attack.

People who work outdoors or are exposed to the sun for much of the day can take pills (Acyclovir) in advance of such exposure.[1]

It is important to note that this disease is not contracted primarily as a result of sexual transmission. The herpes virus can remain in the body from childhood and can reactivate because of stress and other factors. What people may not realize is that it can be passed on through contact with bodily fluids such as saliva. For the family members who are worried about being infected, I usually recommend that during outbreak there be no kissing on the lips (cheeks only), no sharing of cups, plates, utensils, toothbrushes, towels, etc. Many people spread the virus without knowing it or being aware of any bumps. I counsel individuals to pat dry with a towel to avoid spreading the infection to other areas of their body.

The advice I would give to Tammy's mom is to bring up the subject at a relaxed time when they can really talk. Tammy is probably already concerned about her "cold sores" and is self-conscious about them. Tammy's mom can reassure her that God will give her the right man who will love her despite her flaws (physical and spiritual). She can also offer to have her talk with a doctor about medicines to help shorten the course of the outbreaks when they occur.

Genital Herpes

Sue is a gregarious single woman in her late twenties. She has steady dated three times since becoming a disciple but always breaks things off as the relationship becomes more "serious." One night Sue and her friend, Theresa, stay up late talking and Theresa asks questions that finally allow Sue to be open with her deep, dark secret.

The facts: Genital herpes (HSV-2) affects a large number of people (men and women) and the number is growing. Latest statistics show that approximately one out of five of all people over twelve years old in the United States have evidence in their blood that they have been exposed to HSV-2.[2] This is a thirty percent increase since the late 1970s.[3] As one may guess, this rise has to do with more people having more sexual partners and with the prevalence of HIV/AIDS. (People infected with HIV have a weakened immune system so they tend to catch whatever comes their way.) Genital herpes is transmitted sexually and interestingly enough does not cause oral herpes very often. The HSV-2 virus tends to only infect the genital tract and HSV-1 tends to only infect the mouth and lips. This means that people do not generally get oral herpes by performing oral sex. But this does not take away the fact that other diseases, like chlamydia and

---

[1] David Emmert, "Treatment of Common Cutaneous Herpes Simplex Infections," *American Family Physician* (Kansas City, Mo.: American Academy of Family Physicians, March, 2000), 1700.

[2] Emmert, 1700.

[3] Emmert, 1700.

gonorrhea, can cause redness and swelling of the throat, difficulty swallowing and fever if oral sex is performed while someone is infected.

The bad news about genital herpes is that infected persons spread the virus frequently without knowing it—especially women because they can't see the lesions in the vagina. There is no evidence that the medicine we give patients to shorten the course of the outbreaks (Acyclovir) prevents the virus from spreading. Therefore, I recommend that couples use condoms as much as possible except when they are trying to conceive.

Again, limit the sharing of towels to prevent any spreading of the virus. When a woman is pregnant and has a genital herpes flare-up, it is important for her to contact her doctor or midwife especially if she is close to giving birth.

Theresa can be a great friend to Sue if she listens well and encourages her to see a doctor for medicines to help control her outbreaks. Theresa could also share with Sue some scriptures to help her feel better about herself and remind her that the right brother will love her in spite of her herpes. (See chapter 19.) Being open will free Sue to get spiritual and medical help to deal with her condition.

Genital Warts

Susan is a married sister who has three lovely children. She and her husband are happily married, yet there is something missing in their sexual relationship. Whenever they go on marriage retreats, Susan's husband, Larry, knows it will be a difficult weekend. Susan becomes tense, and instead of having a wonderful romantic time, Larry spends the weekend walking on eggshells.

The facts: Genital warts are caused by the Human Papillomavirus (HPV) of which there are about twenty types. Not all twenty varieties produce visible warts. Similar to genital herpes, many people who have genital warts simply do not realize what they are. The virus can infect the mouth of a person who performs oral sex on someone with genital warts. Thankfully several treatments are available to treat this problem. Lesions in the mouth can only be treated by surgery or freezing (cryotherapy with liquid nitrogen). Genital warts can be treated with regular visits to the doctor for acid therapy or freezing treatments, or creams that are applied daily at home.

The main risk of genital warts for women is cervical cancer. Women need a Pap smear every year if they have ever been sexually active. Many single women do not get annual Pap smears, and this places them at high risk for cervical cancer. The HPV infects cells at the lower part of the womb (the cervix) and over time changes the cells. Sometimes the cells start looking precancerous and need to be frozen or cut out so that cancerous cells do not grow.

SEXUALLY TRANSMITTED DISEASE   143

The best thing Larry can do is to show his wife how much he loves her and enjoys being with her, whether or not they are having sex. He should encourage Susan to get help from friends to deal with the feelings she is having. Spiritual women can help her gain a godly perspective of her condition and her role as a wife to Larry.

Chlamydia and Gonorrhea

Christina is sixteen years old. Her parents became disciples a year ago. Christina has seen a great difference in how her parents treat her now—they are more patient and kind. The teens at church reach out to her, but she is not interested in Jesus at all. She prefers to hang out with her friends from school. Christina went to a party three weeks ago and had sex for the first time. Now she has a yellowish discharge on her panties every day and experiences pain in her pelvic area. She is starting to get worried, so she secretly goes to a local clinic for help.

The facts: Chlamydia and gonorrhea are both bacteria that are passed through sexual contact. There are over four million cases of chlamydia diagnosed yearly, and in the United States there has been a huge rise in the number of women infected over the last ten years (as reported to the Centers for Disease Control).[4] Chlamydia can even infect the eyes of a newborn baby when he or she passes through an infected birth canal. Gonorrhea can be passed through oral sex and can cause a nasty sore throat and difficulty swallowing. Usually men notice burning when they urinate and a discharge from the penis. Women might only notice a yellowish-green or bloody vaginal discharge. It is very dangerous when a pregnant woman contracts either of these diseases because it could infect and even kill the baby. This is one of many reasons why God's plan of a monogamous relationship is not only emotionally satisfying, but also safer and healthier.

If a woman feels pelvic discomfort, fever and chills, the bacteria might have traveled up into her womb and fallopian tubes. This is called PID (Pelvic Inflammatory Disease) and may lead to infertility if the tubes are scarred by the infection. When PID is advanced, a woman will need to come into the hospital for IV (intravenous) antibiotics. It is *very* important that the sexual partner be tested and treated. This ensures that the infection is not passed back and forth. This is why these two diseases as well as syphilis and chancroid (a less common STD that causes ulcers) are reportable diseases to the Department of Public Health. The good news is that both chlamydia and gonorrhea are easily cured with antibiotic therapy, unlike several other STDs.

---

[4] Alan DeCherney and Martin Pernoll, eds., *Current Obstetric and Gynecologic Diagnosis and Treatment* (New York: Lange Medical Books/McGraw-Hill, 1994), 759.

Syphilis

Laura and John have been reaching out to their neighbors, Richard and Jayne, for four years. Recently Richard has expressed an interest in coming to church and "getting his life right with God." Jayne seems depressed and withdrawn, and Laura doesn't know how to help her. One day Laura drops by and delivers some fresh cut flowers for Jayne. Jayne starts crying and tells Laura that Richard told her recently that he had an extramarital affair a year ago and had been treated for syphilis. Jayne is angry and afraid.

The facts: Syphilis is one of the oldest STDs. Unfortunately cases of women in their reproductive years with the disease are the highest since the 1940s.[5] It starts off generally in the genital area as chancre (a red, firm, crater-like ulcer that is painless) that disappears after one to five weeks. Early detection is imperative because if untreated over years, it can infect the heart and the brain. If a pregnant woman contracts syphilis and is not treated, forty to fifty percent of the time the baby will be stillborn or be born very ill.[6] Fortunately, syphilis is curable with a series of injections with penicillin.

Trichomoniasis and Gardnerella

Lisa is in ninth grade and she has just started studying the Bible. A girlfriend at school confides in her that she had a Pap smear last month because she has been sexually active for a year. She tells Lisa that she was diagnosed with something called "Trich" and she had to take medicines to cure it. Lisa is glad she has not had sex yet but wants to ask her mom what "Trich" (pronounced "trick") is. After school, she asks her mom how a girl knows if she has an STD.

The facts: Almost fifty percent of women infected with trichomoniasis or gardnerella do not even know they have the bacteria living in their vaginas.[7] Sometimes they notice a thick yellowish vaginal discharge but very rarely are they ill. These infections do not cause PID and are very easily cured by taking an antibiotic by mouth or by using a vaginal cream.

HIV/AIDS

Carmen is a very attractive woman, but recently she has been losing a great deal of weight. Her ministry leader comes up to her at midweek service and asks her if she is on a diet. Carmen says she's been eating well but has had a lot of diarrhea recently and is tired all the time. Her ministry leader asks if she has seen a doctor, and Carmen says she has not. Her ministry leader helps her set up a doctor's appointment for the following week.

[5]DeCherney, 756.
[6]DeCherney, 762.
[7]DeCherney, 757.

The facts: Human Immunodeficiency Virus (HIV) is the virus that causes AIDS. It makes the body's defense system (the immune system) weak so that even a common cold can become a serious health threat. A person can be infected with the virus for several years without knowing it, therefore, anyone who is or has been sexually active should have a blood test to check for the virus. The blood test can be done anonymously at most health clinics.

When a woman first becomes infected, she might have flu-like symptoms and think nothing of it. Years later, she will have difficulty fighting off common infections, feel tired, have sweating at night and lose weight for no reason. It is important to know if you are infected as soon as possible because there are medicines that significantly slow down the virus and help with symptoms. There is no cure for HIV infection or AIDS. As a doctor I see many patients who are not disciples and who are not committed to sexual purity. I encourage them to protect themselves during every sexual encounter with a well made, sufficiently thick condom with spermicide. (It seems that the spermicide will kill the HIV virus.) Of course, God's plan of abstention until marriage and a monogamous relationship is the best plan to protect us from all STDs.

Of note, about one third of women with HIV infection will pass the virus on to their babies if they become pregnant. There is a medicine given to pregnant women to prevent transmission of the virus while the baby is growing inside as well as at the birth. This medicine has been shown to decrease transmission of the virus to the baby to around ten to fifteen percent of the cases. Therefore, most pregnant women are encouraged to have an HIV test when they seek prenatal care.

Something important to realize is that having an STD increases the risk of transmitting HIV/AIDS because of the breaking down of the skin that occurs. This allows HIV to more easily enter the body.

Miscellaneous STDs

There are a few other STDs to mention that are lesser known. One is pubic lice (crabs). They are passed when there is close skin-to-skin contact with someone who is infected. Head lice and body lice tend to stay away from the pubic area, and pubic lice tend to only infect the pubic area. Itchiness and redness in the pubic area are the usual symptoms that bring people to seek medical attention. A cream can be applied to the skin of both partners to kill the lice, but it is very important to wash the clothes, towels and sheets to get rid of all the parasites.

Another STD that is often ignored is Hepatitis B. Within the last ten years a vaccine was developed for Hepatitis B (the inflammation of the liver). In a few generations this disease will be dead and gone. The vaccine is given to all babies at birth, one month and six months of age.

Children who did not receive the vaccine at birth often get the vaccination in their preteen years as this is when many kids start to become sexually active. Hepatitis B is usually transmitted by sexual contact or through receiving blood products (transfusions). The virus that causes Hepatitis B is in most body fluids (saliva, vaginal secretions, semen, etc.), and it can be passed by oral or sexual contact.

Most people do not know they are infected. Some get a flu-like illness. Sometimes the liver is damaged so much the person appears "yellow" in the eyes and skin. There is no definite cure for any of the Hepatitis viruses (A, B or C). Most people fully recover with only one in one thousand people damaging their liver so badly that they die from the infection.[8] The greater problem lies in the fact that five to ten percent of people become carriers of the virus and in time have a greater risk of developing liver cancer.

Oral Sex

Newsmagazines have featured articles regarding the current trend of teens performing oral sex on each other. They have heard the message about "safe sex." They do not want to get pregnant or get an STD, so many have opted for oral sex, thinking it is safer. After a recent "sex scandal" in Washington, unfortunately even newscasts became R-rated as they spoke of oral sex in the Oval Office. After such publicity, it is no wonder that this practice is becoming more and more popular among teens. What so many teens do not realize is that they can contract an STD (HIV/AIDS included) through this exchange of bodily fluids. The consequences can range from annoying to devastating.

The Creator of the human body and its sexual parts has a plan that is the best plan: abstinence until marriage. It is not his will for you to have multiple sex partners or play "musical beds." It is not his will for you to give your body to a person who is not committed to you for life and who does not value the treasure of your virginity. And making the choice to be intimate with someone who is not your spouse leaves you open to painful and even fatal consequences. God's way is always the best way— because he loves us; not because he doesn't want us to have fun.

Supporting Others

To keep me from becoming conceited because of these surpassingly great revelations, there was given me a thorn in my flesh, a messenger of Satan, to torment me. Three times I pleaded with the Lord to take it away from me. But he said to me, "My grace is sufficient for you, for my power is made perfect in weakness." Therefore I will

---

[8]Richard Behrman and Robert Kliegman, eds., *Nelson Essentials of Pediatrics* (Philadelphia: W.B. Saunders Co., 1990), 403.

SEXUALLY TRANSMITTED DISEASE

boast all the more gladly about my weaknesses, so that Christ's power may rest on me. (2 Corinthians 12:7-9)

In the passage above, Paul talks about a thorn in his flesh that tormented him. Biblical scholars debate what the "thorn" was. It is hypothesized that Paul suffered from chronic eye disease, ophthalmia, which would have made him "repulsive in appearance."[9] Paul was one of the major movers and shakers of the early church, yet he suffered from some infirmity that possibly made other people want to avoid him:

Even though my illness was a trial to you, you did not treat me with contempt or scorn. Instead, you welcomed me as if I were an angel of God, as if I were Christ Jesus himself. (Galatians 4:14)

God always uses our suffering to strengthen and teach others. This can be the case with any physical challenge, including STDs. It is how we (individually and as a church) approach these people that demonstrates our true heart for God. In Galatians 5:14 Paul reminds us that "the entire law is summed up in a single command: 'Love your neighbor as yourself.'"

You might be tempted to think, "But in the first century, they didn't have HIV/AIDS." If you are tempted with this thinking, consider the heart of Jesus. He touched lepers so that he could heal them. Leprosy is a highly contagious disease, spread by repeated contact with an infected person's skin. It is not a condition you can easily hide. Eventually a leper's fingers, toes and nose decay and fall off because the small blood vessels to these extremities no longer function. In Biblical times, lepers were outcasts and many people were afraid of them. Yet Jesus touched them, loved them, healed them (Matthew 8:2-3).

In the gospels we also see Jesus healing the blind. It is quite possible that many who were blind had contracted chlamydia in their eyes while coming through the birth canal. Because of the recurring problem of chlamydia, most westernized countries years ago instituted the practice of placing antibiotic ointment in the eyes of every newborn just minutes after the baby is born to prevent possible chlamydial infection. Again, Jesus touched those whom others would not touch.

Certainly we want to be wise and take the precautions mentioned earlier. But we do not want to ostracize or avoid someone who has any disease—STD or another type.

The challenge for us is to follow Jesus' example. We need to touch the people in our lives who have illnesses no matter how repulsive the illness might seem to us. This may be especially difficult for a newlywed whose spouse suffers from genital herpes and therefore has a high risk

---

[9]Henry H. Halley, *Halley's Bible Handbook*, (Grand Rapids, Mich.: Zondervan Publishing House, 1979), 607.

of contracting the disease as well. Spiritual leaders highly recommend that when a disciple enters a steady dating relationship, he or she should sensitively but honestly have a discussion alerting the boy/girlfriend of the condition instead of waiting until premarital counseling. Some people are more affected by this revelation than others. It is only fair to give them time to process and count the cost of making a lifelong commitment. (See chapter 19.)

As a physician, I have been tempted to pull away from patients who had very strong body odor, ugly skin ulcers or who had just vomited or bled all over me. It is a natural reaction. Even more, I have had to pray to love patients who have the self-pitying mindset. I find it more difficult to have compassion on this kind of person. Many times I have witnessed how God places certain people in my life to help me become more humble, more like his Son, Jesus:

> Who, being in very nature God,
>> did not consider equality with God something to be grasped,
> but made himself nothing,
>> taking the very nature of a servant,
>> being made in human likeness.
> And being found in appearance as a man,
>> he humbled himself
>> and became obedient to death—
>>> even death on a cross! (Philippians 2:6-8)

Loving Yourself

A person with a recurring STD can feel cursed by God. The good news is that if you feel cursed, then you are in good company. Jesus was cursed because he died on a cross. (See Deuteronomy 21:22-23.) It was not until recently that I fully understood the shame for Jesus, a Jew, to die hanging on a cross. First of all, this put Jesus in the same category as a murderer. Second, it meant he was cursed by God. Third, Jesus' body would desecrate the land if it were not buried the same day. What a blow! To be the Son of the Most High—and then to be considered a curse and a desecrater. The guilt that we all feel because of our sins is good. It helps us to come humbly to God and ask for forgiveness. Jesus, however, did nothing wrong but voluntarily became cursed for us. Galatians 3:13-14 is a key passage in helping people who feel cursed by God:

> Christ redeemed us from the curse of the law by becoming a curse for us, for it is written: "Cursed is everyone who is hung on a tree." He redeemed us in order that the blessing given to Abraham might

come to the Gentiles through Christ Jesus, so that by faith we might receive the promise of the Spirit.

In most circumstances, disciples who have contracted an STD did so earlier in life. People can think that God should take away their STD since he took away their sins. But God does not owe us anything. He has given us our salvation, and that is the most important thing. Satan will tempt us, however, and at those times we need to go back to 2 Corinthians 12:7-9 and remember Paul's thorn. We do not want to become conceited and self-centered.

Another scripture that I have shared with people facing chronic diseases of all kinds is Romans 8:28, "And we know that in all things God works for the good of those who love him, who have been called according to his purpose." God will use the trials we are undergoing to bring good to ourselves and to others.[10]

As disciples, we should all be grateful to the God who loves us, forgives us and accepts us. Out of that gratitude, we should go and do likewise...with ourselves and with others.

Claudia G. Trombly, M.D.
Boston, USA

---

[10]To help people learn to live victoriously with a physical challenge, I often recommend Tom Jones' book, *Mind Change: The Overcomer's Handbook* (Billerica, Mass.: Discipleship Publications International, 1997). Tom has MS and is a great example of overcoming and seeing God's work in his life.

Living with Herpes

I was sexually active at the age of fourteen. Before becoming a Christian, I had many sexual relationships. For me, the odds of contracting some kind of venereal disease were high—inevitable. Unfortunately, that disease ended up being genital herpes.

I first realized I had herpes when I was eighteen. It wasn't obvious at first because whenever I got the outbreaks, I also had a really bad yeast infection. I had herpes for quite some time before it was diagnosed professionally. I was very fearful when I heard the diagnosis because herpes was highly publicized as a dangerous and fast-growing epidemic. I had always thought that if I got herpes, I would kill myself rather than live with such an embarrassing and devastating virus.

I'll never forget when my doctor gave me the diagnosis. All I could do was fight back my tears and wonder how I would function with this disease. I was in a serious dating relationship at the time, and I had hoped one day to marry the guy. I felt incredibly fearful to tell my boyfriend—I feared that he would think less of me. He took it very well and loved me anyway. Unfortunately, I had already passed the virus to him. Part of me felt like it was inevitable that we would end up getting married since I couldn't imagine anyone else wanting me at that point. We dated for three years and then we got engaged.

Shortly afterwards I decided to become a disciple. I ended the relationship with him because he was not interested in getting to know God. However, this made me confront my fears all over again. What Christian man would want to marry a scarred, blemished, diseased woman?

After becoming a disciple, I dated a brother off and on for three years. I felt intense fear and anxiety at the thought of telling him I had herpes. My ministry leader advised me to tell him before we got engaged, and I agreed. I don't remember the exact words I used to tell him. All I know is that I felt an immense amount of fear, and it took me some time to get the words out of my mouth. When I told him, he was unbelievably kind and understanding and still wanted to be with me. We got engaged but later, for other reasons, broke off our engagement.

At this point I was thinking that I was never going to get married. It took an amazing amount of energy and trust to be so vulnerable with a man. Three years later, I was in another serious relationship with a brother who I was confident I would marry. I had informed my ministry leaders that I needed to tell him about my herpes before he proposed to me—but it never happened! I found myself engaged to a man who did not know

SEXUALLY TRANSMITTED DISEASE   151

that I had herpes. Thankfully, when I finally did tell him, he responded very well and assured me that he still wanted to marry me.

I have been married for almost five years now, and I have had herpes for about fourteen years. My outbreaks are very rare and are usually triggered by stress, poor eating habits, my period or other factors unknown as yet to me. I will "boast" to my husband that I hadn't had an outbreak in many months, and the next thing I know I am feeling the beginnings of one.

For some reason, the location of my outbreaks has moved away from my genital area to my anal area. Though certainly not pleasant, in many ways the fact that the outbreaks are in this area is a blessing. Because of this location my husband has not contracted the disease. (You can only get herpes if you have contact with the affected area.) I believe God has protected him. My life has turned out to be so much better than I thought it could be with this disease, and I am very grateful to God.

When I got pregnant with our first child, I had read that if a woman had an outbreak during the time of her delivery, she would need to give birth by having a C-section. Great! I thought, *One more consequence of my sin.* Fortunately, this didn't happen to me; I was able to give birth naturally.

I asked my husband how he feels herpes has affected our marriage and sexual relationship. He thinks I tend to feel ashamed or embarrassed when I get the sores. Obviously, when I have an outbreak, the prospect of having sex is not at the forefront of my mind. Also, I feel very protective of him. I still fear to this day that I will pass this virus to him. I remind myself of God's love and of my husband's love, and make the decision to bring my fears to God. Then, to be careful, we wait until the sore heals. This can take anywhere from four days to two weeks.

I have found it difficult at times to explain to my husband the fear and pain that I have because of the herpes. To him it is not a big deal. To me, it is a constant reminder of my past. Yet, I am thankful that he doesn't make a big deal out of it. It's difficult enough to live with my own shame, let alone shaming the one I love.

Sometimes I am in a setting in which the shame and embarrassment slam me right in the face again. For example, I was at the dentist's office the other day and had to fill out a medical form. One of the questions on it was "Have you ever had a venereal disease?" It was embarrassing enough having to put down that I had a venereal disease, but when the hygienist asked me to specifically put down what it was, I felt so embarrassed and "branded."

Many things come to people's minds when they hear someone has herpes. Because they don't know about the virus, they fear it. I remember when I was younger, I feared using the bathroom at my friend's aunt's house because I knew she had herpes. I thought I might catch the virus by sitting on her toilet seat. My first instinct was to think less of my friend's aunt...like she was cheap or less of a person. So I realized that when I was at the dentist's office, I was feeling insecure. I thought that perhaps this hygienist would think the same of me. All this reminded me of a passage from Ezekiel:

> "On the day you were born your cord was not cut, nor were you washed with water to make you clean, nor were you rubbed with salt or wrapped in cloths. No one looked on you with pity or had compassion enough to do any of these things for you. Rather, you were thrown out into the open field, for on the day you were born you were despised.
>
> "Then I passed by and saw you kicking about in your blood, and as you lay there in your blood I said to you, 'Live!' I made you grow like a plant of the field. You grew up and developed and became the most beautiful of jewels. Your breasts were formed and your hair grew, you who were naked and bare.
>
> "Later I passed by, and when I looked at you and saw that you were old enough for love, I spread the corner of my garment over you and covered your nakedness. I gave you my solemn oath and entered into a covenant with you," declares the Sovereign Lord, "and you became mine.
>
> "I bathed you with water and washed the blood from you and put ointments on you. I clothed you with an embroidered dress and put leather sandals on you. I dressed you in fine linen and covered you with costly garments. I adorned you with jewelry: I put bracelets on your arms and a necklace around your neck, and I put a ring on your nose, earrings on your ears and a beautiful crown on your head. So you were adorned with gold and silver; your clothes were of fine linen and costly fabric and embroidered cloth. Your food was fine flour, honey and olive oil. You became very beautiful and rose to be a queen. And your fame spread among the nations on account of your beauty, because the splendor I had given you made your beauty perfect, declares the Sovereign LORD." (Ezekiel 16:4-14)

I am so grateful for God's love and tenderness and acceptance in my life.

Recently I had an outbreak. It had been a long time since my last outbreak, and I wasn't even certain if it was herpes because I had been also battling with hemorrhoids. When I get a herpes sore, it feels a bit itchy at first. Then later on, it becomes sore and painful, especially when I urinate. The urine makes it sting. Depending on where I get the sores, I

SEXUALLY TRANSMITTED DISEASE

sometimes find it difficult and painful to sit. Honestly, sometimes it is painful all the time, and no matter what I do I am reminded that it's there. I have learned to bear the pain. To me, it's a constant reminder that I came from the world and that I am a sinner. However, I am grateful that although I have had to deal with the consequences of my sin, it could have been so much worse.

It is sad to realize that herpes is so common. At the same time, there is a comfort in knowing that I am not alone. With the church growing, there are more and more disciples who deal with this disease. I have two other friends who have it. We all come from very different backgrounds—herpes doesn't discriminate. Contracting herpes has nothing to do with educational or ethnic background; rich and poor alike get this virus.

It is unfortunate that I contracted herpes, but it's not the end of the world (as I once thought). God has forgiven me completely of my past sins, and I am eternally thankful for that. As I mentioned earlier, much worse things could have happened to me. There is no way around it: There are consequences for our sin that we need to live with for the rest of our lives. The amazing thing is that it doesn't make our heavenly Father feel differently about us:

"I, yes, I alone am he who blots away your sins for my own sake and will never think of them again." (Isaiah 43:25)

Then one of the elders asked me, "These in white robes—who are they, and where did they come from?"
I answered, "Sir, you know."
And he said, "These are they who have come out of the great tribulation; they have washed their robes and made them white in the blood of the Lamb." (Revelation 7:13-14)

When we are baptized into Christ, we are forgiven of our sins and given new white robes to wear! When we continually repent, our robes are washed through the blood of Jesus. This is always a comforting thought to me—and I hope to you as well!

A Married Disciple
USA

God Is Faithful

It was 1987. We had been living in Columbia, South Carolina, for five years, and Calvin was a full-time elder in the church. We had three sons: Mitchell was a senior at the University of South Carolina, Stephen was a senior at Irmo High School, and Joseph was six years old.

It was a good time in our lives. We knew we were blessed to be part of a growing New Testament church. There were struggles, and the church was being sharpened by persecution, but souls were being saved and the disciples were becoming stronger. We were happy.

Calvin had not been well all spring. The doctor was treating him for an ulcer, but the pain gradually grew worse. Often when I came home in the middle of the afternoon, I would find him lying on the couch. This was so unlike him. Saturday night, May 17, we rushed him to the emergency room. Something was terribly wrong. Monday morning Calvin underwent exploratory surgery at Baptist Hospital in Columbia.

The waiting room at the hospital was filled with friends and family, but the mood was hushed and tense. I think most of the people there knew the news was not going to be good. When I walked down the corridor to talk to the surgeon, I noticed the large clock at the nurse's station. It was 1:20 A.M., Monday, May 19. I told myself then, my life will never be the same again. I felt very cold.

As I listened to Dr. Longacre describe the cancer that had spread throughout Calvin's body, I watched Mitchell, our oldest son, stare at the floor. The veins were throbbing in his temples as tears were dropping to the floor. When the doctor walked away, I took a deep breath, put my arm around him and tried to comfort him. "Remember, God never gives us more than we can handle." I remember thinking if I just kept saying this, it would give me the strength to get through the day. I couldn't be sure that my legs would support me if I took a step.

I can only describe the next four months as an emotional roller coaster. Good news: Calvin would probably have a year to live. Bad news: he had developed blood clots in his lungs. Good news: we could go home. Bad news: the cancer had metastasized to his lungs. He needed radiation. Calvin died September 14, four months after he was diagnosed. Three of those months were spent in the hospital.

Those months, as well as the months following Calvin's death, left me little time for grieving. There were so many decisions to make and details that couldn't be neglected. I can no longer recall all that happened during those times. However, out of the blur, there are certain things that I remember well—ways that God eased the burden and continually took care of us.

But let all who take refuge in you be glad;
>   let them ever sing for joy.
Spread your protection over them,
>   that those who love your name may rejoice in you.
For surely, O LORD, you bless the righteous;
>   you surround them with your favor as with a shield.
(Psalm 5:11-12)

God's Wondrous Church, His Family

Whenever I see women grieving over a lost spouse or a very sick child, I wonder how they get through the pain without God's people holding them up as our brothers and sisters held us up.

I remember Matt who took care of our cocker spaniel on very short notice. He bathed and brushed her because we had promised Joseph he could take his dog to "show and tell" the next day.

I remember Sarah, an old friend, who left her family for a week and drove several hundred miles to lend her support and comfort. She did this more than once.

I remember Susan who picked me up at the hospital at noon one day. We went to a nearby park for a picnic. She spread out an incredible lunch with a beautiful cloth, glassware and flowers. It was cool and quiet. We talked and we both cried. The sun felt warm on my back. I am so grateful for this memory and the love that went into that brief interlude from the hospital walls.

The day we brought Calvin home from the hospital, a large recliner appeared in our den. (Calvin was six-feet four-inches tall.) He spent a month in that wonderful chair.

When Erma learned Calvin craved cold Coca-Cola, she brought a large tin of quarters for the vending machine. Jim lent him his new CD player and we took it to the hospital with Calvin's favorite CDs.

I often think of Jim Long who took Joseph to the YMCA several afternoons a week and taught him to swim. This skill carried him through many rough times for the next fifteen years. Several years later in his senior year he was captain of his swim team.

Two months earlier, Tammy Wieland had asked Calvin about working for the church full-time over the summer. (She was single and working as an oncology nurse.) She had been saving her money to support herself. A week before Calvin's surgery, Tammy became full time in the ministry. Two weeks later she moved into our house. Because she was an experienced oncology nurse, her advice and help was invaluable. She knew our family well and had a natural talent for negotiating with all three of our boys. Tammy could always make Calvin smile with her sweet spirit and her sense of humor. I will always believe God put Tammy there for us because he knew how badly we needed her.

Strength and Reassurance from God

> Preserve my life according to your love,
>> and I will obey the statutes of your mouth. (Psalm 119:88)

I soon realized that God had been preparing me all my life for a time like this. I'm grateful I grew up with a family who had strong convictions about knowing the Scriptures. There were often times when it was hard for me to sit and focus for any length of time, but throughout the days and nights, scriptures would come to mind. Each time, I felt God was putting his hand on my shoulder, talking just to me.

My prayers were uttered almost like breathing. *Lord, help me know how to help Calvin. Help me be sensitive to the needs of our children. Lord, comfort those who love us and are grieving. Thank you, God, for Jim, Paul, Sam, Sheridan, Steve and Lisa, who are always there for us. Thank you for helping us through bad news yesterday. Lord, if it is your will, give Calvin some good days, weeks or months. Lord, thank you for your promises.*

God protected us by giving us our burdens as we could handle them. If all the ramifications, consequences and feelings from Calvin's illness and death had hit us all at once, it would have crushed us. During the time Calvin was ill, I never felt the weight of what it was going to be like without Calvin at Christmas, birthdays, baptisms, graduations, weddings or the birth of our first grandchild. When each "first" time came, God walked us through the sadness, softened by the joy of the occasion. Remember, he never gives us more than we can bear.

Grieving

Since I moved to New York thirteen years ago, I have talked to many women, both young and old, who have lost their husbands, children or parents. Each one has dealt with grief in her own way. There is no time frame or set pattern. Grief is as diverse as the people it envelops; however, below are a few common issues that seem to face us all.

1. Mothers do not want to let their children see them cry. I wanted to be strong. I did not want my boys to see me grieving because I thought that would make it more difficult for them. Hence, they followed my lead. Neither Mitch nor Steve would let themselves talk or show emotion because, after all, their mother wasn't crying. Steve's coaches and teachers knew nothing about his dad's illness until a week before he died. We could have helped each other so much if we had taken time to sit down and talk and cry together.

2. There will be feelings of guilt. If only I had insisted he get a physical every year. If only I had been there when he had his first chest pains. If only I had been more sensitive to the pressures on him. My advice is always, "Don't go there." There is no profit in dwelling on such thinking. Philippians 4:8 teaches us how to think: "Finally, [sisters], whatever is true, whatever is noble, whatever is right, whatever is pure, whatever is lovely, whatever is admirable—if anything is excellent or praiseworthy—think about such things." Satan will only use accusing thoughts to weaken and discourage us.

3. There will be fear and self-doubt. I had been married thirty years— most of my life. Therefore, life without Calvin's strength and love was unimaginable to me. When times were rough, he would often quote Robert Browning's verses to me: "Grow old along with me, the best is yet to be. The last of life for which the first was made."

   I was not given the gift of growing old with Calvin, so I needed to be with someone to talk through my thoughts and feelings. I went into New York City so many times to be with Anita Banadyga. We would walk and talk. She listened to me and acknowledged my feelings. She would remind me of my strengths and then express extreme confidence that my family was going to be fine. This helped me so much because she knew me well.

4. There will be doubts about God's love and power. "Why?" many would ask. Why would God take Calvin at a time when the church needed his maturity so badly? When his children were still young? I didn't know then, and I don't know now. But if I am a disciple, I must let God be God. "Not my will, but yours" takes on a stronger and deeper meaning when heartfelt doubts attack us. Smother the doubts with God's truths, and they will not smother your faith.

5. We must help others help us. Friends and family are unsure how to help. I soon realized I had to think about my needs and talk. I needed to talk about what helped and what didn't help. I made myself think of things I could enjoy—such as a day trip with a friend in Manhattan, walking and talking at the beach and reading the Psalms.

   I began to realize it helped to have something to look forward to. Often I felt tired and getting through the day's schedule was hard. But if I remembered we were having dinner at a friend's house, things were not so hard. Mealtimes were especially difficult for us at first, so to be with a disciple's family meant so much.

6. Outward focus eases the pain. Remember the lost. There were times when it was all I could do to take care of my family. But when I reached out to someone, it helped me. Two weeks after Calvin's funeral, Tammy and I invited all the nurses who took care of us to a brunch. They were such kind people, and we often talked about what great disciples they

would be. As a result of Calvin's great example during his illness our nurse was baptized into Christ. Many others came close to the truth. Most of Calvin's nurses were at the funeral to hear Sam Laing and Steve Johnson speak.
7. Comfort others. Paul says in 2 Corinthians 1:3-4 that we are comforted so we can comfort others. I believe it is invaluable to be able to sit by a sister and say, "I know exactly how you feel and what you are going through." This is one of the blessings (yes, I said "blessings") of working through a tragedy.
8. Some people are very uncomfortable around those who have suffered a tragedy. They do not know what to say. They are dealing with their own fears. One young woman in my discipleship group told me my presence was a constant reminder of her worst fear—losing her husband.

   Two weeks after Calvin died, I went to a meeting at Joseph's school. Even though the women there had known me for years, when I came in, they avoided looking at me. I understood their feelings and tried to set them at ease.

   In contrast, one little first grader knew exactly how to respond. As I was leaving the school, Joseph's first-grade class was coming down the hall single file. As I stopped to hug and say hello to Joseph, I noticed one little boy had stepped out of line and was waiting to speak to me. As Joseph walked away, this child looked up at me with big, sad, brown eyes. "Lady," he said, "I'm sorry your husband died." I will never forget that little guy and what he did for me that day.

I've been a widow thirteen years now. The time has gone by quickly. Mitchell and Steve are married, and I have four wonderful grandchildren. Joseph will be a junior in college this fall. My life is full and content. I love my work with the children in the church. I love working with the single mothers, who in my mind are true heroes.

While writing this chapter and reflecting on all that has happened the past thirteen years, I can say emphatically that God has proven to me that he will never give us more than we can bear…and that he will never leave us.

Joyce Conn
New York, USA

My Grief Will Turn to Joy

Our God is such a genius. Emptiness...formlessness...darkness...nothingness. Then there is something. It is light! The sky appears, then land and seas. Plants and trees fill the land; a sun, moon, and numerous stars fill the sky. Fish and other sea creatures fill the water; birds begin to fly; animals appear on the land...and then the people. God brings order. He doesn't make mistakes. We just need to look at the universe and we see how amazingly brilliant God is. He doesn't make mistakes!

If all that is true...How could God allow the man of my dreams, the love of my life—a healthy, vibrant young man with his whole life ahead of him—to be diagnosed with third-stage skin cancer? He was a committed disciple for more than eighteen years, an amazing dad, a more-than-incredible husband, a best friend to so many, a completely sold-out disciple! Yet, his melanoma was described as "lethal" in February, 1997, and he died in December. Was I sure God never makes mistakes?

All the diagnoses were the same...six months to live!! How could that *be*? Fear gripped me. Unbelief filled my mind, soul and heart. It couldn't be. Not *my* husband. We had an adorable one-year-old boy and a remarkable six-year-old girl. We were disciples and disciples aren't supposed to die so young...at least I had never known any who did. *It just isn't true!* I would cry out late at night...night after night. *There must be a mistake. God made a mistake. What is he doing? Why is this happening?* I was in shock...unbelief...not *my* healthy husband. I felt as though I was walking in the shadow of death.

A Difficult Test

I was in for the test of my life...would I pass? The first six months I was failing. I felt like a spiritual failure in my heart, in my trust for God, with my husband, with my children. Psalm 23:4 says, "Even though I walk through the valley of the shadow of death, I will fear no evil, for you are with me; your rod and your staff, they comfort me." I, however, was filled with fear. I felt as though God had deserted me forever. I had absolutely no comfort in my heart. What was I to do! Could it be true that I could become a single mom? Bob did everything for me...bathed the children, disciplined the children, took care of our household needs, auto needs, financial needs. He was there to help me up when I was down spiritually. He was there to make me feel secure when I was feeling insecure. He was there to help me through my bad attitudes! What in the world would I do without him? I couldn't understand what God was doing. (See John 13:7.)

This diagnosis, I soon realized, was very real! Bob's cancer continued to spread throughout his body and finally to his brain. He was amazing, though. He was always joyful and very evangelistic. I put my husband into the hospital on November 11, 1997. He would never return home. That was a life-changing day for me.

A brother sat me down in the hospital and told me that I must "face the truth, and the truth would set me free." Another sister said, "Jayne, you must obey the Bible." Ah...that all-too-well-known scripture in John 8:31-32. How many times had I taught that to other women? It was now time to live it out in my life like never before. It was time for me to get on the soul train and start depending on God like never before. It was time for me to believe the Bible like no other time in my spiritual life. I knew I must walk closely with God if I was going to get through this.

God Doesn't Make Mistakes

My spiritual eyes began to open. The scales fell off and I could see Jesus again. "You see, at just the right time, when we were still powerless, Christ died..." (Romans 5:6). At just the right time, my husband died. God doesn't make mistakes.

I was ready, by this time, to stop fighting with God. I was tired. I finally accepted his plan for my life. That acceptance and surrender has brought me peace that surpasses understanding! It was exhilarating; it was freeing. I realized that it was time to stop feeling sorry for myself and make God and my husband proud of our children and me. It was time to continue his legacy of faithfulness, fruitfulness and happiness. I sought the kingdom like never before. Disciples were amazed. Neighbors were dumbfounded. I started living a life pleasing to God and without excuses because I decided to trust God and his word.

I started having amazing quiet times. I had always had the mindset that we would live forever and ever. The people of Jesus' day did too. It says in John 12:34 that "we have heard from the Law that Christ will remain forever, so how can you say, 'The Son of Man must be lifted up'? Who is this 'Son of Man'?" When I thought we would live forever, I didn't know Jesus! I didn't know this Son of Man.

For so many years I had a fear of death...yes, even as a disciple! That is so opposite of what the Bible says. (See Hebrews 2:14-15.) I started to study out (and continue to this day studying) the teachings and thoughts of Jesus regarding the death of disciples. It is an amazing study. These studies continue to set me free. We are but a mist! (See James 4:13-17.)

I gained insights from the Bible that I would have probably never gained if I hadn't experienced my husband's death. God says that my husband was receiving the goal of his faith, the salvation of his soul. He was about to enter heaven—the place God began preparing for us since before time—a place where there would be no more tears, fears, pain and worries for my husband. He would be face to face with Jesus. He was going to the land of the living. We are in the land of the dying! Isaiah 33:17-24 says that my husband "will see the king in his beauty and view a land that stretches afar." There will be no more arrogant people. It will be a peaceful abode. "There the Lord will be our Mighty One....No one living in Zion will say 'I am ill'; and the sins of those who dwell there will be forgiven."

I learned what Jesus taught in John 14:28: "You heard me say, 'I am going away and I am coming back to you.' If you loved me, you would be glad that I am going to the Father, for the Father is greater than I." I need to rejoice daily that my husband is with God in heaven…and I have learned to rejoice!

Jesus explains to his disciples in John 16:20 that their "grief will to turn to joy." That is exactly what happened to me. Sure, I grieved (Psalm 30:5). I would cry out at night, but in the morning I rejoiced! I believed the Word, though. God promises that if we believe his word, we will cross over from death to life (John 5:24). John 11:25 says, "He who believes in me [Jesus] will live, even though he dies; and whoever lives and believes in me will never die. Do you believe this?" You bet I do! Yes, my grief turned to joy (John 16:20). I was joyful when the world would have been mourning because disciples do not die!

Because of the Scriptures, I can see how, through my husband's death, he became more like Jesus. Jesus said in John 16:28 that he came from the Father and entered the world; now he was leaving the world and going back to the Father. That is what Bob did.

God Is with Me

God promises that he will not leave us as orphans (John 14:28). I am not alone. I was never alone. Satan wanted me to think that I was. God was with me the entire time. Nothing will separate me from the love of God (Romans 8:38), not even my husband's death. God promises that I have the Holy Spirit to fill my every need. All I need to do is to ask him! (See John 16:5-7, 23-24.) Jesus said that it was for our good that he went to heaven. He promises that good will come from my husband's death, and I have seen good come. My husband has won the ultimate prize…heaven! He is with his Maker. Good continues to happen. My children and I are more focused on heaven than ever before—God waiting for us and now their dad is as well.

Jesus has told us these things so that in *him* we will have peace because in this world we will have troubles. I need to take heart, though, because Jesus has overcome the world (John 16:33). Yes, my days do have troubles. My son puts an M&M up his nose. Mom, who has sopping wet hair one hour before a date, needs to rush him to the emergency room (yes, I have begun to date). As we are driving, my son says, "Mom, please forgive me. I am only a little kid." Jesus has overcome the world.

My daughter has a question about her algebra. Yes, Mom has to figure it out. I become closer to my daughter each time. Jesus has overcome the world.

Mom needs to go without her husband to the school open house. Ah yes, half the people are divorced, and I am ready to share my faith with them. Jesus has overcome the world!

Mom needs to take the kids to their soccer games while being the team mom for *both* teams. There are soccer moms on *both* teams who are so open to studying and coming to church that one of them invites herself. Jesus has overcome the world!

Immediately after soccer, Mom needs to drive both Rachel and John to tennis. Yes, the tennis coach is open and coming to church. Jesus has overcome the world.

Mom has to take both kids to school, very early in the morning. Ah yes, a handful of moms would love to come to church and they, too, want to study the Bible. Jesus has overcome the world.

I have to wipe the tears from my son's eyes when he falls down and console my daughter because she has had kids at school being mean to her...after which time they both say, "Mom, you are a great mom." Jesus has overcome the world. You see, God is my husband and brings me peace because Jesus has overcome the world!

I have had the privilege of hearing my son pray and ask God to help him be a great disciple when he gets older and thank God that his dad is in heaven. I have the honor of seeing my daughter enter the preteen ministry, and I have the privilege, once again, to date brothers in God's kingdom...because Jesus has overcome the world!

In John 16:29, the disciples finally understood that they didn't need to ask any questions because Jesus knew all things (John 16:30). The same for me...I do not have to ask "why" anymore. God knows better than I. His thoughts are not my thoughts. His ways are not like mine. As high as heaven is from me so high are his thoughts from my thoughts. (See Isaiah 55:8-9.)

Jesus was so fired up in John 16:31 that he exclaimed to his disciples, "You believe at last!" I know that Jesus was saying the same thing about me—at last she believes that I am in control. She believes that I do not make mistakes. She believes that she will do even greater things in her life.

God continues to pour down his blessings and allows Bob's legacy to live on. John 12:24 says that if a seed dies, it produces many seeds. God is allowing Bob to continue to produce spiritual fruit. Two months after Bob died, his barber and his barber's wife became disciples. They are now on staff and have been personally fruitful many times!

God has made me more aware of Satan. I am sure that Satan must have thought he would pull me down with this one. No way! I wasn't going to let it happen. I was going to defeat Satan and become more spiritual. Jesus told his disciples that when he went into heaven, they were going to do even greater things. And they did greater things. They were more spiritual after he died. I want to follow their examples of faith and courage.

Ironically, after Bob's death, there were deaths in each region of our church. I was able to help in these situations and share with them the victories that I had in Jesus when I finally understood how precious God's tests are in our lives (2 Corinthians 1:3-4). I was able to share with others the deep conviction I have about what really matters in life (2 Corinthians 4:16-18).

My husband continues to disciple me today. I remember everything that he taught me, and I try my best to live by those teachings day to day. He taught me to always be happy, always seek first the kingdom and always save souls.

Today our hope is in heaven (Colossians 1:3-5) because "no eye has seen, no ear has heard, no mind has conceived what God has prepared for us who love him" (1 Corinthians 2:9).

I will be forever changed. I am not the same person that I was four years ago. Today I am happily bathing my children, disciplining my children, taking care of the auto needs, financial needs and household needs while God is keeping me spiritual and plugged into him.

Jayne Ricker
San Diego, USA

God Knows What He Is Doing

It was a phone call I'm sure the caller didn't want to make. On January 12, 1994, while I was at work, Dean Kerman called me from Rutgers Law School. My husband Paul, one of his law students, had collapsed while playing basketball with his colleagues. Paul was being taken via ambulance to the nearby hospital, and I was encouraged to bring someone with me and to meet them there.

The events that took place the rest of that day are etched in my mind. It was a long drive in a snowstorm to the hospital. My dear friend, Deborah Wright, came with me. I was hoping for the best, yet preparing myself for the worst. We walked into the ER and saw the saddened faces of Paul's colleagues who had tried desperately to resuscitate him when he collapsed with a heart attack. The doctors pulled me into a room to tell me that their efforts to save Paul had failed. I prayed, cried and thought to myself, "I'm widowed—he was only 37!" (Paul and I had just celebrated our fifteenth wedding anniversary.)

As most people facing a sudden death, I never expected this to happen. I remember that evening telling our two girls, Elizabeth, then eleven years old (who has Down's Syndrome), and Marilisa, five years old. Elizabeth's response was, "Oh, mommy, I'm so sorry." She was responding to my sadness. Marilisa asked, "Will I get a new daddy?"

I knew Paul was in a better place. He had received the goal of his faith. That was very comforting. I got through the following days, weeks and months with tremendous support and encouragement. God truly is a God of all comfort. The kingdom of God is a family.

Keeping Perspective

How did I deal with losing Paul? What helped me through that difficult time?

First and foremost was my conviction that God loves me. Nothing that happened changed that fact. Nothing would separate me from God's love. I resolved that the only way to face each day and make it through victoriously would be to start it with God, in his word and in prayer. I would begin each day at 5:30 A.M. in meditation, Bible study and prayer. That one decision to start each day that way made the first year after Paul's death life-changing for me.

Keeping a daily journal was one of the most helpful things for me. It was certainly difficult to write out my feelings, fears and thoughts. It made them more starkly real, but on the other hand, it helped me deal with them honestly. It kept me from stuffing and going on...only to have to deal with stuffed feelings years later.

Something else that helped me through this time was being consistently open with someone who was strong and spiritual. Satan wanted to make the grieving process unbearable and insurmountable. Facing the death of someone you love is one of life's greatest struggles. Only by my being close to God and to others could I be an overcomer. I knew that for sure.

Remarriage?

I suppose I believed early on that I needed to be open to the possibility of remarriage. One reason was that Paul and I had discussed with each other that if something happened to one of us, the other one should remarry. Another reason was that having experienced fifteen wonderful years of marriage, I wanted to experience that type of relationship again. Also I wanted my two girls to have a daddy again. Finally, I wanted to remarry because I believed that I would do better spiritually with a husband. I knew myself pretty well. My sinful nature is to be self-sufficient, independent, prideful and just plain selfish. Being married calls me to deal with my character day in and day out.

I did desire to marry. However, my desire to marry again couldn't overshadow my contentment with being single. I had to be content being alone. This took surrendering to God's will daily. I'm thankful I can say that I struggled honestly with God, and he gave me the victory and the peace that comes with being content in any and every situation (Philippians 4:7,12).

I certainly had concerns and fears regarding the possibility of remarriage. Top on my list was the fact that I had two children, one with special needs. Any person who was willing to take on this responsibility would be very special and unique. How would my girls feel about my dating someone? How would they feel about that person? When my mom dated again after her divorce from my dad, I didn't really know the new man in her life. It wasn't until after they married that I got to know my new dad. I didn't want that to be the case for my daughters. I wanted them to feel great about someone I would consider in their future. What if they didn't?

Then, of course, there was the fear of not finding the right man. My conviction was that I would only consider a relationship with someone who was godly and could help me and my girls get to heaven. That was my main desire. I was thirty-eight when Paul died. My biological clock was ticking. Are there any older, spiritual and attractive men available? With God, all things are possible! God helped me face and deal with my fears by trusting him.

Ron Cicerchia and I were introduced to each other on July 4, 1994. Ron was in town from Boston visiting his good friends, Clyde and Jane Whitworth. I was having a cookout with friends. The Whitworths just "happened to drop by" so Ron could meet me. After our casual meeting, Ron decided to accompany the girls and me to watch the Fourth of July fireworks. (Ron has fun telling people he saw "fireworks" the first time we met!) It was good having someone to talk to who could relate to losing a loved one. Ron's wife, Jane, had passed away two months before Paul, after her courageous battle with cancer. Ron was easy to talk to and we both wanted to stay in touch. We became friends. Then we dated. It wasn't easy maintaining a long distance relationship—Ron lived about four hours away. But God can overcome any obstacle. Over the next twenty months, we fell in love and got married.

Building Our Marriage

The transition during the first few years of marriage had its challenges. I expected the difficult part to be Ron's adjustment to parenthood. He actually handled fatherhood rather well. The greater challenge came with us bringing our own list of expectations into this new marriage—not good! I think we both felt that our previous mates were nearly perfect, so we naturally fell into comparing each other to either Paul or Jane. This was not a good dynamic in our marriage. Comparing people is unfair, unhealthy and unproductive. People are different. No one likes being compared (negatively) to someone else. Especially in our situation, it was imperative for me to accept Ron for himself, appreciate all his great qualities and strengths and be patient as God helped us build a great marriage over time.

One thing we have learned is that we need to feel free to talk about Paul or Jane with each other. Rather than feeling insecure or uncomfortable, being open with each other has built greater closeness and intimacy.

Going through those newlywed years again was hard for me. I thought, *I have done this before; why should it be so hard?* But building a great marriage takes work. I knew that intellectually, but fought it on an emotional level. God knew exactly what I needed in giving me Ron. Over the past five years of our marriage, God has helped me grow to become more faithful, open, vulnerable and secure. Satan always tries to attack our faith. When times were hard, he tried to make me doubt God's plan. He made me question whether I had made a mistake. What I was really doing was questioning whether God made a mistake. When things were going great, it was clear that Ron was the right one. But I needed to be faithful through the bumps and realize that God knew exactly what I needed to grow spiritually and to get to heaven.

Ron is an awesome man of God. He's a wonderful husband and father. I feel so blessed that God brought our lives together. And then he showered a surprise blessing upon us almost three years ago with the birth of our baby, Lauren Deborah Cicerchia!

Every chapter in the book of my life has had its blessings and its difficulties, but with faith, God works incredible miracles. God knows what he's doing. God loves me more than I can comprehend. He is able to do anything. Knowing this about God makes me feel very secure in any situation.

Melanie Cicerchia
New York, USA

When All I Can Do Is Not Enough

> A hot-tempered man must pay the penalty;
> if you rescue him, you will have to do it again.
> Proverbs 19:19

When I read the above proverb, I picture a wife scurrying around behind her husband, making excuses for his rudeness, cleaning up the lamps and dishes he has smashed, and anxiously tiptoeing around him for fear of his unpredictable fits of rage. I also picture the mother who makes excuses for her children who are whiney and rude and cold, saying that they are tired, not feeling well or just shy. I see a husband meticulously covering up the evidence of his wife's prescription medication addiction so that they will look like a "normal" family to others. I also see a well-meaning disciple who drops whatever she is doing to go "rescue" a young disciple who has missed the bus to work for the fifth time.

No Pain, No Gain

All these behaviors can be described as "codependent," which has become a fairly familiar word to us as women in the past decade. But how do I know if I'm being codependent or being a patient "helper"? (Genesis 2:18, Colossians 1:28-29). In *Some Sat in Darkness*, Joanne Randall defines a codependent from a Biblical standpoint as "a person who prevents others from feeling the consequences of their decisions through control, manipulation, enabling and rescuing."[1] Over and over again in Scripture, God tells us that the people who are out of control are the ones who need to pay their own consequences. And he says that if others pay for them, others will have to pay over and over again (Proverbs 19:19)—simply because he uses the consequences to teach them to change. When we clean up their messes, make amends to those whom they have hurt and insulted, or just make excuses for them, we are paying their penalty, which leaves God with nothing left to use to discipline them. We are therefore interfering with God's plan to bring them back to him, and the resulting behaviors in our lives can be harmful to our character, even deadly to our faith.

God Spells It Out

Thankfully, God gives us the perfect example in the Bible of someone who could have been codependent, but chose not to be. In Luke 15 in the

---

[1] Mike Leatherwood, Brenda Leatherwood, Declan Joyce and Joanne Randall, *Some Sat in Darkness*, (Billerica, Mass.: Discipleship Publications International, 1997), 107.

CODEPENDENCE   169

Parable of the Prodigal Son, the father firmly resists the temptation to control, manipulate, enable or rescue his son. He not only lets his son go, but he agrees to give him his inheritance. In verse 16, we read that in his new country, after he had squandered all his money, "no one gave him anything." The very next verse says that "when he came to his senses," he decided to go home. What brought him to his senses? Very simply, it was hunger. God used a famine, fickle friends and filthy pigs to bring him to his knees. God can do that—he will do that. He loves us enough to do or to allow whatever it takes to bring us back to him.

Imagine if someone had been there to feed this boy. In spite of the famine and all that God was doing, he would not have been hungry. Would he have gone home? Perhaps, but let us not forget that this is a parable, an earthly story, with a heavenly message. What is Jesus teaching? At least one lesson is that God uses pain to bring us to him.

Additionally, I always wondered why the father let him have the money. He must have known his son's character well enough to know that the money would be wasted, squandered and lost. But imagine if the father had not given it to him. The son would have most certainly ended up in the same pigpen, but he could have blamed his father, thinking to himself, "I never had a chance." But sitting in that pigpen, he knew that he had no one to blame but himself. It was this pain that brought him to his senses.

We know the Bible teaches us over and over that pain produces character (James 1:2-4, Romans 5:3-4, and Hebrews 12:2-11). Even Jesus learned obedience from what he suffered (Hebrews 5:8). However, when it is our children, our husbands, our friends who are suffering, this often does not feel right. We may feel compelled to relieve their pain. We want to clean up our drunk husbands' vomit, make excuses to their bosses, hide their bottles from the children, minimize the problems or keep the peace, thus keeping them from having to pay the penalty for their own actions. The Bible says that we will have to do this over and over.

I Can Relate

What I know about codependence, I have learned from personal experience. I remember what it was like to live suspended between the fantasy world of denial and the nightmare of reality. Before my husband was in recovery from alcoholism, I often thought I was losing my mind. I was fearful, isolated from my friends, deceitful and faithless. Resentment came when my husband blamed me over and over for being late, being broke, being undisciplined and being unspiritual. But in fact, I was doing everything in my power to not only manage my own life, but also the lives of the people in my family—unrighteously paying consequences that were not mine. It became an overwhelming responsibility to do everything, much less to do it well (Mark 7:37). Therefore, I was afraid to take on any more responsibility.

I was also isolated from my friends because I had this terrible secret, this thing in my family's life that made me different. I became deceitful because the truth was too horrible to look at. I hated the truth. Even when I could look it in the eye, it would scare me so badly that I would deny it and tell myself that it was not real. How could I have faith in God in this state? I didn't, and God slipped out of my mind. I prayed, but felt that my situation was impossible even for him to fix.

Because denial is an integral part of addiction, the one who is abusing drugs does not readily see his or her problem. Addicts are manipulative, insulting and often downright abusive to their friends and families, especially when they are confronted about their addiction to mood-altering substances.

When my husband was drinking, he was very manipulative. When I told him I was concerned about how much he drank, he would tell me it would be a good idea for me to talk to someone about it. But then he would tell me that he didn't know anyone whom I could talk to because no one else in the church knew as much about substance abuse as he did. No one else had his experience in the field. No one else had even been married as long or had children as old as ours. So, even though he told me to talk to someone, I felt as if I had no one to talk to. I usually felt that I was the one with the problem, since I did not know anything about addiction. He was the substance abuse counselor—wouldn't he know if there was a problem? I would conclude that I was being a nagging wife, critical and untrusting. I thought I just needed to try harder to make him happy. By thinking this way, I set myself up to pay his penalties over and over until I became very resentful and bitter. Then I felt like it was my fault that our marriage was not working because I knew my heart was filled with sin. So I tried harder, but only became more resentful. I could not find a way out of this cycle.

The Codependent Triangle

There is a way out of this sin, and I am so grateful that God allowed me to find it. Let's look at the example of a wife being codependent with her alcoholic husband. Her life can be mapped in the shape of a triangle because there are three distinct roles in which she may find herself: rescuer, victim or persecutor. (See diagram below.)

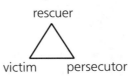

CODEPENDENCE

She may be at the top of the triangle in the role of the rescuer, being the one who pays her husband's penalty. She may rescue him out of pity or out of fear, but the bottom line is a desire to make everything all better. But she doesn't make things better. She then becomes the victim—one-hundred percent of the time: she cleans up his vomit, makes excuses to people for his bad behavior, and takes another job to pay for his expensive habits. She takes on more and more responsibility with the children, the yard and the finances until she is overwhelmed. Eventually she will move from the role of victim into the role of persecutor: "That's it! I've had it! I'm leaving! I hate him! I wish he would die!" She says and does sinful things out of anger and feels guilty afterward. She knows it was wrong. The regret she feels gets her ready to step back into the role of rescuer the next time he needs us. Then she will be the victim again, then the persecutor, then the rescuer again. As Proverbs 19:19 essentially says, if she pays his penalty for him, she will have to do it again and again.

The only point at which codependents can exit this triangle is at the point of rescuer. We may feel like we are ready to get off at the point of the persecutor because this is when we are angry and want to hurt them. Others looking in from the outside can be very frustrated with us because we say we are ready to do something, to make changes, to take a stand. But when this passes, we move right back into the role of rescuer, leaving others to wonder what happened to our determination.

If you are the one in this situation, you may feel that you are going crazy—I certainly did. You are not crazy! You are just trying to get off the bus at the wrong stop. When you can sit down and think through the situation rationally and calmly make decisions that are in the best interest of yourself, your husband and your children, then you are much more likely to be able to carry out these decisions.

Getting Practical

Let's look at some examples of getting off at the wrong stop and at the right one. A woman is married to a man who has been drinking more and more. One night as they are leaving a party, the wife says to her husband, "I don't think you should drive." The husband insists, however, that he is able to drive, although she feels that he has had too much to drink. What does she do? It is embarrassing to go back into the party and tell their friends that she needs a ride. He is furious that she would even consider this option. Should she risk her own safety in order to be a submissive wife? Is this the best thing to do for him? Sometimes a situation like this can escalate into a major confrontation in which both say things that are cruel. Then, the wife will most likely feel ashamed of her behavior, ride home with him and try harder the next day to make it up to him.

Another option is for her to think ahead. She knows that he drinks too much at times, so she never leaves home without cab money. When they leave the party and her husband insists on driving, she simply says, "I don't feel safe riding with you when you have had this much to drink, so I am going to take a cab. Be careful. I'll see you at home." Then whether he likes it or not, she has given him the message that he drinks too much for her to feel safe with him. There is no need to argue. Because she did not rescue him, she will not be his victim; then she does not need to become a persecutor. She simply refused to put herself in a position where she would have to pay his penalty.

But what if he had an accident on the way home? I have felt that I had to be there to somehow prevent anything like this from happening, as if I had the power to do that. God knows whether an accident will help him or not. Leave it in his hands. He is God, and we are not. Don't forget that God uses pain to bring us to our senses. Pray that the pain of you not riding home with him will be enough, but be grateful that God is working in his life as well.

God Is Able

Daniel 4:37 is good news: "Everything [God] does is right and all his ways are just. And those who walk in pride he is able to humble." This means that when my husband was drinking, I didn't have to punish him. I didn't have to try to make him change. God did that. Now I've learned and I no longer have to suffer the insanity of trying to control the uncontrollable. I am not God, which is a good thing. What happened when Herod played God? He was eaten by worms (Acts 12:23).

Breaking free from codependence means that I can forgive my husband. But I also *have* to forgive him, because if I don't forgive him when he sins against me, God won't forgive me when I sin (Matthew 6:15). But neither do I have to be a victim of his sin. I can be a strong, victorious woman of God who lives a happy, abundant life. This is God's plan for me.

God never promised us a pain-free life. He has promised us that everything that happens to us he will use to work for our good (Romans 8:28). And he has promised to never leave us (Matthew 28:20). He wants us to live fulfilled, victorious lives and with his help, we can.

Brenda Leatherwood
New York, USA

Godliness

Your Body Is God's Temple

"The holy of holies." To even say the name of the dwelling place of God was enough to cause a devout Jew to tremble in reverent fear. Only once a year could the high priest enter this most sacred place, hidden in the center of the temple of the living God. He went before the ark of the covenant and encountered the presence of the King of the universe. Only priests and Levites could enter the area immediately outside the most holy place in the temple. Awe, respect and consecration accompanied them into this house of God with its splendor and intricate golden designs.

This is the glorious context of Paul's statement in the New Testament:

> Do you not know that your body is a temple of the Holy Spirit, who is in you, whom you have received from God? You are not your own. (1 Corinthians 6:19)

Paul says that each of our bodies is God's holy temple. Think about how the Jews respected and revered the temple...the meeting place of God and man. God through his Spirit actually takes up residence in our bodies. Each of our bodies becomes the holy of holies. In order to bring glory to God, we should take care of our earthly bodies, his temple, thus, place our bodies in submission to God's Spirit.

Being the dwelling place of the Spirit of God is an incredible honor and privilege. It is also an incredible responsibility. As Paul says in Romans 12:1 we should offer ourselves as "living sacrifices, holy and pleasing to God." Only by taking care of our bodies can we truly be holy and pleasing to God—at the same time we can be optimally effective and productive in our walk with him and in other areas of our lives.[1]

Practical Applications for Everyday Life

Discipleship Times

During my fourteen years as a disciple, I have observed that the majority of "discipling times" are spent sitting...often sitting and eating. We all need to sit and eat, and certainly these activities offer a convenient time to get with people. However, we can and should be more creative and active in the times we spend together as disciples.

---

[1] U.S. Surgeon General's report says that people need to have at least thirty minutes of moderate physical activity on most days of the week—walking, cycling, dancing, running, etc.—to maintain a healthy body.

A great way to incorporate physical activity into our lives is to walk with discipleship partners while we talk. Many of us have health or weight problems that would cause us to benefit from this. As we look to our Lord as an example, we see Jesus walking with his disciples from town to town, or hiking with them in the hills and mountains. He spent valuable time with them and taught them in the process:

> As Jesus was walking beside the Sea of Galilee, he saw two brothers, Simon called Peter and his brother Andrew. They were casting a net into the lake, for they were fishermen. "Come follow me," Jesus said, "and I will make you fishers of men." At once they left their nets and followed him. (Matthew 4:18-22)

> After six days Jesus took Peter, James and John with him and led them up a high mountain, where they were all alone. (Mark 9:2)

Of course, we understand that during the first century the primary mode of transportation was walking. Accordingly, Jesus had a very physically active way of life. He didn't have a car, a phone, a fax machine. To see people, to communicate he had to walk. In this day of busy lifestyles and increased reliance on technology, we have to make a conscious effort to incorporate activity into our lives. For most of us, we only have physical activity because we plan to. If we are going to walk with someone, for instance, we have to plan it. And it will most likely be recreational walking because most of us cannot walk to work or to the mall. Long commutes and suburban locations prohibit that. We have to be reminded that walking and talking with someone is an encouraging way to share our hearts and our lives.

Some of my favorite "bonding" times have been while hiking, walking, biking or running with someone. A mutual sharing of God's creation can reveal our hearts as we are humbled to see his majesty and power:

> When I consider your heavens,
>   the work of your fingers,
> the moon and the stars,
>   which you have set in place,
> what is man that you are mindful of him,
>   the son of man that you care for him? (Psalm 8:3-4)

Joining a health club or gym with another disciple is a wise use of time and money. As you work out, you can encourage each other to not give up...and to have fun. Almost everything is more enjoyable when we do it with someone else.

Evangelism

Another product of exercising together is the opportunity to share our faith with others. In Philemon 6 Paul writes, "I pray that you may be active in sharing your faith, so that you will have a full understanding of every good thing we have in Christ." It is doubtful that Paul was referring to "exercising together" in using the word "active." But it is an added bonus to be active as we are actively sharing our faith.

Being on sports teams and going to parks are great ways to get out and meet new people, build relationships and share our faith. Jim Fulcher, an evangelist in San Diego, refers to the club where he works out as his "fishing hole." Jim recently shared his faith with a nationally ranked athlete whom he met at his fishing hole. He was thrilled to baptize his new friend as a disciple of Jesus. I encourage you to find a place where you can bring glory to God by taking care of your body *and* sharing your faith.

Walking or playing tennis or racquetball with a neighbor or coworker is a great way to reach out and share your faith. You can build a meaningful friendship on common, non-threatening ground.

I remember a singles household in Cincinnati that would hold summer volleyball Bible Talks every Thursday night at their apartment's sand volleyball court. Friends and neighbors would come to the volleyball games on a regular basis. Afterwards we would go back to the apartment and have a group Bible study. This was an innovative way to build great relationships with friends and neighbors.

Developing Perseverance and Endurance

As disciples, we all have to persevere through tough times; they come to everyone in one form or another. We also need the quality of perseverance to stick with a commitment to exercise. Perseverance carries over from one area of our lives into another...for good or for bad. Peter encourages us to "make every effort to add to [our] faith goodness; and to goodness, knowledge; and to knowledge, self-control; and to self-control, perseverance; and to perseverance, godliness; and to godliness, brotherly kindness; and to brotherly kindness, love" (2 Peter 1:5-7). If we persevere with an exercise program it will build our character and help us persevere and be consistent in other areas of our lives.

Personal Times with God

As I said earlier, one of my favorite ways to spend time with God is to be outside admiring his glory in nature. I love to go on prayer walks, runs, bike rides, hikes or swims (great meditative times). I am continually amazed and delighted at the beauty he places in my path, whether it is during runs at dawn, hikes at sunset or walks on a starry night. Nature truly does speak to me:

> The heavens declare the glory of God;
>> the skies proclaim the work of his hands.
> Day after day they pour forth speech;
>> night after night they display knowledge.
> There is no speech or language
>> where their voice is not heard.
> Their voice goes out into all the earth,
>> their words to the ends of the world.
> In the heavens he has pitched a tent for the sun,
>> which is like a bridegroom coming forth from his pavilion,
>> like a champion rejoicing to run his course. (Psalm 19:1-5)

I use these times to meditate on what I have been studying in his word and to pray. Afterwards—the peace that God provides is unsurpassed.

> Rejoice in the Lord always. I will say it again: Rejoice! Let your gentleness be evident to all. The Lord is near. Do not be anxious about anything, but in everything, by prayer and petition, with thanksgiving, present your requests to God. And the peace of God, which transcends all understanding, will guard your hearts and your minds in Christ Jesus. (Philippians 4:4-7)

Go to a park or place where you can study the Scriptures and meditate on God. You will be imitating our Lord and getting in closer touch with yourself and with God's character. Jesus loved to go to the Mount of Olives, away from the hustle and bustle of Jerusalem to be alone with his Father:

> But Jesus went to the Mount of Olives. At dawn he appeared again in the temple courts, where all the people gathered around him, and he sat down to teach them. (John 8:1-2)

Key Points

- Develop a plan to be active in your times with God and with people.
- Use your time wisely in bringing God glory and taking care of his holy temple, your body.
- You can imitate Jesus by being active with other disciples and active in sharing your faith.
- You can get in touch with God and his character as you are physically active in his glorious creation.

Action Plan

- Study the Scriptures to convict your heart about the need to bring glory to God through his "flesh and blood" temple. Study what the temple meant to the Jews.
- Seek advice from others if you need help with a plan or inspiration.
- Put together a plan on how you will incorporate physical activity and exercise into your daily life as a disciple.
- Encourage others to join with you in your new commitment (friends, discipleship partners, family members).

Whether we are building relationships, sharing our faith or spending special time with God, we can effectively incorporate physical activity into our Christian life. We will inspire others by our lives as we grow closer to God, imitate his Son and "transform" our earthly bodies. By incorporating daily physical activity we will make ourselves healthier, happier and more energetic for serving him throughout our lives.

Barbara N. Campaigne, Ph.D.
Indianapolis, USA

Dealing with Emotions

The following notes can be used for a personal, one-on-one or group Bible study. At first I planned to write out the notes in a normal chapter format. But I decided to retain the outline format because it causes the reader to think more about the answers to the questions posed. After most of the questions I offer possible answers, but certainly they are not the only answers. It is my hope that you will add your answers to the ones I have given.

Introduction
- Think of a one-word description of emotions. (confusing, happy, uncontrolled, bonkers, roller-coaster)

Through the years I have been confused at times about the role that my emotions are to play in my life. Often it seems that all they do is get me in trouble and that I am better off without them. Are emotions friends or fiends?

Imagine the following scene: You are sitting at the table drinking tea with a friend. She says something really hurtful like, "You have a really big nose, and it makes that hat look silly on you." But you just sit there and smile. You say pleasantly, "Would you like some more tea?" You are enjoying the cooling breeze and the warmth of the jasmine tea. Her mean comment didn't even bother you because you are not affected by any negative emotion. You are not hurt or angry. You do not question your value or your worth. You do not flash back to mean comments from the kids in your elementary school like, "Hey big nose, save some air for the rest of us!" You feel happy, blessed and full of self-esteem.

Wouldn't it be wonderful if life were that way? And yet, we cannot have it both ways. If we no longer had capacity for negative emotions, the same would be true about positive emotions.

We would be unable to appreciate and enjoy loving someone, witnessing the glowing embers of a sunset, holding a newborn baby. If we throw a blanket over our negative emotions, we will find that it falls over our positive ones too.

We must decide to "make peace" with our emotions.

1. Made in the Image of God...Emotionally
- What does the fact that we have emotions tell us about the character and nature of God?

EMOTIONS

> Then God said, "Let us make man in our image, in our like-
> ness, and let them rule over the fish of the sea and the birds
> of the air, over the livestock, over all the earth, and over all the
> creatures that move along the ground."
>
> So God created man in his own image,
> > in the image of God he created him;
> > male and female he created them. (Genesis 1:26-27)

He said that all his creation was good. As human beings we are capable of complex emotions. Animals know fear and the desire for safety
and comfort, but they do not understand unconditional love, and they do
not understand humor (as smart as she is, my dog never thinks anything
is funny!). We are emotional beings because God is an emotional being,
and he made us in his image.

- He made us capable of feeling what he feels and expressing what
  he expresses.
- The reasons for emotions:
  1. to experience and express the nature of God
  2. to experience and realize our need for the power of God
     (to control those emotions)

2. God's Emotions versus Our Emotions

   A.   Emotions that God shows

- What are some of the emotions that the Scriptures ascribe to
  God? (See some examples below and use your concordance to
  look up others.)

anger	jealousy
joy	hate
sadness	love
grief	longing

- How can learning about Jesus help us know the emotions of
  God? (We can come to know God's emotions by knowing Jesus'
  emotions: Colossians 1:15 says that Jesus is the "image of the
  invisible God." Colossians 2:9 says that "in Christ all the fullness of the Deity lives in bodily form.")
- Can you think of some examples of times that Jesus showed
  his emotions?
  1. John 11:32-36—Death of Lazarus:
     love—Jesus loved his friends Lazarus, Mary and Martha.
     grief, sorrow—He wept because of the hurt that especially
     Mary was going through (even though he knew he was go-
     ing to raise Lazarus).

2. John 2:13-17—In the temple:
anger
indignation
hurt
3. Matthew 20:29-34—Healing two blind men:
compassion
4. Matthew 26:36-41—Praying in the garden before arrest and crucifixion:
sorrow
loneliness
5. Luke 6:23—Teaching his followers:
joy

B. Why God shows emotion versus why we show emotion
- What was the motivation for God showing emotions? (love for us, our best interest) That is his nature and he can do nothing apart from his nature.
Let us look at the situations that caused God's/Jesus' emotions:
1. Anger:
Jesus in the temple (John 2:13-17)
- Why was he angry?
- Why types of situations usually bring up anger in us?
- Is it possible to have righteous anger the way Jesus did?
- What is often true about the anger that we think is righteous?
- How does our anger tend to be different from God's anger?
- How can our expression of anger be sinful?
2. Jealousy:
God's jealousy:

> Do not worship any other god, for the LORD, whose name is Jealous, is a jealous God. (Exodus 34:14)

> This is what the LORD Almighty says: "I am very jealous for Zion; I am burning with jealousy for her." (Zechariah 8:2)

Paul's jealousy (a godly human expression of jealousy):

> I am jealous for you with a godly jealousy. I promised you to one husband, to Christ, so that I might present you as a pure virgin to him. (2 Corinthians 11:2)

EMOTIONS   183

- Why was God jealous? (He made his people to be in a relationship with him; that is how our needs are met, that is how we find true meaning; that is how we will be with him forever. If we are worshiping other gods, we are being destructive to ourselves.)
- What types of situations usually bring up jealousy in us?
- Is it possible to have godly jealousy the way God does and Paul did?
- What is often true about the jealousy that we think is righteous?
- How does our jealousy tend to be different from God's jealousy?
- How can our expression of jealousy be sinful?

Paul said he was "jealous" in 2 Corinthians 11:2, but he is careful to distinguish jealousy that is a sin, as in the verse below:

> For I am afraid that when I come I may not find you as I want you to be, and you may not find me as you want me to be. I fear that there may be quarreling, jealousy, outbursts of anger, factions, slander, gossip, arrogance and disorder. (2 Corinthians 12:20)

- Think of other examples of God's and Jesus' emotions.

3. Our Need for God-Controlled Emotions

A. Strong emotions tempt us to sin, we have already seen this with anger and jealousy.
- What are some other ways that strong emotions can lead us into sin?

B. Since God made us to be in his emotional image, we need to seek to be like him, to express his emotions, not to be led into sin by our emotions. We must seek to have the "mind of Christ."

> The mind of sinful man is death, but the mind controlled by the Spirit is life and peace. (Romans 8:6)

> Your attitude (mind) should be the same as that of Christ Jesus. (Philippians 2:5)

> But we have the mind of Christ. (1 Corinthians 2:16b)

> Now the Lord is the Spirit, and where the Spirit of the Lord is, there is freedom. And we, who with unveiled faces all reflect the Lord's glory, are being transformed into his likeness with ever-increasing glory, which comes from the Lord, who is the Spirit. (2 Corinthians 3:17-18)

- What does it mean to you to "have the mind of Christ"? If we take on the mind/thinking/attitude of Christ, we will also respond with his emotions. To follow Christ, then, is to take on the mind of Christ. To take on the mind of Christ is to take on the emotions of Christ. God did not give us emotions for them to control us. Instead, he gave us emotions so we could experience and express his nature—that is what following Jesus is all about.
- Give examples of ways that emotions control us.
- How do we allow God to control our emotions…how does this take place in our lives?
- What is the outcome of God-controlled emotions?
- What is the message we need to hear if our emotions are controlling us?

Conclusion

A. So we see that we have emotions to
  1. experience and express the nature of God
  2. experience and realize our need for the power of God (to control those emotions)

B. If we don't look to God for his power to control our emotions we go one of two ways:
  1. we are controlled by emotions
  2. we shut down all emotions (which is still a form of being controlled!)
     - Either way, what is the result in our lives?

To sum up what you learned about emotions:
1. God created us to be like him emotionally.
2. He will not program us or make our emotions line up with his.
3. He reveals himself to us so we know what godly emotions are.
4. He calls us to follow Jesus and to take on his mind and his emotions.
5. We are only fulfilled in life if we make this decision.

EMOTIONS

6. If we do not follow Jesus, our emotions will control us and lead us into sin.
7. If we do not follow Jesus, we will miss out on the life God has prepared for us...here and for eternity.

I leave you with this question to test yourselves when strong emotion comes up in you:

- If I give in to this emotion, will it bring about the purpose of God (if so...totally give in) or will it cause me to sin? (if so, do not give in)

Decide to follow Jesus and look to his power to bring godly control to your emotions.

Sheila Jones
Boston, USA

Controlling My Emotions

> The end of all things is near. Therefore be clear minded and self-controlled so that you can pray.
> 1 Peter 4:7

Throughout my life I have had little control over worry, fear, depression and sadness. I would cry and read the following scripture over and over when I was consumed with these emotions:

> Rejoice in the Lord always. I will say it again: Rejoice! Let your gentleness be evident to all. The Lord is near. Do not be anxious about anything, but in everything, by prayer and petition, with thanksgiving, present your requests to God. And the peace of God, which transcends all understanding, will guard your hearts and your minds in Christ Jesus. (Philippians 4:4-7)

I would pray to God as it says, but afterwards I did not feel the peace this passage said I should feel. I would feel frustrated and think, *What's wrong with me?*

Finally, I connected Romans 8:28 with Philippians 4:4-7:

> And we know that in all things God works for the good of those who love him, who have been called according to his purpose. (Romans 8:28)

This verse is a promise to me from God. I believe what God says. I love God, so Romans 8:28 assures me that no matter what is happening in my life, God is working for my good. It all comes down to my trusting and believing God's promise. It means even when things aren't going the way I think they should and even when bad things are happening, I need to trust God is working for my good.

From the smallest things to the biggest things—from traffic jams causing me to be late for an appointment to my husband's job security, from forgetting if I turned the oven off to wondering if we will have a check to pay for food and housing next month—I need to trust God is working for my good in the situation. When I am believing this promise, then I can pray to God as Philippians 4:4-7 says and turn it over to God and have that peace instead of worrying and losing control of my emotions.

It all comes down to accepting God's promise in Romans 8:28 and not trying to control everything myself.

EMOTIONS

Amazingly, several months ago I realized that I had come from being a woman with little control of her emotions to one who can shut down all emotions. Neither of these extremes is being self-controlled as 1 Peter 4:7 says. This happened when my second daughter, Anna, moved out of the house into downtown Boston to go to college. I felt it was more than I could bear to feel the pain of her leaving home. I had been through this when our first daughter, Sarah, moved away to college, and then moved to Macedonia and Bosnia. I knew what the pain felt like, and I didn't think I could bear it again. I shut down so much I felt no emotional connection with anyone—not even my husband. It was scary! I had to work and pray to get in touch with my emotions again. I needed to let myself feel the pain and hurt of losing Anna. I also needed to remember another promise of God in 1 Corinthians 10:13:

No temptation has seized you except what is common to man. And God is faithful; he will not let you be tempted beyond what you can bear. But when you are tempted, he will also provide a way out so that you can stand up under it. (1 Corinthians 10:13)

God did help me through the pain; it was not more than I could bear. His promise was fulfilled once again. I learned that I am not being self-controlled to let my emotions fly loose and control me or to let them shut down and disconnect me from God and others.

I can be self-controlled in my emotions as Peter says to be only if I remember to hold on to God's promises. Romans 8:28 and 1 Corinthians 10:13 are the two that help me the most. There are certainly many other promises. I would simply encourage you to find the promises of God and hold on to them. Our God is a faithful God and is worthy of our trust.

Gail Frederick
Boston, USA

God and Only God

"I wanted to change the world, but I couldn't find a babysitter."
Ultra Woman

I feel pressure to excel in all areas of my life, don't you? I want to be an effective builder, a wise counselor, a Christlike discipler, a compassionate servant, a gracious hostess and a brave warrior like Joan of Arc. Can I do it? Can you do it?

In Luke 10:38-42, Jesus reminds Martha that life is not about performance and roles. Life is about relying on God. And it is not just letting God help you; it's letting God do it all for you! Hopefully this chapter will help convince you that God is more than able to make you and me the women he needs us to be: adventurous, God-reliant disciples. One thing is needed: God—and only God!

Effective Builders

Have you ever tried to build something? Big designs can often lead to big disappointments. Like a great architect, we imagine the perfect structure. Even though we have great vision, when we do it on our own power we are often frustrated by failure.

Last year I wanted to build an addition to our front porch. My idea was to surprise Scott and do it while he was out of town. I took him to the airport and went straight to the supply store to get started. I had the right idea, but doing it on my own power was a mistake! I realized halfway through that I lacked the skill and experience to lay the right foundation. Scott came home to a mess and he had to get an engineer friend to lay the foundation for us. Then I was able to fill in the rest. The result is quite pleasing, but doing it on my own power almost had disastrous results!

In Isaiah 48:13 God says,

> "My own hand laid the foundations of the earth,
> and my right hand spread out the heavens."

In building God's kingdom, I desperately need God's power and strength in the planning and execution. When I think that I can build on my own "wisdom" I am being foolish and will end up becoming frustrated and humbled. (Prayerfully God will step in, fix my mistakes and build it correctly!) If I will simply rely on God from the beginning, the pressure is off and the result is glorious.

Wise Counselors

Have you ever felt short of wisdom when asked for advice? Do you feel the pressure to give the "right" answers? Have you ever been baffled by a problem? Too many of us (myself included) just tear into a situation and try to solve it with our own wisdom.

A few months ago I found a huge water spot in my kitchen. I was ready to tear up the floor and find the problem. I was sure the problem was right under the wet spot. Fortunately for me (and the floor) I thought to call an expert before I ripped open my floor. I learned that the spot was a symptom of a leaky pipe three feet away!

When we counsel others we can also make faulty assumptions. We see a problem and want to tear into it, not realizing we have got to go to God and seek his advice and wisdom or we will just leave a huge gaping hole in someone's life and heart. As Psalm 20:6-7 says,

Now I know that the LORD saves his anointed;
    he answers him from his holy heaven
    with the saving power of his right hand.
Some trust in chariots and some in horses,
    but we trust in the name of the LORD our God.

Christlike Disciplers

I need to raise up young women and train older women as well. The way to do this can seem obscure and difficult at times. I have seen, though, over and over again that it is God who sends the right people into our lives and that he is the one who disciples these people. He is the one working in the church to raise up leaders—if we will pray to him for guidance. I have seen this happen repeatedly in Hong Kong and now in Seattle as we try to raise up Bible Talk leaders and full-time staff. God has a plan and we need to follow him to figure it out. The pressure is off!

Return to us, O God Almighty!
    Look down from heaven and see!
Watch over this vine,
    the root your right hand has planted,
    the son you have raised up for yourself. (Psalm 80:14-15)

Compassionate Servants

It is always God's heart to do whatever he can to help. But do you ever feel overwhelmed by the needs of the poor? Often in Third World countries, I have felt so pulled and torn by the vast needs. At the same time, I am so proud of the work of HOPE *worldwide* and the many needs being addressed through all the efforts of disciples. In my heart I feel called to care more and be more and do more. God cares, too, and he can help us do that. "For he stands at the right hand of the needy one" (Psalm 109:31a).

Recently, a single sister in our congregation wanted to adopt and I was surprised at the number of disciples who were quite negative about the idea. This sister had to work through all the input and make her own decision. She did adopt, and I have seen how God has blessed her life and been there at her right hand to help her and give her incredible opportunities to share about her life and faith. If we will just do what we can, when we can, God will be our strength and help us to meet those needs. But only one thing is needed: God and only God!

Gracious Hostesses

I like to cook. I like to use cooking as a way to serve my husband, family and friends. However, cooking takes work and can put pressure on an already busy life. But Jesus cared about meals with people (Matthew 14:13-21; Luke 7:36, 10:38, 22:7-8; John 21:4-14). Jesus can help us cook and serve. In Isaiah 62:8-9, God promises to provide for his people "by his right hand and by his mighty arm." If we will just let God help, we can relax and enjoy feeding others!

Brave Warriors

I frequently feel that I am in the midst of a battle. There are many days that it's not a pretty picture! This is reality. Christianity is a battle and it is well worth fighting—but keeping in the fight is not easy and we should not expect it to be. Each day is a battle for personal righteousness, for souls and for perseverance. But only one thing is needed—God and only God! God's people understand this:

It was not by their sword that they won the land,
　　nor did their arm bring them victory;
it was your right hand, your arm,
　　and the light of your face, for you loved them. (Psalm 44:3)

So that feeling that we have to do it all, do it well and never have a hair out of place—is it impossible? Well, the hair part probably is, but the rest of it—the building, counseling, discipling, serving, fighting—it can be done. But there's only one way: with God and only God! He'll stoop down to make us great! (See Psalm 18:31-36.) We need to give up on the arm of self-reliance (it's useless anyway) and rely instead on God and his powerful right arm. He can do it all—with one arm tied behind his back!

Lynne Green
Seattle, USA

Be Still and Listen

"Be still, and know that I am God."
Psalm 46:10

How does it feel to talk openly and vulnerably with another person, only to realize they are not really listening? Perhaps they are looking other places, changing the subject or…the ultimate crusher…they bluntly admit, "I wasn't listening; what did you say?" Doesn't your heart sink? Listening is vital in relationships; it reflects your love and respect for the other person. This skill (or lack of) transfers into our relationship with God. We expect God to listen to us—but how good are we at listening to God? Here are a few scriptures to consider.

Luke 10:38-42

- Martha—the hyperactive hostess; Mary—the humble listener. Both women were honored to have Jesus in their home, yet they showed it in two very different ways. Martha showed her excitement by performing duties; Mary sat still and listened to Jesus.
- Consider Martha's interaction with Jesus. Apply it to yourself:
    What are my daily distractions? What do I worry about? Do I accuse other people of not helping me? Do I feel like Jesus does not care about my situation? Do I get security from performing duties?
- Now consider Mary. She was sitting and listening to Jesus, and he commended her for it. She wasn't distracted, and she didn't change the subject or perform duties. Apply this to yourself:
    What does it take to be a good listener? How can I be a better listener to Jesus? Do I rush through my times with God? Am I easily distracted? Is it hard for me to sit still and meditate on the word of God? Am I more consumed with my "to do" list than with God's "to be" list?
- I'm sure you have been told, "God will direct you," or "God will show you the answer." These are right and true statements—but how can we expect to *hear* God's direction for our lives if we are running around, tired, busy, complaining? Does God's heart sink because you are not listening to him?

1 Kings 4:29-34

- Several kings sent their men long distances to listen to Solomon's wisdom. Think about the time, money, sacrifice and desire this required. How do you think these men felt about the opportunity to go hear Solomon? When they stood in Solomon's presence, how attentive do you think they were? Apply this to your relationship with God:

> Am I excited and honored to "go" spend time with God? Do I make extra effort and sacrifice in order to ensure quality time with God? During that time, am I attentive to his incredible words of wisdom?

- We need to sit and meditate on God, focus on his character, dig deeply into the Scriptures, seek his wisdom. It is an honor to sit at his feet!

1 Kings 10:1-9

- Rather than sending her men, the queen of Sheba came personally to listen to Solomon. She tested him "with hard questions" and talked "about all that she had on her mind." After soaking everything in, she was overwhelmed and grateful! Apply this to yourself:

> Do I actively pursue God, or do I wait to be spoon-fed scriptures? Do I ask God hard questions and talk to him about all that is on my mind? Do I take the time to listen to his answers? When was the last time I was overwhelmed by God's wisdom and grateful for his direction in my life?

Matthew 12:42

- The queen of Sheba's heart and attitude condemns us if the effort she made to listen to Solomon (the son of David) is greater than the effort we make to listen to Jesus (the Son of God)!

James 1:22-25

Listening to the Word leads to obedience. We must look intently (no distractions) into the Word so that we will know how to obey. I am sure God realizes our schedules are packed with activities and appointments. I am also sure God is aware that society is constantly rushing. He has prepared good works for us to do (Ephesians 2:10). It is not, however, our busy lifestyles that impress God. Are we busy for the sake of being busy? Are we too tired to listen? What God wants more than anything is for our hearts to be focused on him. He desires our love, respect, trust, time and our full attention. He loves it when we stop our "duties," sit at his feet...and listen!

These verses have transformed my relationship with God. I studied my Bible on the topics of "listening" and "meditating" (which I highly recommend), and it melted my heart to see how much God desires to communicate with me. I used to feel guilty if I took "extra" time for my Bible study. I fell into the trap of thinking my spirituality was proven primarily by getting with people, going to activities and performing my duties. I don't believe that anymore! I believe God is tickled when I block out chunks of time especially for him...not just time in the morning, but throughout the day and week. I also regularly plan dates and retreats with God.[1] These uninterrupted, special times with my Father have become precious to me. By listening to God and his word, my actions are more balanced and focused. Because of this, my security and trust in God have grown immeasurably.

I am inspired by Jesus, our perfect example. In John 12:50 and 14:31 he informs us that he says and does *exactly* what God has told him. He listened intently to his Father!

"He who has ears, let him hear." (Matthew 13:9)

Vickie Boone
Boston, USA

---

[1] To inspire and increase your wonder and awe of God, I suggest reading Henry Kriete's book *Worship the King* (Billerica, Mass.: Discipleship Publications International, 2000). The chapter "Treasure" lists forty-five ideas to "enrich your walk with God and deepen your personal worship experience."

Using Time Well: The Noble Path

But the noble man makes noble plans,
and by noble deeds he stands.
Isaiah 32:8

1. **A Light for My Path: Psalm 119:105, Proverbs 20:24**
   A. Make the effort to look ahead
   B. Practical planning times needed:
      1. Daily planning—take fifteen minutes at the end of your quiet time
      2. Weekly planning—get together with your husband/co-leader/discipler for at least an hour
      3. Monthly planning—pray for vision and attack the month with faith for your life and ministry
      4. Yearly planning—especially important when you are a leader in the church, but do the others first
   C. Develop routines. Building routines in our lives keeps us from being overwhelmed.
   D. Practical routines to develop:
      1. Morning routine—the most important (read, pray, plan, etc.)
      2. Lunchtime routine—various appointments
      3. Dinnertime routine—helpful for your family (dinner, talk/pray after)
      4. Evening routine—Bible studies, discipling times, times to encourage others, family times
      5. Discipling times routine—so you don't have to think through it every week, but only occasionally
      6. Bible study routine—with someone who wants to become a Christian, same time each day or week
      7. Phone call routine—important for generating momentum in your ministry and encouraging your friends
      8. Exercise routine—hard to do, but so needed (See chapter 24 for ideas.)

2. **The Path Ahead: Psalm 139:3**
   A. Hold yourself accountable (example: personal finances and getting out of debt)
   B. Develop personal accountability:

1. Make your schedule plan and then record the actual events to see if you are following through with your plans
2. Develop a list of priorities

3. Diligence: Proverbs 21:5
   A. How hard do you work at your schedule...really? (That shows your faith.)
   B. What was the last thing you held yourself strictly accountable to changing?
   C. Do you have a list of priorities? What would your schedule say about these?

Jesus had the most noble path. Do we have the faith to schedule as Jesus did? Jesus had incredible mornings: he worked hard for the weak, getting up early for time with God (Mark 1:32-39). Jesus had incredible fruitfulness. He was a leader who was not too busy to share his faith with others (Mark 2:13-14). Jesus had strong convictions with his family. They criticized his schedule, but he stuck to his priorities (Mark 3:20-21, 31-35). Jesus had the incredible ability to train others, taking time to build life-changing relationships (Mark 6:6b-13).

Gail Ewell
San Francisco, USA

Order in Your Home

Our God is an ordered God, and he calls us to imitate his character. In our fast-paced society we can allow ourselves to become accustomed to disorder in our lives and in our homes. We excuse ourselves by saying, "I am just too busy to keep things neat." But, if we decide that order is a priority, can't we find the time to train our character to clean as we go and keep clutter in its place?

The two women who wrote the following articles would answer a resounding *Yes* to this question. They will help you not only to desire order, but to do a better job of maintaining it.

Ordered, but Not Obsessive

After each step of the creation process, "God saw that it was good." As he created order from the formless and empty earth, he was pleased. Throughout the first chapter of Genesis we can see God's plan emerge. We see how he put things together, making each part work beautifully with all the other parts. We see an order that reflects the nature of God in the petals of flowers, in the feathers of birds, and in the consistency of the sunrise. The challenge for us is to reflect that same penchant for detail and order in our houses.

Another great example of God's order can be found in his instructions to the children of Israel as they were wandering in the wilderness. Exodus 25-27 records his plan for the building of the tabernacle. Every aspect of the building was exact and precise. No facet of this great undertaking was overlooked or considered unimportant. Then in Numbers 2 God gives specific instructions about the arrangement of the different tribes as they camped together. In Numbers 4 he gives instructions to the different Levite clans for moving the tabernacle from place to place. Each person had his particular task. Every time the Israelites pulled up camp, each Levite knew exactly what his responsibility was, exactly what he needed to carry to the new location. They weren't grabbing curtains and altars and scrambling to take the tent down. Even to the detail of carrying the tent pegs, they had their specific assignments.

Let's also look at God's ordered plan for the coming of Jesus. He began way back in Abraham's day (around 2000 B.C.), giving him the promise that he would bless the whole world through his seed. Then through the prophets Isaiah, Daniel, Joel and others, he predicted specifics about the coming of the Messiah. God kept following his plan through the birth and life of

Jesus, and all the prophecies culminated at the resurrection. Because it is God's nature to stay with his plan, we thankfully now have salvation!

Order in Our Homes

As we look at these examples of order from the Scriptures, we see that if we are to have order in our lives and in our houses, we must also have a plan. Even though many of us today work outside of our homes, proper planning can enable us to accomplish efficiently whatever needs to be done at home. Just as every office has its ordered way to get things done, so should every home.

Of course, even with the best efforts things do not always go according to our plans. Children get sick, parents get sick, or something comes up that needs immediate attention. All these things can distract us, but if we have a plan, we have something to go back to which will get us on track once more.

For the most part, setting up specific things to do on specific days seems to be the best way to get started. This way we commit ourselves to accomplishing at least one or two tasks each day. For example, on Monday there always seems to be a lot of laundry after the weekend, so the laundry can be washed, folded and ironed, if needed, and clothes put away. The house usually needs a rather major cleaning each week, especially if there are children, so that could be the focus on another day. Grocery shopping could be accomplished on yet another day. For some people, making a daily list of things to be accomplished is a help. Beware: Too long of a list can be overwhelming and too short of a list can be limiting.

Of course with any plan there needs to be flexibility, but not so much flexibility that work is not accomplished or that we make excuses about the lack of order in our homes. On the other hand, if we are too rigid, we can easily sin against our friends and family or anyone else who "interferes" with our routine. It is very important to have a joyful balance and to make sure that lack of order is not the norm. If we err in either direction, maintaining our homes becomes a burden, and we become grumblers and complainers, unable to rejoice in our responsibilities.

My Personal Plan Through the Years

When our five children were little, keeping the house neat and orderly was a challenge. Each evening after they were all in bed, I picked up anything out of place, cleaned the bathroom (after all those bedtime baths!), and only then would I sit down. Had I been a disciple then, planning would have been even more crucial, as it is for disciples with families today. With very busy ministry schedules, our houses could look like children's playrooms much of the time if we are not consistent.

Taking time to think through my meals for the week helped me to write out a very specific grocery-shopping list. Therefore, I usually only went to the grocery store (with all my children) once a week. This helped not only in stress management, but in budget management as well.

I also needed a plan to keep the kitchen clean. I washed dishes as soon as dinner was over. When I got a dishwasher, I rinsed dishes and immediately put them into the dishwasher, washing the pots and pans and putting everything away in the cabinets. Now this is sometimes hard to do because of a group or one-on-one Bible study scheduled right after dinner. But the good thing about having a plan is that I can return to it before going to bed. That way I can always start the day with a clean kitchen.

Character Development

To take advantage of every opportunity, we must have two definite aspects of character: (1) a trained eye to see the chaos and (2) a mindset that wants order in the home. Since I was trained by my mother in both of these areas, the only really difficult part for me was to do it and not to be lazy and indifferent. Becoming pregnant within the first year of our marriage, I discovered how quickly I could become self-indulgent and lazy. Morning sickness became my excuse not to get up. The excuse extended into the evening mealtime, so no dinner was prepared. For a while the sickness was legitimate, but as I look back, I know I should have held myself to some degree of order and productivity.

When I was growing up, my parents held me accountable; they taught and expected me to push through until the work was done...then I could rest. Isn't that God's way? He worked six days and rested on the seventh. Fortunately as disciples we have people in our lives to correct us if we are becoming lazy and to encourage us to push through and get our work done. It is then that rest is truly rewarding.

Be Open to Discipling

As disciples, even after learning how ordered God is and how we are to reflect his nature to others, we can rebel and be indifferent in the way we manage our homes. We may even have people in our lives giving us input and advice, but we consider it unimportant or intrusive. Some of us can think that those who disciple us are being too picky about unimportant details. But if this is the case, we need to go back and read Exodus 25-27 and Numbers 2 and 4 to see just how detailed God was in his instructions to the Israelites. And if we just do not seem to be able to get it together, we should keep asking for help. God will bless a heart that is willing, open and wants to learn.

ORDERED LIFE

Order is important to God; therefore, it must be important to us. There are many ways to get the work done, and it is up to us to find the best way, always being mindful that everything we do in our lives is to bring glory to God and to his kingdom.

Helen Wooten
Los Angeles, USA

Consistent, but Not Compulsive

God is "the same yesterday and today and forever" (Hebrews 13:8). Everything God is and does demonstrates his constancy and consistency. The flow of the seasons year after year, the coming of every new day, the utter reliability of his promises—God is always there, always working for our good, always working to sustain and maintain this world in which we live.

We are all greatly affected by our environment. Too many days of darkness and dreariness will depress even the most positive and cheerful among us. On the other hand, a bright, clear spring day lightens our steps and lifts our spirits! The same is true of the places we live. How do you feel when you arrive home only to be greeted by dirty dishes all over the counter and in the sink, piles of dirty laundry in every room, unmade beds and filthy bathrooms? I don't know about you, but just the thought of this scene makes me feel burdened and depressed. We do not have to live like this, and in fact, disciples *must* not live like this! The real challenge, however, is not the great, inevitable clean-up; it is to *keep* it clean.

A Change of Mind and Heart

As the years have gone by I have become more convicted of God's desire for order and discipline. As God's child, everything in my life is a reflection of God himself. What a privilege and what an incredible challenge! My home is my little bit of creation, and the way I keep it speaks volumes about my view of God, of myself, and of my family and guests.

Most of us are able to at least straighten up our homes, apartments or rooms. Perhaps we do it under the duress of expected company, or maybe we have just reached the point of "I can't stand this mess any longer!" The frustration comes because, once we have everything cleaned up, we cannot seem to keep it that way. The great challenge is to keep a home that is clean and neat while still allowing those who live there the freedom to do just that—*live*. We are a people of extremes: We either don't care enough about creating homes that are neat, clean and attractive, or we are obsessed with the state of our surroundings, becoming selfish, greedy and unloving. God made a beautiful world and he keeps it that way. Why? So we can live in it and enjoy it. The same is true of our personal surroundings, our homes.

I asked my children how they felt about having a clean house. They talked about how important it was for them to be able to bring their friends to a neat and attractive home. We tend to think children don't care about these things, but in fact, they do. Their friends have often commented that our home seemed so nice and "cleaned up." My children also went on to describe how they felt when they visited other people's homes that were messy or dirty. They all expressed embarrassment for their friends and their friends' families.

Once we are convinced that cleanliness and order should be maintained on a consistent, daily basis, what are some of the practical things we can do to bring this about?

Every Day

Make your bed first thing in the morning!

It's amazing how much nicer a bedroom can look by just making the bed. It only takes a few minutes, but it is one of those things that is hard to get back to once the day begins.

Keep the kitchen cleaned up and uncluttered.

Get into the habit of cleaning up after every meal. Keep dishes washed and put away or rinsed and in a dishwasher whenever they are used, and teach your entire family to do the same. Teach everyone to clean "as they go," keeping crumbs and spills wiped and swept up. Does the microwave need cleaning or the stovetop wiping? Do these things when you notice them; it takes about thirty seconds when we do them as we go.

I keep only a few decorative things on my kitchen counters. Most of the small appliances that cover our countertops are not very attractive, and we really do not use them as often as we might think. The only appliance I leave out is my coffeemaker. Everything else I store under counters or in drawers. This goes a long way toward making a kitchen look clean and in order.

Straighten up before you go to bed.

Pick up the little odds and ends still lying around at the end of the day: children's toys, cast-off shoes and unclaimed clothes. No one wants to greet a fresh new day with clutter and confusion. It makes me feel burdened and overwhelmed before the day has even begun.

Don't forget the dirty clothes.

For those with small families, laundry may not be a tremendous burden and can be done once or twice a week. However, for those with larger families the laundry can be one of the most overwhelming tasks of the week. As soon as everything is finally washed, dried, folded and put away, several more loads appear out of nowhere. These suggestions may help:

- Teach everyone to bring their dirty clothes, sheets or towels to a laundry room or designated place at the end of the day.
- Start a load of wash first thing in the morning and sort out the next load.
- Folding clothes is a great job for older children, especially when they are sitting and watching television.
- Teach them to fold and put the clean clothes and laundry in the appropriate rooms.

Every Week

Get rid of the dust and dirt.

Most houses need a good dusting once a week and a thorough vacuuming once or twice a week. Keep up with it and it's a breeze; let it go and it's miserable.

Clean those bathrooms!

Bathrooms that are cleaned well once a week tend to stay clean and don't take nearly the time to clean as those that are only dealt with when the slime of mildew and the scum of neglect have begun to grow.

Again, teach everyone to clean and wipe up as they go. Dirty clothes should be taken to the laundry basket, towels hung, toothbrushes and toothpaste put away, floors swept. As in the kitchen, organize so that very little is left out on the counters and everything has a specific storage place.

If you need help, get it.

Maintaining a home is a challenge to the most disciplined among us! Keeping a clean home seems next to impossible for mothers who juggle both families and jobs. I have often hired an older high school student or a college student to clean for two or three hours each week. It takes a load off me to have my bathrooms thoroughly cleaned and my house dusted. If she has time, she may run the vacuum cleaner. When those things are done, I can keep up with the rest fairly comfortably. I pay her more than she can make babysitting or even at a minimum-wage job, so it's worth it for her, and yet I still pay less than I would pay a cleaning service.

Every So Often

Get rid of the things you don't need or use.

My rule of thumb is: If you haven't used it, worn it or looked at it for close to a year, toss it, sell it or give it away. You'll never miss it! It is uncanny; we can regularly pare down our possessions, but they always seem to "grow back." Several times a year, I go through closets and cabinets searching for what is outgrown, never used, worn-out or broken. My children and husband have sometimes thought me to be a bit heartless as I threw away rubber-band balls, torn T-shirts, two-year-old schoolwork, paper-clip chains, fossilized Halloween candy and various other sentimental items, but even God declares that there is "a time to keep and a time to throw away" (Ecclesiastes 3:6).

Everyone Helps

As I have often told my children, "We all live here, we all make the mess, so we all clean it up." It is amazing how much easier it is to maintain a home when everyone helps. Children can do much more than we often expect of them, and it is important for them to learn to be responsible and to do things well. From a young age children can be taught where toys belong and be expected to put them there. Older children can do many things, from keeping their own rooms clean and straightened, to doing the dishes and cleaning up the kitchen, folding clothes, dusting and vacuuming. (Just remember that they are not slaves or indentured servants, but rather loved and cherished members of a family!) The same principle applies to singles' households and married couples without children. This builds unity, communication and character.

Put these things into practice and watch as chaos begins to subside, laughter is restored, and your blood pressure returns to normal. As you begin to enjoy the results of these changes, however, be careful that the pendulum does not swing too far in the *other* direction! Just as I once was irresponsible and undisciplined, which was reflected in my surroundings, I now struggle with a different problem: I sometimes care *too* much about our home's appearance. God's world reflects his heart of love, and my home also expresses my heart. I therefore want it to be a testament of my love and care for people, rather than a mirror of frustration and impatience. Unfortunately, developing this balance is much easier said than done.

There are a few things that I have had to accept and continually remember about the work of running a home and a household:

1. It will *never* be *all* done.
2. It will *never* be perfect.
3. It will *never* stay that way.

ORDERED LIFE

Accept these facts, and it will be so much easier for you to relax and enjoy life!

Our homes are for living and living is for people. We must not ever forget that. One day our children will be grown and gone. Yes, they will remember and appreciate all the ways we physically took care of them and met their needs (probably more than they do now). But above all, they will remember and cherish the things we did together in our homes: the laughter, the hugs, the jokes, the good times. They will remember the family times more than the family room, the bedtime talks and stories more than the bedroom, and the meal times together more than the meals themselves. The same is true of all those who will have come through our homes. The love and joy they experienced there will be remembered long after the messes are cleaned up and order is restored. If I could add a verse on to 1 Corinthians 13, God's chapter on love, it would be: "If I am able to clean my house until it shines and polish it until it sparkles, but have not love, it is no more than an empty shell and is worth nothing!"

Let us, therefore, imitate our awesome Creator and loving Father by reflecting in our own tiny pieces of creation the love, compassion and beauty he has lavished upon us.

Geri Laing
Raleigh/Durham, USA

These articles are reprinted from the hardback *The Fine Art of Hospitality* (Billerica, Mass.: Discipleship Publications International, 1995), 19-28. (no longer in print)

The Role of Women in the Church

Does the Bible really teach that women are inferior to men? Was the apostle Paul a blatant woman-hater? And after all, wasn't the Bible a product of a male chauvinist society? Unfortunately there is great confusion in the minds of men and women concerning the woman's role in Christianity. Misapplication of Scripture, coupled with the secular campaign for female liberation, has intensified the confusion, leading many women into fear, discontent or rebellion.

We need to learn God's will about the woman's role so that we can be free from the confusion and thus be free to follow God's plan for our lives. Matthew 11:28-30 tells us that God's plan is not burdensome, but rather, a flight of freedom for our souls. Still, we often find it difficult to trust God's word and practice it in our lives.

Our article aims to correct common misunderstandings about women and the Bible, and to present the truth about the woman's role. As we will see, there is no reason whatever to reject the authority of the Bible because of its teaching on women. Actually, this is one of the strongest arguments for accepting its inspiration!

The Honor of Women in the Bible

Contrary to the claims of some, women in the Bible have generally been highly honored. Let's discuss the theme of the dignity and honor of women in the Bible, beginning with God, moving on to Jesus, then considering the general commendation women receive in the Scriptures.

God the Father

The source of the high honor given to women is found in God himself. God makes no distinction between man and woman as far as their basic dignity goes. He created both. Both have rebelled equally against his will, and he lovingly receives both back to himself on the same conditions of faith and repentance. Jesus died on the cross for *all* people, and Christians have been given a commission to share the good news with both men and women (Mark 16:15). Moreover, God expects total commitment from all alike. Truly, God shows no favoritism (Acts 10:34).

Scripture makes it perfectly clear that the creation of woman was not an afterthought. Woman is just as much a special part of God's creation as man. However, it is tragic that the prevailing attitude in the world toward women has been negative and even demeaning. A popular Chinese proverb calls baby girls "maggots in the rice bowl," and the government cruelly translates this belief into policy in this nation of 1.2 billion. The

Apocrypha (officially accepted as an inspired addition to the Bible by nearly a billion people today) states, "...the birth of a daughter is a loss."[1] Hundreds of millions of women on earth are routinely abused, shouted at, sworn at, bullied and beaten every day. What a contrast the Bible presents, from the very first page.

People will ask, "Is God male or female?" Interestingly, in one sense the answer to the question is yes! Genesis 1:27 says

So God created man in his own image,
>   in the image of God he created him;
>   male and female he created them.

The "image" of God is reflected in both male and female! We are taught to address God as "Father," and certainly this is appropriate, but did you know that our heavenly Father's personality has all of the best attributes of male and female? God has the perfect blend of love, power, sensitivity, strength, emotion, rationality, concern, decisiveness, patience and thoughtfulness. This is why men and women are complementary. God never intended for them to stand *independent* of each other. On the contrary, he created them to be *interdependent* (1 Corinthians 11:11).

Jesus Christ

No one has done more to liberate women than Jesus Christ. In an age when many females were ranked as equal to slaves, Jesus acknowledged their worth and elevated their status to equality with males before God. The Gospels record numerous accounts of Christ interacting with women on the same level as he did with men.

Jesus had close relationships with women (John 11:5), supported them when others put them down (Luke 7:36-50, Mark 14:3-9) and taught them personally (Luke 10:39). Jesus' ministry was financed by women (Luke 8:3). His first post-resurrection appearance was to women (Matthew 28:1-10). Jesus Christ did not hesitate to break through racial, traditional and sexual barriers—to the utter amazement of his followers (John 4:9, 27). Though not compromising on the need for women to repent, Jesus upheld the honor and dignity of womanhood. Let it never be said that the Christian religion robs women of their dignity!

Of Heroes and Heroines

The Bible is full of heroes—great men of faith—but it is also full of heroines. The Old Testament has Sarah, Rebecca, Rachel, Deborah, Ruth, Hannah, Esther and a host of others. In the New Testament, we quickly recall Mary (the mother of Jesus) and Mary Magdalene. But there are so

---

[1]Sirach 22:3. See also 25:13-26:18.

many more heroines—for example, the Samaritan woman (John 4), Priscilla (Acts 18), Lydia (Acts 16) and the woman who anointed Jesus with perfume (Mark 14). The Bible writers weren't afraid to give women the credit they deserved.

Men Have Much to Learn

Some people have interpreted the Bible to mean that men have nothing to learn from women. It is true that the New Testament does not allow women to usurp (or wrongfully take) authority from men in teaching or preaching (1 Timothy 2), but nothing could be further from the truth than to say that men have nothing to learn from women.

For example, in Genesis 21:12, God told Abraham to "Listen to whatever Sarah tells you...." Sarah was his wife and was commended for her submissive attitude toward him (1 Peter 3), but in that instance God told Abraham to listen to his wife. Deborah was a judge over Israel, and through her wisdom many difficult issues were decided (Judges 4:5). Priscilla was a trusted companion in the apostle Paul's ministry (Acts 18) and several times received his commendation. These examples could be multiplied many times over. The point is clear: Men are not considered intellectually, morally or spiritually better than women in the Bible.

Christian Chauvinism?

Is it true that women are degraded or downgraded in the Bible? Middle Eastern society today is much the same as Jesus' society was two thousand years ago. Most Middle Eastern nations today are Muslim, so for the sake of illustration, let's consider the position of the Koran on women:

> Men have authority over women because Allah has made the one superior to the other, and because they spend their wealth to maintain them. Good women are obedient. (Surah 4)

Mohammed goes on to reprimand disobedient wives—they are to be rebuked, beaten and sent to bed! In most mosques the women are hidden behind a screen. Heaven in Islam is "a band of brothers," and little thought is given to women. This is degrading, but thankfully, this is not the teaching of the Bible. Pakistan severely restricts the rights of women, not allowing them on the streets at night. This is a radical Islamic republic. In another Muslim nation, Saudi Arabia, women are not allowed to drive cars. If these comments are hard to relate to, rent a copy of *Not Without My Daughter* and prepare to see how women are treated in many countries of the world (in this case, the fundamentalist Islamic republic of

WOMEN'S ROLE 207

Iran). Women's rights are virtually nonexistent. And the sad stories can easily be multiplied worldwide.[2]

If the Bible were really only the product of men, we would expect it to treat women in the manner of first century society. Instead, we find a nice surprise: women in Jesus' day would have enjoyed *more,* not *less,* honor if their husbands and society followed the principles of God's word. The same holds true today.

Submission

Our society instinctively distrusts authority and submission. That's why so many people dislike the Bible's teaching on marriage. Marriage is designed to operate on the principle of loving "submission" (the wife's side) and loving "leadership" (the husband's side). This is God's plan. No wonder the state of marriage in the world is such a disaster! People have tried every way but God's way.

The Dirty Word

"Submission" has become the dirty word in our society. Men and women simply do not *want* to submit, and signs of rebellion are everywhere. Students disrespect teachers, citizens hold police and other authorities in contempt, and children disobey parents. It shouldn't surprise us that our society, with its selfish emphasis on "me," has rejected God's plan for submission within marriage. God never said it is easy to give up our rights and put the needs of others ahead of our own, but he commanded us to do that because he knows that it is only through self-denial that we will find self-fulfillment (Philippians 2:4-7). He has created us "to do good works" and to function on the fuel of sacrificial love (Ephesians 2:10, 5:1-2). Selfish ambition is on the Galatians 5 list of sins because it destroys love and relationships.

Submission does not mean domination or oppression. The Bible teaches very clearly against abuse of authority (Matthew 20:25, Colossians 3:18-19). There are two correct meanings of submission, and neither of them usually settles very well when we hear it for the first time.

---

[2]In "democratic" India, which is more than eighty percent Hindu, opportunities for its half a billion women are limited indeed. Hinduism teaches that you get in this life what you earned in the last; a certain fatalism and passivity are not, therefore, entirely unexpected. Wife-beating and spousal abuse are rampant. A disgrace in the history of India is *suttee* (the burning alive of a Hindu widow on her husband's pyre).

With their official "one-child policy," Chinese authorities often force women to abort or "terminate" the newborn and exact fines from persons exceeding the one-child limit. China is officially atheist, though Taoism-Buddhism survives in many parts. Until the Revolution of 1911, women's feet were commonly "bound" (wrapped so tightly that they became grossly deformed, useless for walking).

Female circumcision is an international issue. Such nations as Chad, Somalia and the Sudan show unspeakable cruelty toward their female citizens in continuing this barbaric practice of cutting out the female genital organ, first recorded in Egypt more than four thousand years ago. Much of Muslim or tribal Africa enforces this rite of passage.

The first is to willingly put the needs of another (male or female) ahead of our own, as in Ephesians 5:21: "Submit to one another out of reverence for Christ." The second meaning is to willingly subject ourselves to another's authority, as in the Hebrews 13:17 command of submission to the authority of church leaders. This also applies to the relationship of wives to husbands.

This last area tends to be the most difficult to digest. Today's society interprets the submission of a woman to a man as an admission of inferiority. To make things worse, some men have abused their positions in leadership and have become tyrants. Still others lack confidence in gaining female respect. The result can be rebellion at the seeming unfairness of the woman's role.

Viewing the situation from God's perspective, however, puts submission in a positive light. The Lord, not man, has designed marriage, knowing what will make it work best. He put submission into the relationship to create order, not inferiority. Someone has to be the leader, and God gave that responsibility to the husband. A man's authority over his wife is not earned; it is assigned by God. Submitting to that authority does not mean he is superior and she is inferior; it simply fulfills responsibility within the different roles God has assigned both.

One more thing: while most women do not like having to "submit" to a man, it is also true that many women find it even *more* difficult to submit to a woman. The real issue is submission, not gender. (Of course, at the bottom of it all lies rebellion against the authority of God himself.)

Equality = Equalization?

Does equality mean that men and women should be the same in every respect? Consider a soccer team: since everyone is "equal," should we erase the distinction between the positions and let *everyone* play goalkeeper? Or let everyone play any position he likes? This would not increase the chance of winning in the slightest! Teamwork is essential, and this is possible only when all the players operate within the roles assigned to them. "Equalization" would destroy any hope of victory.

There are several basic differences between men and women (physical size and strength, voice, childbearing, emotional makeup), but the differences between the sexes go even further: we have different roles as well. We certainly need to accept the basic differences, but we also need to understand the difference in roles. God's plan, especially in the marriage relationship, is for men and women to complement one another. We must remember that men and women were never intended to stand independent of each other. God's word clearly teaches that the husband is to be the spiritual leader of the family (Genesis 3:16). The Bible says, "Wives, submit to your husbands as to the Lord" (Ephesians 5:22).

WOMEN'S ROLE   209

On the other hand, the husband is not free to be uncaring, lazy or disrespectful (Ephesians 5:25-33). In fact, he is commanded to love his wife "just as Christ loved the church and gave himself up for her" (Ephesians 5:25). We seriously wonder if a wife would object to following her husband's lead if his attitude was one of sensitive, sacrificial, selfless devotion to her.

Differences in roles absolutely do *not* imply inferiority or superiority. Of course, we are all equal in one sense in our standing before God, but *equality* before God does not mean *equalization* of our different God-assigned roles. We can fill different roles and functions and still remain "equal." All church members share one sort of equality (the ground is level at the foot of the cross), but it would be incorrect to say everyone is equally a leader. In the same way, the Bible teaches that men and women are equal (Galatians 3:28), but that does not override the role differences between husband and wife.

Summary

Submission does not mean inferiority. Rather, it is the means to harmonious relationships. Our society is totally fixated on individual rights and has overreacted to the Biblical concept of submission. The right balance is what will bring the harmony and depth of friendship we all seek.

The 'Woman Hater'

The mistaken notion that Paul was a woman hater is based on a very few passages from his letters and a whole lot of bad will on the part of people with an ax to grind. Before we examine the passages taken to show Paul's "male chauvinism," let's examine his general attitude toward women from the evidence.

If Paul were negative toward women, his own writings should be highly incriminating. Yet when we study those writings, we find a character exactly opposite to that which we have been led to expect! He made his appreciation and praise of women clear in every letter he wrote:

- *Rome:* Paul's warm feelings toward women friends and colleagues exude from the printed page (Romans 16).
- *Corinth:* He allows women to pray and prophesy in the assembly (1 Corinthians 11) and says all apostles have a right to marry (1 Corinthians 9:5). The demand for a celibate clergy is vigorously rejected! (See 1 Timothy 4:3.)
- *Galatia:* Paul strongly upholds the equality of all believers: "There is neither...male nor female, for you are all one in Christ Jesus" (Galatians 3:28).

- *Philippi:* Paul urges the men to support the female leadership in the church (Philippians 4:3).
- *Colosse:* Paul teaches husbands to sacrificially love their wives (Ephesians 5). To the Colossians he says, "Husbands, love your wives and do not be harsh with them" (Colossians 3:19).
- *Thessalonica:* Paul encourages the Christians to respect everyone who works hard in the church—not just the men (1 Thessalonians 5:12).
- *Ephesus and Crete:* When Paul writes to male leaders, he is fully supportive of the women's role. Men are to expect a high standard of commitment from the women, just as from the men (Titus 2:3-5), and yet they need to treat them with sensitivity and respect (1 Timothy 5:2). In fact, Paul reserves the highest leadership positions in the local church for *married* men with well-behaved children (1 Timothy 3, Titus 1). Clearly he appreciated the invaluable experience and insight that come only from a smoothly running Christian marriage in which both partners communicate, love each other (love God even more) and fill the roles God has assigned them.

It is obvious that, far from being insensitive to women, Paul was extremely considerate. In fact, when we tally all of Paul's personal greetings in his letters, *a full forty percent are to women*—that's better than most men do today. Some woman hater!

Of course, it is possible to say one thing in a letter and yet be different in person. Exactly what was Paul's personal effect on the women of his day? Consider the upper-class Greek women in his society—the ones most likely to be offended if he was "down on women." As we read Acts, which records the growth of the early church, we see many noblewomen coming to faith and following Paul (Acts 16:13-14, 17:4, 17:12, 17:34, etc.). They weren't offended by the "woman hater"—instead, they accepted him and his message.

Problematic Passages?

Now that we have an accurate view of Paul's attitude toward women, we can examine the passages problematic for those who have been offended by him. People have taken 1 Corinthians 14:34 to mean that women must keep absolutely silent in the church. The situation was that some women were embarrassing their husbands and violating order and decorum by arguing with men over the interpretation of prophecies. (This is the context of 1 Corinthians 14.) Paul tells them to take up their questions *outside* the assembly, once they have gone home. The difficulty with the view that Paul prohibits women to speak at all is that in chapter 11, he evidently has no objection to women praying and talking out loud in the services.

WOMEN'S ROLE

1 Timothy 2:11 teaches the same principle. Verse 12, however, deserves comment: "I do not permit a woman to teach or to have authority over a man; she must be silent." As we have seen, Paul is not commanding total silence. Nor does he say this because men are superior to women. He does, however, uphold the Biblical principle that in the church, the men are to lead. What a shame that in most churches today there are few men who attend, and even fewer who take on leadership responsibility. Far from liking to dominate in the church, most men have little or no desire to be spiritual leaders. In such a setting, it is easy for a woman to want to take over the leadership. God commands that she not do so.

Paul's Insight and God's

It is God's word that pierces our inner being and lays bare our thoughts and attitudes (Hebrews 4). Paul's writings (thirteen of the twenty-seven New Testament books) are *all* inspired. Paul had a profound understanding of human character, including female character. He was right when he commented on the weak will and lack of self-control on the part of many women (2 Timothy 3:6-7). Women on the average *are* much more emotional than men are. This is possibly one reason God entrusted the leadership of the church to men.

We notice also that Paul is extremely hard-line with those who don't want to work (2 Thessalonians 3:6-13), as well as with those who are critical and divisive (Titus 3:9-11). In a tense situation, men tend to withdraw (stop working), while women tend to manipulate and take over the leadership from the withdrawn brother, which does not bring about the spiritual balance that God commands. Women who do take over leadership do not like Paul and his no-nonsense approach as to how the church should be governed. (And critical and divisive women, or men, certainly do not appreciate Paul's challenge to them…unless they truly have a heart for God and want to change.)

Far from having a poor evaluation of women, Paul understands them—and men—all too well! Paul was neither a woman hater nor a man hater; he was, however, a sin hater. We must realize that Paul's insight is not his own; it is *God's* insight into our characters. God's word is true, on target and always penetrating.

How About a Retrial?

Paul did not misunderstand women, but women have misunderstood Paul—and all the more as amazingly few have read what he actually said. We have found that good-hearted women—those who are really serious about giving God control of their lives and "crucifying the sinful nature"—are not the ones who stumble on Paul's teaching. Rather, the women who fight against Paul are the ones who tend to be critical, emotional and rebellious.

Why the Confusion?

We do not deny that women were misunderstood or oppressed in Jesus' day. They certainly were, and this has been the case in every generation.[3] Treatment of women isn't much better today: in many Third World countries women are worked like slaves, and in developed countries they are treated as sex objects, misunderstood by men too selfish to listen and really care. In any and every society the position of women would be radically improved if men—and women—would put the principles of God's word into practice.

All men and women share in the same mission: to spread the word of God to a world without love (Matthew 28). As long as we keep that straight, we will have true unity between sexes. Gratitude and sincere appreciation for hard work (1 Thessalonians 5:12) will replace critical attitudes and competitive feelings.

Instead of reading what the Bible really says, most women have listened to their friends' ill-informed opinions about the Bible's oppression of women and Paul the "woman hater." Uncritically they have swallowed these negative attitudes hook, line and sinker. Sadly, many people are looking for issues to campaign against. They simply would not have time for this if they were about their mission—if they could say, with the apostle Paul, that they are being "poured out" for the cause of Christ (2 Timothy 4:6).

The massive confusion results from *ignorance* and *selfishness*. Only when men and women make time to study God's word and deny themselves (Luke 9:23) will we be united in our purpose and find what we were striving for all along: meaning and happiness in life.

Douglas Jacoby and Pat Gempel
Washington, D.C. and Philadelphia, USA

---

[3]Contemporary sociology recognizes the abysmal status and treatment of women in the ancient world and the utter contrast in which the Christian religion held out true hope to women. In *The Rise of Christianity*, (Princeton University Press, 1996), page 118, sociologist Rodney Stark writes:

> Both Plato [Republic 5 (1941 ed.)] and Aristotle [Politics 2, 7 (1986 ed.)] recommended infanticide as legitimate state policy. The Twelve Tables—the earliest known Roman legal code, written about 450 BC—permitted a father to expose any female infant and any deformed or weak male infant (Gorman 1982:25). During recent excavations of a villa in the port city of Ashkelon, Lawrence E. Stager and his colleagues made a gruesome discovery in the sewer that ran under the bathhouse. "This sewer had been clogged with refuse sometime in the sixth century AD. When we excavated and dry-sieved the desiccated sewage, we found [the] bones...of nearly one hundred little babies apparently murdered and thrown into the sewer (1991:47)." Examination of the bones revealed them to be newborns, probably day-olds (Smith and Kahila, 1991).

NOTE: This material is reprinted from *Q & A: Answers to Bible Questions You Have Asked* by Douglas Jacoby (Billerica, Mass.: Discipleship Publications International, 2001), 150-160.

LIFE & GODLINESS FOR EVERYWOMAN
VOLUME 1 (COMPANION VOLUME TO THIS BOOK)

CONTENTS

LIFE

Single
1. Single Women and Sexuality *Sheila Jones*
2. Supporting the Brothers *Vickie Boone, Bethany Jones*
3. Life to the Full *Dr. Karen Kolarik*
4. Dating, Courtship and Engagement *Sam and Geri Laing*

Wife
5. Respecting Your Husband *Geri Laing*
6. Building Up Your Husband *Sheila Jones*

Mom
7. New Mothers: Quiet Times *Sandy Drenner*
8. Teaching Your Children to Respect *Sheila Jones*
9. Parenting Older Children *Tom and Sheila Jones*
10. Deciding Whether to Work Full Time *Sheila Jones*
11. Business at Home *Loretta Berndt*

Single Mom
12. Our Children's Fathers *Joan Lapointe*

Non-Disciple Husband
13. Esther: Winning Your Husband *Jennifer Lambert*
14. Never Compromise *Lori Kotkowski*
15. Encouragement from the Scriptures *Irene Gurganus*

Divorce
16. My Maker Is My Husband *Kayren Carter, Pam Riddell*

Aging
17. Menopause: Am I Going Crazy or What? *Dr. Helen Salsbury*
18. 40+ Is Positive *Sheila Jones, Gloria Baird, Marcia Lamb, Sally Hooper, Jeannie Fredrick, Linda Brumley, Joyce Conn, Pat Gempel, Lois Schmitt*
19. Empty Nest–Happy Nest *Gordon and Theresa Ferguson*

Death
20. Ministering to the Dying and Their Families   *Dennis Young*

Miscarriage
21. Dealing with Miscarriage   *Gloria Baird*

Infertility
22. Victory in Contentment   *Debbie McDaniel*

Abuse
23. Healing from Past Abuse   *Marcia Lamb*

Adoption
24. What to Expect When You Adopt   *Julia Hannon, Lea Wood, Jennifer Radl*

Surgery
25. When You Gotta Have It   *Sheila Jones*

GODLINESS

Emotions
26. Godly Emotions   *Linda Brumley*
27. Contentment Vs. Worry   *Gloria Baird*
28. From Fear to Faith   *Sheila Jones*

Mountainside Visits
29. Mountainside Visits: The Teachings of Jesus   *Kay McKean*
30. Humility   *Kay McKean*
31. Purity   *Kay McKean*
32. Speech   *Kay McKean*
33. Relationships   *Kay McKean*
34. Benevolence   *Jeanie Shaw*
35. Prayer   *Kay McKean*
36. Forgiveness   *Theresa Ferguson*
37. Contentment   *Debbie McDaniel*
38. Golden Rule   *Bernadine Bellmor*

Spiritual Potpourri
39. Helping Someone to Forgive   *Theresa Ferguson*
40. God's Wisdom in Our Lives   *Pat Gempel*
41. Read the Bible in a Year
42. Topical Index to Women's Writings in DPI Books

Suggested Reading for Parents

Published by DPI

A Heart to Teach (edited by Tom Jones and Kelly Petre) This book contains two weeks of quiet times and fifteen chapters of resource ideas designed to prepare children's ministry teachers for a new rotation of service. It is also a valuable resource for parents as they are taught the "big picture" of their child's future as they grow in God's church.

As for Me and My House (Tom and Lori Ziegler) A treasury of fifty devotionals along with ideas of how to make family devotionals fun and memorable. These are tried and tested by experienced parents.

Raising Awesome Kids in Troubled Times (Sam and Geri Laing) A book to train, convict and inspire. The authors share their experience and conviction on raising an entire family to know and love God in an ungodly world.

Scriptures to Grow On (foreword by Sam Laing) A quick Scripture reference designed topically to help you find practical verses that apply to everyday life situations. Great for discipling times, family devotionals, conflict resolution and the day-to-day need to have God's words on our hearts and to impress them on our children.

The Wonder Years (Sam and Geri Laing, Elizabeth Laing Thompson) Godly wisdom written to help parents navigate the preteen and teen years with confidence and success. Extra power and understanding come as a result of having both the view of the parent and of the child. This book is full of hope and practical suggestions.

Not Published by DPI, but Highly Recommended

Age of Opportunity (Paul David Tripp, Presbyterian and Reformed Publishing Co.) Tripp inspires a "mind change" from the traditional dread and fear of being the parent of a teenager to the "opportunity" of this time of life to mold and influence a young adult to live a lifetime for God. It will encourage your heart and lift your standards.

Boundaries with Kids (Henry Cloud and John Townsend, Zondervan Publishing House) This book gives real-life examples of behavior and consequences to guide parents to raise responsible, self-controlled children who then become mature, confident adults. It gives very practical suggestions and teaches parents to think of the natural progression of a certain behavior and how that will continue into adulthood.

Child-Sensitive Teaching (Karyn Henley, Standard Publishing) An educator with more than twenty-five years experience walks you through our world through the eyes of a child. This book will help both teachers and parents to communicate more effectively and enjoyably with children. It encourages adults to have the heart of a little child.

Dare to Discipline (Dr. James Dobson, Tyndale House Publishing) A straightforward, practical, tough love approach to making the parent-child relationship the best it can be. It focuses on appropriate discipline, building security through boundaries and ultimately real love.

Fun Excuses to Talk about God (Joani Schultz, Group Publishing, Inc.) Forty-eight devotionals using natural events in everyday life to teach children to see God in their world. These are especially written for children age 4 to 11, but everyone will have fun with them. It will inspire you to become young at heart.

52 Simple Ways to Teach Your Child to Pray (Roberta Hromas, Thomas Nelson Publishers) Practical and easy suggestions to train your child (and yourself) how to "pray without ceasing" and bring their relationship with God to a very real level.

How to Really Love Your Child (Ross Campbell, Chariot Victor Books) Campbell simply and clearly describes to parents how to fill up their child's "emotional tank" so that the child feels and knows the love of the parent. The principles he teaches will change your way of thinking about meeting your child's needs.

How to Really Love Your Teenager (Ross Campbell, Chariot Victor Books) Campbell continues the theme of his first book, now dealing with communicating love during the teenage years. He strongly believes many difficulties occurring during this time of life can be avoided if parents know how to hear what their teen is saying and communicate effectively back to them.

Parenting Adolescents (Kevin Huggins, NavPress) Disciples of Jesus are always growing, and Huggins shows parents of adolescents how they can raise their children to have a godly character...while they, as parents, are continuing to develop theirs.

Shepherding a Child's Heart (Tedd Tripp, Shepherd Press) More than correct behavior children need to have the right heart motivating their actions. Tripp clearly helps parents develop deep convictions in their children through everyday interactions.

OTHER HELPS   217

The Story of Me (Stan and Brenna Jones, NavPress) Another beautifully illustrated picture book, the first in a five-part series. This book talks to children age 3 to 5 about sexuality and how they came to be. It lets parents begin to discuss sexuality at a very early age, thus removing much of the awkwardness of the topic.

Before I Was Born (Carolyn Nystrom, NavPress) Number two in a five-part series. This picture book is geared for ages 5 to 8 and is tastefully and beautifully illustrated to help this age group deal with sexuality at their level of understanding. It encourages a continuous honest and open communication with your child about sex beginning in their early years.

What's the Big Deal? (Stan and Brenna Jones, NavPress) Number three in a five-part series. This book is written for ages 8 to 11, dealing with sexuality and God's design in the maturing lives of adolescents. It is very easy to understand and familiarizes kids with what could be an uncomfortable topic.

Facing the Facts (Stan and Brenna Jones, NavPress) Number four in a five-part series. This book is written to children ages 11 to 14. It describes the changes taking place in the adolescence body, mind and relationships both at home and in the world around them. It gives them a spiritual perspective on why God designed their bodies this way and encourages an openness about sex in the parent-child relationship.

How & When to Tell Your Kids About Sex (Stan and Brenna Jones, NavPress) This is the final book in a five-part series and the only one written specifically for adults. It helps parents give their children a healthy understanding of sexuality by guiding parents back to the basics of developing a strong, healthy character in their child.

The Five Love Languages of Children (Gary Chapman & Ross Campbell, Northfield Publishing) This simple, enlightening book describes the "languages" of quality time, physical touch, acts of service, words of affirmation and gifts. Both authors show how every unique child "hears" a certain "language" more clearly than the others and therefore responds and feels loved with some languages more than others.

The Five Love Languages of Teenagers (Gary Chapman, Northfield Publishing) The author continues his theme into the teenage years, but with a new perspective on gaining influence instead of having authority. This is an excellent book on leadership both inside and outside of family bonds.

Lea Wood
Boston, USA

Things Not to Say to Single Women

As married women, all of us want to encourage our single sisters in the church, right? Well, in order to do that, many of us need some helpful input. In talking with single women I have found that the married people in their lives do not always come up with the most encouraging comments. Certainly no one is out to say inappropriate and hurtful things. (And the single women say, "Amen. Just think what they would say if they were *trying* to be inappropriate and hurtful!")

In Volume One of *Life and Godliness for Everywoman*, I wrote at the end of my chapter on "Single Women and Sexuality" the following statement:

> Sometimes people who love us and want us to be married are the very ones who make comments that hurt us and tempt us with discontentment and despair. One single sister told me that sometimes she is content with where she is in life, and then other times she is tempted with deep discontentment. She realized that there was a correlation between her feelings of discontentment and the well-meaning but inappropriate comments of her married friends.

I think most singles receive these comments from people they are not close to—people they meet in passing or who casually talk with them in fellowship (or at weddings!). Certainly those who are close to them are talking more deeply with them and know what they are thinking and feeling. These friends make comments to help them get perspective, and any faithful single woman wants that kind of input. It is just the offhand comments that jab them...meanwhile, the perpetrator is going happily on his or her own way, smiling and "encouraging" countless others in their path of emotional destruction.

Top Ten Comments That Make Single Sisters Cringe

To help rectify this situation, I have polled some of the single women in my life to determine the most unappreciated comments. I share the results with you below.

10. "Jesus was single." (Obviously that doesn't mean that we should all be single.)
9. "How's the dating life?" (Sounds like an innocent question, but if anything exciting were happening, she'd tell you.)
8. "How come you're not married yet?" (She starts thinking there must be something wrong with her.)

OTHER HELPS

7. "What's wrong with the single brothers?" (Maybe she is finally convinced there is nothing wrong with her, and then she gets a huge attitude toward the brothers.)
6. "I'm sure there is someone out there for you somewhere (in a patronizing tone)." (*Yeah*, she thinks, *so where is he?*)
5. "Since you are probably not doing anything this Saturday night, would you keep our kids so my husband and I can go out on a date?" (How about maybe finding her a date so you can double?)
4. "You run around and take care of everybody else. You need someone to take care of you." (So, what does she do with that?)
3. "What do you do with all your free time?" (What free time?)
2. "Don't worry, I was single for three lo-o-o-ong years before I met my sweetie." (This is a killer statement when you are talking to a single woman who's been a disciple for eight, ten, fifteen years. Ouch! One woman told me she ran to the bathroom and wept after receiving a comment like this!)
1. And the #1 top unappreciated comment from a married person: "I don't know how you do it. I couldn't stay pure that long. I'm so thankful I'm married."

Top Ten Comments That Single Women Long to Hear from Married Sisters

As Jesus reminds us in Luke 11:24-26, when we sweep the negative out of our lives, we need to replace it with the positive. Here are the top ten encouraging statements people can make to single women.

10. "I always pray for you." (Just letting her know she is on your heart.)
9. "I know God is working in your life." (Give specific instances if possible!)
8. "Thank you for doing [fill in the blank]. You are so valuable to the kingdom." (Hebrews 6:10)
7. "You are so beautiful." (Some single women haven't heard that from anyone since their mom or dad said it to them in the first grade.)
6. "I'd be so happy if my daughter grew up to be like you."
5. "You are a great friend. I admire the way you build meaningful and close relationships."
4. "I would never want you to marry anyone who didn't realize how special you are."
3. "I have a great brother I'd like to set you up with." (Then actually do it.)
2. "It would be fun to do a double date with you. When are you available?" (Again—actually make it happen.)
1. And the # 1 statement that single women long to hear: "Faithful single women like you are my heroes."

The writer of Hebrews charges us to "consider how we may spur one another on toward love and good deeds (Hebrews 10:24). *Strong's Greek Dictionary* defines "consider" as "to observe fully: behold, consider, discover, perceive." So, with the single women in our lives, let us observe fully, behold, consider, discover, perceive how to encourage them and help them be the best they can be for their Lord.

And single women everywhere say, "Amen!"

May our Lord Jesus Christ himself and God our Father, who loved us and by his grace gave us eternal encouragement and good hope, encourage your hearts and strengthen you in every good deed and word. (2 Thessalonians 2:16-17)

Sheila Jones
Boston, USA

Contributors

Gloria Baird—world sector leader, congregational elder's wife, Los Angeles Church of Christ, coauthor of *Love Your Husband*

Vickie Boone—copyeditor with DPI, teen ministry leader, Boston Church of Christ

Melanie Breitenbach—registered dietitian, nutrition therapist, family group leader, Detroit Church of Christ

Linda Brumley—women's ministry leader, elder's wife, Seattle Church of Christ

Dr. Barbara Campaigne—doctorate in exercise physiology, medical writer, family group leader

Melanie Cicerchia—Bible talk leader, New York City Church of Christ

Joyce Conn—children's ministry leader, New York City Church of Christ

Mary Lou Craig—women's ministry leader, Columbia S.C. Church of Christ

Gail Ewell—world sector leader, women's ministry leader, San Diego Church of Christ

Theresa Ferguson— women's ministry leader, congregational elder's wife, Boston Church of Christ

Gail Frederick—regional elder's wife, Boston Church of Christ

Pat Gempel—world sector leader, women's ministry leader, elder's wife, Executive Vice President of HOPE *worldwide*, Philadelphia Church of Christ

Lynne Green—world sector leader, women's ministry leader, Seattle Church of Christ

Linda Howard—spiritual-strengthening ministry leader, San Diego Church of Christ

Douglas Jacoby—kingdom teacher, Washington D.C. Church of Christ, author of *Q & A: Answers to Bible Questions You Have Asked, Shining Like Stars, Life to the Full, The God Who Dared, True & Reasonable*

Sheila Jones—women's editor with DPI, regional elder's wife, Boston Church of Christ, author of *9 to 5 and Spiritually Alive*, coauthor of *To Live Is Christ*, editor of *The Fine Art of Hospitality, Life & Godliness for Everywoman, Volume 1*

Geri Laing—women's ministry leader, Triangle Church of Christ, coauthor of *The Wonder Years, Raising Awesome Kids in Troubled Times, Friends & Lovers*

Brenda Leatherwood—chemical recovery ministry leader, New York City Church of Christ, coauthor of *Some Sat in Darkness*

Kay Summers McKean—world sector leader, women's ministry leader, Boston Church of Christ, author of *Our Beginning,* coauthor of *Love Your Husband*

Shelley Metten—associate professor of anatomy, UCLA Medical School, elder's wife, spiritual recovery leader, AMS region, Los Angeles Church of Christ

Lisa Morris—editorial assistant with DPI, family group leader, Boston Church of Christ

Jayne Ricker—children's ministry leader, San Diego Church of Christ

Debbie Rosness—women's congregational leader, Greater Reno Church of Christ

Pamela Roy—set decorator for feature films and television, Bible talk leader, AMS ministry, Los Angeles Church of Christ

Brian and Mary Scott—regional administrator, teen ministry leaders, Boston Church of Christ

Elizabeth Laing Thompson—campus ministry leader, Atlanta Church of Christ, author of *Glory Days,* coauthor of *The Wonder Years*

Dr. Claudia Trombly—MD, family physician, family group leader, Boston Church of Christ

Donna Western—ultrasound technologist, families ministry, Greater Philadelphia Church of Christ

Lea Wood—children's ministry leader, Boston Church of Christ

Helen Wooten—OASIS (Older Active Singles in the Spirit) ministry, Los Angeles Church of Christ